MW00964863

Windows 2000 and Mainframe Integration

William H. Zack

MACMILLAN
TECHNICAL
PUBLISHING
· U·S·A

Windows 2000 and Mainframe Integration

William H. Zack

Published by:
Macmillan Technical Publishing
201 West 103rd Street
Indianapolis, Indiana 46290

Copyright © 1999 by Macmillan Technical Publishing

FIRST EDITION

International Standard Book Number: 1-57870-200-3

Library of Congress Catalog Card Number: 99-60205

Printed in the United States of America

03 02 01 00 99   7 6 5 4 3 2 1

Interpretation of the printing code: The rightmost double-digit number is the year of the book's printing; the rightmost single-digit number is the number of the book's printing. For example, the printing code 99-1 shows that the first printing of the book occurred in 1999.

Composed in XXX and MCPdigital by Macmillan Technical Publishing

Trademark Acknowledgments

All terms mentioned in this book that are known to be trademarks or service marks have been appropriately capitalized. Macmillan Technical Publishing cannot attest to the accuracy of this information. Use of a term in this book should not be regarded as affecting the validity of any trademark or service mark.

Warning and Disclaimer

This book is designed to provide information about Windows 2000. Every effort has been made to make this book as complete and as accurate as possible, but no warranty or fitness is implied.

The information is provided on an as-is basis. The authors and Macmillan Technical Publishing shall have neither liability nor responsibility to any person or entity with respect to any loss or damages arising from the information contained in this book or from the use of the disks or programs that may accompany it.

Feedback Information

At Macmillan Technical Publishing, our goal is to create in-depth technical books of the highest quality and value. Each book is crafted with care and precision, undergoing rigorous development that involves the unique expertise of members from the professional technical community.

Readers' feedback is a natural continuation of this process. If you have any comments regarding how we could improve the quality of this book or otherwise alter it to better suit your needs, you can contact us at networktech@mcp.com. Please make sure to include the book title and ISBN in your message.

We greatly appreciate your assistance.

Publisher
David Dwyer

Executive Editor
Linda Ratts Engelman

Managing Editor
Gina Brown

Acquisitions Editor
Karen Wachs

Development Editor
Katherine Pendergast

Project Editor
Alissa Cayton

Copy Editor
Keith Cline

Indexer
Nadia Ibrahim

Team Coordinator
Jennifer Garrett

Manufacturing Coordinator
Chris Moos

Book Designer
Louisa Klucznik

Cover Designer
Aren Howell

Compositor
Wil Cruz

About the Author

William H. Zack has been the Chairman of the New York Windows NT/2000 User Group for more than five years. He has more than 30 years of experience developing mainframe batch, transaction-processing, client/server, and Internet systems. In his current position, Bill assists clients in the conversion of legacy mainframe transaction and client/server systems to Windows NT and Internet Information Server. He has served as a beta tester for numerous versions of Windows NT, including Windows 2000, and has been working with Windows NT systems for more than six years. He is a Microsoft Certified Professional Product Specialist in Windows NT Installation and Support. Bill is the author of three previous books: *Fast Access OS/2* (1990, Brady); *The OS/2 2.0 Handbook* (1992, Van Nostrand Reinhold); and *The OS/2 Handbook, Second Edition* (1994, Van Nostrand Reinhold).

About the Technical Reviewers

These reviewers contributed their considerable practical, hands-on expertise to the entire development process for *Windows 2000 and Mainframe Integration*. As the book was being written, these folks reviewed all the material for technical content, organization, and flow. Their feedback was critical to ensuring that *Windows 2000 and Mainframe Integration* fits our readers' need for the highest-quality technical information.

Farhaad Nero is an internal Information Center Consultant with Time-Warner. He has more than 13 years of experience in the IT industry both as an applications and systems software developer as well as a systems administrator. He has worked at Citicorp, Tupperware, and Bankers Trust. His experience includes systems management in DEC VAX cluster environments, computer programming using COBOL on the IBM mainframe and MicroFocus COBOL on the PC, Visual Basic and C, SQL databases, including Oracle and Sybase. He most recently completed a successful Windows NT 4 deployment from Windows 3.11 in a Novell NetWare network environment.

Joel L. Rosenblatt has more than 25 years of experience in programming mainframe and PC systems. He is currently the manager of IBM VM Systems for the Academic Information Systems at Columbia University. In this capacity, he provides systems programming, application programming, support and consulting services to the university, its faculty, and students. In addition, he is responsible for the Windows NT systems at the Electronic Data Service Library at Columbia University. As an independent consultant, he has written many software packages that have been licensed to clients for their use. He is a principal consultant for the firm DVS International Inc., which supplies depreciation and valuation studies and software for the utility industry. He also custom builds personal computer systems to meet the specific requirements for some of his clients. He is a graduate of Columbia School of Engineering and Applied Science with a Bachelor of Science degree in Materials Science, with a minor in Computer Science and Electrical Engineering, and he has completed all the postgraduate courses for a Masters in Materials Science.

Dedication

This book is dedicated to a family that, once again, has lived with my mental absence for the past eight months so that I could write yet another computer book. To my beautiful and talented daughter Amy Cheryl, to my fine and talented young sons David Allan and Steven Michael, and most of all to my wife Marcia whom I love dearly and who has stood by me for richer or poorer, in sickness and in health, I dedicate this book.

Acknowledgments

I would like to thank the entire staff at Macmillan Technical Publishing for making the production of this book possible and one of the best publishing experiences of my career. To Linda Ratts Engelman, for believing in the project and convincing Macmillan to publish the book. To Karen Wachs for constant encouragement and advice (and sometimes a little well-deserved nagging). To Jennifer Garrett for orchestrating the whole show, to Alissa Cayton for an excellent job editing the final work for production, and to Katie Pendergast, one of the best Development Editors whom I have ever worked with. To you, and all the many others working behind the scenes at Macmillan Technical Publishing, I owe my sincerest thanks.

I also want to thank the technical reviewers who were unbelievably quick with feedback and unfailingly helpful in suggesting areas for improvement. Many of their suggestions have found their way into the book in one form or another.

Contents at a Glance

Table of Contents

Introduction

At the time this book is being written, there is great debate as to whether Windows NT and its successor Windows 2000 are enterprise ready in terms of scalability and reliability. Recent technology demonstrations by NCR Compaq and others have show that they can indeed support databases in terabyte sizes with hundreds of transactions per second. This performance, previously thought possible only by mainframes, is achievable today. Nevertheless I do not expect the mainframe to just go away. Rather, I expect a healthy coexistence between mainframes, Windows 2000 systems, and even other computer systems running other operating systems.

Who This Book Is For

This book was written for you if you are a professional with an IBM mainframe background. It will bring you up to speed quickly on Windows 2000 and its use in an enterprise, which includes both mainframes and Windows 2000 systems. It will do this by leveraging your experience working with IBM mainframe hardware and software and related features of Windows 2000 in terms already familiar to you.

In this book, I use my personal experience working with OS/390 and its predecessors to help you learn about Windows NT and Windows 2000.

The second purpose this book is to act as a sort of "reverse translator" for Windows NT and Windows 2000 people who know nothing about mainframes. This book will help you to understand the mainframe environment and how features in Windows 2000 either do or do not map to features in OS/390.

Chapter Structure

Rather than organizing the material in the book in the order of other books written about Windows 2000, I have chosen to structure it based on the features that OS/390 provides, and the equivalent Windows 2000 features. In those cases where Windows 2000 has no equivalent feature, I point out where Windows 2000 is deficient or where third-party products can be used with Windows 2000 to achieve the missing functionality. In those cases where Windows 2000 has superior functionality, I point that out as well.

I hope that this approach gives you an appreciation for Windows 2000 by itself, as well as Windows 2000 in a mixed environment where it coexists with IBM mainframes. There is also an ulterior motive in beginning each chapter with material on OS/390. Those of us who have been working in mainframes for 30+ years think that we know everything that there is to know about our working environment. In reality we have been working with it for so long that we take for granted the subset of operating system features that we use most of the time. Furthermore, jobs in the mainframe world are highly specialized. You may be a programmer proficient in COBOL, but you have never IPL'ed a Parallel Sysplex or acted as the "Console Commander" of an OS/390 system. You may work as a printer pool operator and understand how to issue JES2 commands to control the routing of job output to printers, but be totally unfamiliar with the work that a systems programmer does to install new versions of OS/390 and apply fixes to the operating system.

This book may even teach you a thing of two about OS/390 that will be useful to know over and above what it teaches you about Windows 2000!

Origins and Evolution of OS/390 and Windows 2000

In the 1960s, IBM announced a new operating system, OS/360, to go with a new hardware architecture, System/360. OS/360 evolved through many, sometimes overlapping, incarnations to reach what is known today as OS/390.

Windows 2000 had its earliest origins in the MS-DOS and PC-DOS operating systems. This chapter briefly reviews the history of OS/390 and Windows 2000 to help you understand the design differences between OS/390 and Windows 2000 that are explained throughout the book.

The Evolution of OS/390

OS/390 started life more than 30 years ago. It began as a single-tasking operating system—just as MS-DOS, the predecessor of Windows 2000, did. Since the 1960s, it has evolved through many different versions to reach its current state of functionality as a multitasking, multiprocessing operating system.

This discussion doesn't attempt to catalog every variation and dialect of the operating system that became OS/390 because this is, after all, a book about Windows 2000 and not OS/390. Therefore, this chapter takes the liberty of compressing some of the history of IBM's operating systems. You should bear in mind that IBM had many operating systems and even had different versions of the same operating system in production at the same time.

OS/PCP

The earliest predecessor of OS/390 was a version called the *OS/Primary Control Program* (OS/PCP). OS/PCP, released in 1966, was a single-tasking operating system. Instructions were given to this operating system on decks of punched cards read in by slow-speed card readers. These card decks contained data and control statements in a *Job Control Language* (JCL). Output from these jobs was often printed on relatively slow-speed line printers. Assuming 60 lines a page, for instance, a 1,200 line-per-minute line printer would only print 20 pages a minute.

As discussed in Chapter 5, "Multiprogramming," running a single job on modern computer equipment is wasteful of resources. Modern processor speeds are so fast and input/output device speeds so slow that a processor would spend most of its time in a "wait" or "idle" state if you ran only a single job at a time. Through proper operating system design, it is possible for administrative and utility functions to be performed by the operating system using these wasted CPU cycles.

Functions such as reading in new jobs to be executed and/or buffering printer output to disk and from disks to printers are likely candidates. This led IBM to produce the first multitasking version of the operating system, *Multiprogramming with a Fixed Number of Tasks* (MFT), in the mid-1960s.

OS/MFT and HASP

OS/MFT appeared in 1972. It featured a fixed number of fixed-size memory partitions in which independent applications could be run. This operating system also used other partitions for performing utility functions to read input transactions and dispose of output data.

OS/MFT was IBM's first attempt to produce a multitasking operating system. Although this was a big step forward, it was somewhat awkward to start and stop jobs in multiple OS/MFT partitions, and control the distribution of printed output. A group of IBM'ers in Houston subsequently developed an add-on software package to improve on-the-job scheduling and printer output management of MFT. They named this software *Houston Automatic Spooling Priority* system (HASP).

HASP included features to handle input job spooling, job scheduling, and output spooling. The significance of HASP is that it eventually became the basis for the *Job Entry System 2* (JES2), which is now an integral part of OS/390. In fact, many of the operator messages from OS/390 still begin with HASP.

OS/VS1

The MFT operating system and HASP evolved into an operating system IBM called OS/VS1 later in 1972. OS/VS1 still featured multiprogramming with fixed-memory partitions. This was the first operating system in the OS/360 family to support the use of virtual memory.

Up until this point, IBM's operating systems were real-memory operating systems. If more memory was needed than the memory size of the computer, a job could not run. To relax this restriction, IBM used a technique called virtual memory. Virtual memory makes memory appear to be larger than it actually is by using a disk-backing store to act as an extension of memory. This allows the operating system to simulate a memory address space larger than the physical memory in the machine.

OS/VS1 still used the concept of running jobs in fixed-size partitions. This was considered wasteful because each partition had to be large enough to fit the largest job run in it. To relax this requirement, IBM produced another operating system that would support the running of a variable number of jobs in variable-sized regions of memory.

OS/MVT

In 1967, IBM delivered OS/MVT. This operating system had more features than VS1; however, it could only run on IBM's larger mainframes. IBM continued to support VS1 in parallel with this operating system.

MVT used variable-sized partitions called regions that could be sized to fit the job to be run in them. OS/MVT was not a virtual memory operating system. It was, however, the basis for the SVS and MVS operating systems that followed it.

OS/VS2-SVS and MVS

OS/VS2-*SVS* (Single Virtual Storage), developed in 1972, featured a single virtual memory address space. Like MVT (and unlike OS/VS1), it could run jobs in variable-sized regions of memory rather than fixed-size partitions.

Two years later, IBM modified this design to support the execution of multiple jobs, each running in its own address space; the result was OS/VS2-*MVS* (Multiple Virtual Storage). MVS then went through several incarnations such as MVS/XA and MVS/ESA in its evolution into today's OS/390.

OS/390

In the 1990s, IBM decided to repackage MVS together with many of its separate products, such as CICS and DB/2, and to call the result OS/390.

Further Historical Information on OS/390

This chapter's historical summary does not do justice to the development of the original OS/360 operating system. For more details on its development, together with an outstanding treatment of software development principles, you should, by all means, read The Mythical Man Month *by Fred Brooks (Addison Wesley, Anniversary Edition, 1995).*

Fred Brooks was in charge of the development of this operating system and is considered by many to be the "father" of OS/360, just as Dave Cutler is considered by many to be the "father" of Windows 2000. (The history of Windows 2000 is discussed later in this chapter.) ◆

The Evolution of Windows 2000

When IBM wanted to cash in on the microcomputer market in the early 1980s, they realized they had lots of experience building large-scale hardware and software. They did not, however, have experience with small computers. In addition, there was a great deal of internal resistance to IBM's entry into this market. It was thought by many within IBM that the sale of small, relatively inexpensive computers might, in some way, undermine the sale of IBM's bread-and-butter mainframes. IBM therefore decided to go outside the corporation for both the hardware and the software for its new Personal Computer.

Subsequently Intel was chosen to provide the hardware and Microsoft was chosen to provide the operating system (PC-DOS) for the new IBM Personal Computer. Although the story of how this all came to pass is fascinating reading, this discussion concentrates on the history as it bears on Windows 2000. Therefore, the detailed story is not covered here.

Further Historical Information on Windows 2000

For those interested in more on this subject, you should read Hard Drive: Bill Gates and the Making of the Microsoft Empire *(Wallace et al., Harperbusiness, 1983).* ◆

Microsoft later marketed its own version of PC-DOS, called MS-DOS. Because these operating systems were nearly identical, the remainder of this chapter refers to them just as DOS. The rest of this chapter discusses how DOS led to the development of Microsoft Windows, Windows NT, and Windows 2000.

DOS

The original IBM PC operating system supported a single-user task at a time. As processors got faster, however, the same need to utilize wasted CPU cycles that led to multitasking in mainframes began to become a factor. This led to various techniques to make use of these wasted cycles.

Originally, applications that had to print output did so directly to an attached printer. Later versions of DOS added a primitive output spooling capability implemented by the DOS PRINT command. The PRINT command intercepted program output destined for a printer. It then stored the output on disk. It subsequently used idle processor cycles to print the output. The PRINT command was implemented using undocumented features of DOS, which allowed programmers to write *Terminate and Stay Resident* programs (TSRs). With TSRs a program could arrange to be reactivated when either a hotkey keyboard sequence or some external event occurred. The program would then end without being removed from memory. When the hotkey sequence or event subsequently occurred, the program would then resume operation.

Later, software vendors such as Quarterdeck, with its DeskView multitasking software, made use of this technique to add additional multitasking capabilities to DOS. This did result in the ability to run more than one program at the same time, but it also resulted in a lack of stability, which often caused the operating system to fail (usually at a critical point before you saved that important document that you were working on!). The reason for this instability was, of course, that the underlying operating system (DOS) was never designed to support multitasking.

Windows

Multitasking finally took the stage in a limited form in 1985, when Microsoft introduced Windows. Based on ideas developed at Xerox and originally implemented by Apple, Microsoft was able to take DOS from a single user interface in the form of a black screen to a mouse-driven, icon-based *graphical user interface* (GUI). Windows made its debut in 1985.

Windows also integrated TSR techniques to support a limited degree of multitasking. This enabled multiple applications to run in windows on the desktop. Although it did support multitasking, weaknesses in the underlying DOS operating system limited its success. Although it did work (most of the time), it was not extremely reliable and often resulted in operating system failures, such as the infamous *General Protection Fault* (GPF) and the *General Application Error* (GAE) so familiar to users of Windows today.

Windows subsequently went through the following incarnations:

- Windows 2.0 in 1987
- Windows 286 and 386, both in 1989
- Windows 3.0 in 1990
- Windows 3.1 in 1992
- Windows for Workgroups 3.1 in 1992
- Windows 3.11 in 1994
- Windows for Workgroups 3.11 in 1994

About the time of Windows 3.1, Windows began to be accepted widely in businesses as a desktop operating system, but the multitasking problem remained.

OS/2

Because the DOS/Windows combination was based originally on nonmultitasking technology, both IBM and Microsoft thought that a need existed for a new operating system to be designed from the ground up to support multitasking in a robust fashion. Accordingly, IBM and Microsoft entered into a partnership to develop a new operating system, OS/2. The first version of this new operating system was delivered in 1987.

OS/2 was an all-new operating system with a multitasking Kernel and a GUI, the *Presentation Manager* (PM). The OS/2 PM had its roots in the Windows GUI, a previous GUI developed by IBM called TopView, and a graphical rendering system taken from one of IBM's mainframe products.

OS/2 1.0 lacked the PM GUI interface, which was produced with version 1.1 of the operating system. Unfortunately this version of the operating system suffered from a number of problems that limited its initial acceptance. It required a significantly larger amount of memory than was required to support the DOS/Windows combination. In addition, it was not completely compatible with its DOS/Windows predecessor. Many DOS/Windows applications refused to run under the new operating system as a result.

Although at first OS/2 was not widely accepted by businesses, later versions of OS/2 began to be accepted to a larger degree. Throughout this process, OS/2 went through several incarnations:

- OS/2 1.3 in 1990
- OS/2 2.0 in 1992
- OS/2 2.1 in 1993

The Durability of Early Versions of OS/2

Many years later, several of these early versions of OS/2 are still in use by some of my clients even though two or more newer versions of the operating system have since superceded them. This is a testament to the reliability of these early versions, as well as to the loyalty of early OS/2 adopters. ◆

The Rise of Network Operating Systems

About the same time that DOS and Windows were gaining acceptance in corporations, network operating systems (such as Novel NetWare) were also becoming accepted as a means of sharing data among multiple work-stations. Microsoft produced Windows for Workgroups, a variation of Windows geared toward supporting this feature in small workgroups.

For larger groups of users, Microsoft produced an OS/2 add-on package called LAN Manager. LAN Manager ran under OS/2 and added the same kind of file-sharing capabilities provided by NetWare. At the same time, LAN Manager also enabled users to run applications on remote servers. IBM adopted this product, which, with modifications, they released as IBM LAN Server.

OS/2 and the IBM/Microsoft Divorce

After OS/2 2.0 was released, Microsoft also released Windows 3.1. It was not long before Windows 3.1 began to be widely accepted by businesses. Microsoft and IBM soon began to differ in their objectives. Microsoft wanted to push the use of Windows. IBM wanted Microsoft to downplay the use of Windows and to emphasize OS/2.

Although they did initially begin to develop the next generation of OS/2 (to be known as OS/2 Version 3), things did not really work out between them. This acrimony resulted in a divorce between the two parties and the end of their collaboration on OS/2. Each party took with it the unfinished core of OS/2 Version 3. IBM went on to complete the development of this product as its next operating system, OS/2 Version 3.0 (OS/2 Warp). Microsoft, in turn, took the work in progress and incorporated some of it in its new operating system, Windows NT.

Dave Cutler and Windows NT

To complete the development of their next-generation operating system, Microsoft hired Dave Cutler from *Digital Equipment Corporation* (DEC). At DEC Dave had been one of the primary architects of DEC's extremely successful minicomputer operating systems, including VMS. Dave brought several associates and many ideas on operating system design from DEC, and the result of his involvement was Windows NT (New Technology).

> ### The Relationship of Windows NT to VMS
>
> *Much of the internal architecture of Windows NT is patterned after VMS. The file systems are so similar, for example, that the first defragmentation utility for NT (DiskKeeper) was produced by Executive Software, the company marketing the premier VMS defragmentation utility.* ◆

As in the case of early versions of OS/2, the new operating system had larger memory requirements and ran slower than the DOS/Windows combination. It was also not completely compatible with all earlier applications. This prompted jokes about what NT stood for (Nice Try, Not There, Next Time, and so on). Windows NT Workstation and Windows NT Server 3.1 were shipped in 1993, followed by Windows NT 3.5 in 1994, Windows NT 3.51 in 1995, and Windows NT 4.0 in 1996.

By the advent of Windows NT 3.51 and Windows NT 4.0, the meteoric spread of NT in businesses had begun. This was also helped by a decline in memory prices, which fortunately happened at the same time.

Windows 95

To capitalize on the acceptance of DOS/Windows in business, and because initial versions of Windows NT were met with resistance as discussed earlier, Microsoft subsequently reworked DOS and Windows into a new packaging as Windows 95 (delivered, of course, in 1995). This version had a prettier interface than its predecessor, but still suffered from the instability of its predecessors (except that GPFs were cleverly renamed GAEs so that Microsoft could claim that GPFs were things of the past).

Windows 98

As a follow up to Windows 95, Microsoft made minor interface and internal improvements and released Windows 98 in 1998. About the time that Windows 98 was released, Windows NT 4.0 was making strong corporate inroads as both a workstation and a server operating system.

Windows NT 4.0

When Windows 98 was released, Microsoft admitted that Windows 98 would be the last generation of the venerable Microsoft DOS/Windows duo. Because Windows NT 4.0 Workstation and Server were starting to make major inroads in the corporate world at about the same time, Microsoft began to adopt the position that corporations would be better served by moving to Windows NT rather than to Windows 98.

Windows NT 4.0 existed in both Workstation and Server versions. Windows NT Workstation was sold as a desktop operating system for individual corporate users. Windows NT Server and Windows NT Advanced Server were sold as servers supporting file, print, and application services.

As Windows NT 4.0 began to be accepted in corporations, it was observed that it had certain deficiencies that limited its enterprise-wide usefulness. Windows NT 4.0 was criticized in the following areas:

- Scalability
- Ease of administration
- Availability
- Security

Scalability

Scalability refers to the capability of a system to grow to handle any necessary workload.

Windows NT was widely accepted at the department and workgroup level. Even though it was available in a multiprocessor version, many users thought that Windows NT did not scale well enough to handle the transaction volumes supported by mainframes and large multiprocessor UNIX systems.

To dispel this impression, Microsoft held a Scalability Day event in 1998. During the event, Microsoft demonstrated 40 Windows NT Servers performing one billion transactions per day in a highly tuned and optimized system. Despite this, the perception still existed that Windows NT did not scale to the levels supported by IBM mainframes or the larger multiprocessor UNIX systems. Although NT Server was available off the shelf with Symmetric Multiprocessor support for up to eight CPUs and custom OEM support for up to 32 processors, independent studies showed diminishing returns when more than three processors were added to a single system.

To answer this criticism, Microsoft introduced clustering in Windows NT 4.0. This form of clustering (code-named WolfPack) is currently quite primitive compared to the clustering supported by other operating systems such as OS/390, UNIX, and Digital's VMS operating system. More advanced forms of clustering are expected to be released in later versions of Windows 2000.

Ease of Administration

Windows NT was viewed as being weak in its capability to be managed, especially in corporations with hundreds of users and a large number of servers. The GUI of Windows NT was attractive and easy to use when making a small number of changes. When making a large number of changes, however, the GUI was found to be inadequate. Administrators longed for a command-line interface that would enable them to automate mass updates with batch files. Chapter 9, "Job and Task Management," shows how many of these command-line capabilities have been included in Windows 2000. Windows 2000 still has a way to go in this area; these deficiencies will be pointed out and discussed in later chapters.

In the Windows NT (and Windows 2000) administration model, resources (such as files, directories, and printers) are protected by *access control lists* (ACLs). These ACLs contain *System IDs* (SIDs) that uniquely identify users and groups of users who can access each resource.

The main security and administration entity in Windows NT is a logical grouping of computers that can be managed as a single entity with a single administrative database of user accounts. This grouping is called a *domain*.

Windows NT and Windows 2000 Administration

This book covers only the use of Windows NT and Windows 2000 in a network domain architecture. There is another administration model, the Workgroup model, which was inherited from Windows for Workgroups. It is not suitable for enterprises involving large numbers of servers and workstations. Because even a network of a few computers can benefit from the domain model, this book does not cover the Workgroup model. ◆

In Windows NT, users and groups containing users are defined in a Security Accounts database located on a system acting as a domain controller. When a user logs on to the domain, the domain controller (or another system acting as a backup domain controller) authenticates that user. This authentication process retrieves a unique Security ID for the user. This then gives the user the right to access resources anywhere in the domain, subject to the permissions for that resource as defined by the presence of the user's Security ID and/or group Security ID in the ACLs of the resource.

Windows NT supports two types of groups: local groups and global groups. (Windows 2000 supports additional types of groups and a more flexible administration model, as shown in Chapter 2, "Operating System Architecture.") This present chapter, however, focuses primarily on the Windows NT administration and security model.

Local groups contain the Security IDs of users and any global groups from other domains. If these Security IDs exist in the ACLs of a resource on a local system, that user has privileges to access that resource.

Global groups are used to export the Security IDs of local users to another domain. Normally administrators assign users to global groups in their logon domain and then define these global groups in a local group on a remote domain. Then, if they have access permissions to resources in that domain, they can access the resource.

In the single domain model, administration is relatively simple. In cases where multiple domains need to be set up, Windows NT provides one of several additional models:

- The master domain model
- The multiple master domain model
- The complete trust model

Normally in Windows NT, multiple domains need to be set up to allow separate organizational units to administer their own accounts and resources. Chapter 2 discusses how Windows 2000 improves on these models.

The Master Domain Model

To simplify the administration of multiple domains, the *master domain model* can be used. In the master domain model, a trust relationship can be established between two domains. Trust relationships between domains are one-way. If Domain A trusts Domain B, for example, Domain A can rely on Domain B to authenticate all users of resources in Domain A. However, access to resources in Domain A is still subject to the ACLs on the Domain A resources.

In the master domain model, the authenticating domain is normally called the *administrative domain* and the domain owning the resource is called the *resource domain*. As mentioned earlier, trust relationships are one-way. To establish a two-way trust relationship, two one-way trusts have to be set up.

The Multiple Master Domain Model

In the *multiple master domain model*, there are normally multiple master domains and multiple resource domains. All the master domains trust each other with two-way trusts. All the resource domains, in turn, trust all the master domains. This allows the administration of resources to be more decentralized.

The Complete Trust Model

The *complete trust model* is like the multiple master model; however, every domain trusts every other domain. This opens up the security infrastructure completely (subject, of course, to access restrictions on the resources in the domains).

It is easy to see how the number of trust relationships that need to be set up escalate exponentially in this model as the number of domains increases. Chapter 10, "Catalogs and Directories," explains how this administration model has been enhanced, simplified, and made more powerful in Windows 2000.

Availability

Windows NT was a more robust operating system than its DOS/Windows ancestors were. Even so, it had nowhere near the reliability of the IBM mainframes and larger UNIX systems of its day. It is widely accepted that IBM mainframes can achieve 99.999% uptime. This translates to only minutes of downtime per year! Less than this may not be acceptable for some mission-critical, bet-the-business applications, such as high-volume transaction processing and large database-access applications.

This degree of availability normally requires some form of clustering and fault tolerance as implemented by IBM mainframes in the Parallel Sysplex architecture and other UNIX-based clustering techniques. Windows NT does support disk fault tolerance in the form of mirroring and several levels of *Redundant Array of Inexpensive Disks* (RAID). Until recently, however, Windows NT did not support any form of clustering. The current version of Windows NT clustering (WolfPack) is extremely primitive and not yet fully featured enough to help much in this area. Currently, it provides only a hot-standby, fail-over capability. It does not yet provide any kind of load-sharing or distributed-processing support.

Of course, a number of third-party add-ons can be used to improve Windows NT in this area. Chapter, 19 "Scalability," discusses some of these solutions. That chapter also shows how Windows 2000 will address these deficiencies with more advanced clustering options in subsequent versions beyond its initial release.

Another criticism of Windows NT's availability was that changes to most operating system and disk configuration parameters required a reboot for the change to take effect. This contributed to lower system availability.

Security

In the 1990s, thanks to the explosion of the Internet, the industry developed an obsession with security. IBM mainframes had long been used to move large amounts of financial data with extreme security. UNIX, having been more or less in the public domain, had received so much scrutiny and analysis that it was widely accepted as being a very secure operating system. Windows NT was mistrusted somewhat on this score despite the fact that early versions of Windows NT had received a Government C-2 security rating as a secure operating system. Although critics were quick to point out that Windows NT's C-2 security rating covered only the use of Windows NT when not connected to a network, this C-2 rating still helped to support the claim that Windows NT was a reasonably secure operating system.

In addition, Windows NT's Challenge/Response authentication, based on that of the earlier LAN Manager product, was not considered strong enough to thwart intruders. Chapter 13, "Security," discusses how Windows 2000 addresses this weakness.

Windows NT 5.0—aka Windows 2000

About the same time that Microsoft released the first beta version of Windows NT 5.0, it told the world that it was "betting the corporation" on Windows NT and that Microsoft planned to spend billions of dollars on the development of a next-generation, enterprise-ready version of Windows NT, Version 5.0.

Although originally this new operating system was to be called Windows NT just like its predecessors, most people shortened the name to just NT. Microsoft was concerned that the marketing impact of the name Windows would be lost. In keeping with the use of the year-of-release naming convention used for the previous two operating systems (Window 95, Windows 98) and the impending arrival of the year 2000, Microsoft renamed the operating system Windows 2000. As homage to Windows NT, the box will state, "Based on Windows NT technology."

Another reason for changing the name was to highlight that this version of NT is a major upgrade from its predecessor. Windows 2000 is reported to have 60% more code than the previous version. Therefore, Windows 2000 is better equipped to handle enterprise functions such as security, deployment, and scalability. The name change was, of course, applied to all four versions of Windows 2000.

1. **Windows 2000 Professional.** The workstation version of Windows 2000. It follows in the footsteps of Windows NT Workstation 4.0 as Microsoft's premier desktop operating system.

2. **Windows 2000 Server.** The entry-level version of the server product line. It comes with support for up to four-way Symmetric Multiprocessing (SMP).

3. **Windows 2000 Advanced Server.** A more powerful departmental and application server. It supports up to eight-way SMP and larger physical memories than Windows 2000 Server does. It is also the first version that supports clustering.

4. **Windows 2000 Datacenter Server.** Microsoft's assault on the IBM mainframe and large UNIX systems world. It supports 32-way SMP and up to 64GB of addressable memory for specially written applications. It also continues to support clustering and load balancing as integral features.

The next chapter compares the architectures of OS/390 and Windows 2000. That comparison provides the basis needed to examine the features of these two operating systems in subsequent chapters.

2

Operating System Architecture

This chapter presents a functional overview of the architectures of OS/390 and Windows 2000. This explanation of the architectures will give you a framework within which to understand and appreciate the differences between OS/390 and Windows 2000.

The Architecture of OS/390

OS/390 consists of a monolithic operating system kernel called the nucleus, and assorted subsystems that run on top of the nucleus. Subsequent chapters cover some of these subsystems, such as CICS and RACF.

Subsystems and applications make calls to nucleus routines for system services. The nucleus in turn accesses the hardware directly, or through a layer of microcode that interfaces with the hardware.

As you will see in Chapter 3, "Central Processing Units," a mainframe can be operating in one of two states: problem program state or supervisor state. Application programs normally execute in problem program state. In this state, they cannot execute protected instructions. Operating system routines execute in supervisor state and can execute any instructions that they want. Figure 2.1 shows this architecture. The "Architecture of Windows 2000" section compares this to the use of User and Kernel modes in Windows 2000.

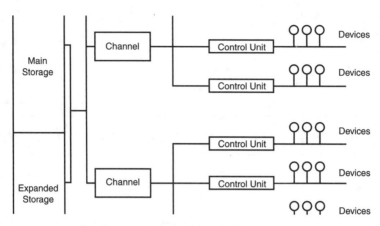

Figure 2.1 *OS/390 architecture.*

Although early versions of this operating system were written in assembly language, the operating system was eventually rewritten in an internal dialect of PL/1, called PLS (PL/1 for Systems).

The Operating System Nucleus

The operating system nucleus sits below the application program layer as shown in Figure 2.1. It operates in supervisor state and provides all operating system services to the application programs and subsystems. Nucleus routines run in supervisor state, unlike application programs and subsystems, which normally run in problem program state. The nucleus contains the following components:

- Memory Management
- Job and Task Management
- Interrupt Management
- Input/Output Management
- Program Management
- Inter Address Space Communications

The following sections discuss the key features of these components.

Memory Management

Memory Management is responsible for handling all operating system, subsystem, and application program requests for memory. This also includes setting up the initial address space for an application, managing virtual to real-memory address translation, and the paging of memory pages to external page files on disk.

The Memory Management component of the operating system is covered in more detail in Chapter 4, "Memory Management."

Job and Task Management

As you will see in Chapter 9, "Job and Task Management," units of work in OS/390 are grouped into logical entities called jobs and tasks.

A *job* is the execution of one or more programs or an interactive time-sharing session under TSO. A job normally consists of a sequence of JCL statements submitted to the JES for execution. The following example illustrates this:

```
//ZACKA    JOB  (1648666,34567-A),'WEEKLY AR REPORT',
//              CLASS=1,NOTIFY=ZACK,MSGCLASS=X
//OUTPUT01 OUTPUT COPIES=10
//STEP1    EXEC PGM=IGHRCO00,REGION=4096K
//STEPLIB  DD  DSN=SM01.LOADLIB,DISP=SHR
//SORTLIB  DD  DSN=SM01.SORTLIB,DISP=SHR
//SYSUDUMP DD  SYSOUT=*
//SYSOUT   DD  SYSOUT=*,OUTPUT=*.OUTPUT01
//SORTWK01 DD  UNIT=SYSDA,SPACE=(CYL,(10,10),RLSE)
//SORTWK02 DD  UNIT=SYSDA,SPACE=(CYL,(10,10),RLSE)
//SORTWK03 DD  UNIT=SYSDA,SPACE=(CYL,(10,10),RLSE)
//SORTIN   DD  DSN=ZACK.RAWARDAT,DISP=SHR
//SORTOUT  DD  DSN=ZACK.SRTARDAT,DISP=(NEW,CATLG,DELETE),
//              UNIT=DISK,
//              SPACE=(CYL,(16,6),RLSE),VOL=SER=ARVOL1
//SYSPRINT DD  SYSOUT=*,OUTPUT=*.OUTPUT01
//SYSIN    DD  *
SORT FIELDS=(1,9,CH,A,17,25,CH,A)
/*
//STEP2    EXEC PGM=ARREPORT,PARM='01-01-1999',COND=(0,EQ,STEP1)
//STEPLIB  DD  DSN=PROD.PROD.AR.LOADLIB,DISP=SHR
//SYSUDUMP DD  SYSOUT=*
//SYSPRINT DD  SYSOUT=*,OUTPUT=*.OUTPUT01
//INFILE   DD  DSNAME=ZACK.SRTARDAT,DISP=OLD
//WORK2    DD  DSN=&&TEMP,UNIT=VIO,SPACE=(1700,(300,50))
//OUTFILE  DD  DSNAME=ARREPT.LIST,DISP=(,CATLG,DELETE),
//              UNIT=DISK,VOL=SER=ARVOL1,SPACE=(CYL,(70,50),RLSE),
//              DCB=(RECFM=FB,LRECL=120,BLKSIZE=12000)
//
```

A Job statement defines the overall operating parameters for a job, such as time limits, initiator classes, output classes, and accounting information for charge-back purposes. This is followed by one or more Job Step definitions. Each Job Step identifies a program to be run and the data sets to be used by that step. In the example shown, the operating system assigns a different-sized memory region for each Job Step. The first Job Step specifies the region size explicitly. The second one defaults to an installation-specified value. Chapter 9 discusses this subject in more detail.

In OS/390, a program consists of one or more units of work called tasks. A *task*, like a thread in Windows 2000, is the primary dispatchable unit of work. When OS/390 starts the execution of a program, it creates a main task control block for that program. The program, in turn, may create other subtasks using the ATTACH operating system request. (The operating system can also create additional tasks within the region to support the execution of the program.)

Although OS/390 application and system programs can create subtasks during their processing, this act involves a large degree of overhead. This led to two interesting developments. Early in the life of the operating system, IBM and others developed teleprocessing monitors such as the *Customer Information Control System* (CICS) that do their own internal subtasking. More recently IBM added a streamlined sub-subtask called a *System Resource Block* (SRB). SRBs, however, are only used internally within OS/390. They are not available to user programs.

This component of the operating system also includes the Master Scheduler, which dispatches operating system and application tasks based on priority.

Interrupt Management

The operating system must be responsive to interrupts generated by I/O devices and program errors. The Interrupt Handler is responsible for handling interruptions caused by program errors (such as illegal instructions), input/output device interrupts, as well as program-generated requests for service in the form of *Supervisor Call Instructions* (SVCs).

Input/Output Management

The Input/Output Management component of OS/390 nucleus is responsible for providing low-level support for external input/output.

When a systems programmer customizes a new version of the operating system for a particular hardware configuration (a process called a SYSGEN), the programmer prepares an *Input/Output Configuration Dataset* (IOCDS), defining the input/output devices attached to the computer. The nucleus uses this table to control the input/output devices.

Chapter 6, "Input/Output Device Management," discusses the management of input/output devices under OS/390 and Windows 2000 in more detail.

Program Management

This component of OS/390 is responsible for loading programs into memory and controlling the sharing of these programs. Chapter 8, "Program Management," discusses program management in more detail.

Inter Address Space Communications

Because subsystems and applications run in separate address spaces, they cannot normally communicate with each other. This component of the operating system provides services that allow communications between tasks running in different address spaces.

Nucleus Initialization and System Startup

When the operating system is started, all the previously discussed components have to be loaded and initialized. These components are loaded and initialized by the operating system *Initial Program Load* (IPL) procedure.

This process starts when the computer operator enters instructions to load the IPL program from a fixed hardware address. This address will be the address of the device that holds the resident operating system (the SYSRES device). From this point on, the process is similar to the process used to boot Windows 2000.

The IPL program loads and initializes the nucleus. Then it loads and initializes all subsystems such as the JES, Initiator/Terminators, and TSO.

Operating System Subsystems

Subsystems are those components of the operating system that run in their own address spaces outside of the nucleus.

Major subsystems of OS/390 include the following:

- JES
- Initiators
- Multiple Console Support
- Security Subsystem
- Time-Sharing Option
- Communications Device Management
- Transaction Processing
- Database Management

The following sections explain each of these subsystems.

The Job Entry System (JES)

OS/390 supports two Job Entry Systems (JES2 and JES3). Chapter 9 discusses JES2, the most often used version of JES. The JES performs the following functions:

- Reading JCL input
- Converting JCL statements into internal tables

- Placing these tables in execution queues to be run
- Intercepting output requests to print data
- Routing print data to the appropriate printer
- Purging the job from the system when it is complete

Initiators

The Initiators run in each region and are responsible for starting the subsystem or user job in that region. Each Initiator examines a set of input queues to decide the job to execute next. When it finds a job to run, it initializes an address region and starts the first step of the job. As each Job Step completes, the Initiator starts the next step. At the end of the job, the Initiator examines the input queues looking for another job to run.

Multiple Console Support

The OS/390 nucleus also includes support for multiple operator consoles. This is important because the central processing unit may be in a different room or on a different floor from the printer pool and other external devices!

Security Subsystem

Security under OS/390 is managed either by IBM's *Resource Access Control Facility* (RACF) or by *Computer Associates Access Control Facility* (ACF). IBM provides RACF as part of OS/390. ACF is a popular third-party alternative, which many OS/390 installations use. ACF has additional features above and beyond those provided by RACF. These security subsystems enable an administrator to set up user accounts and define the access privileges that control access to resources such as data sets.

  Windows 2000, in contrast, uses two industry-standard security architectures, Kerberos Private Key security and *Secure Sockets Layer* (SSL) Public Key security. See Chapter 13, "Security," for more information about Windows 2000 security.

Time-Sharing Option

In the early days, OS/390 supported only batch processing. When IBM eventually started making terminals, they needed to add support for interactive users. To support this requirement, IBM added the *Time-Sharing Option* (TSO) to the operating system. TSO provided only a primitive command-line interface much like the one provided by the DOS-PC operating system discussed in the preceding chapter. IBM subsequently enhanced this capability with an add-on component called the *Structured*

Programming Facility (SPF). SPF provided a pseudo–full-screen interface with input and output panels. IBM provides a predefined set of panels for common functions such as program development (hence its name) and other utility functions. Users and third-party vendors subsequently created and linked-in additional panels to seamlessly integrate additional applications into this interface.

Not a GUI!

It is well to remember that when a full-screen interface is mentioned here, the reference is to a graphical user interface (GUI). A GUI (such as the Windows 2000 Explorer shell) allows direct mouse and keyboard manipulation of programs, directories, and files represented by icons on a metaphorical desktop. Most IBM terminals are character based and send and receive data in block mode. These terminals are only capable of limited local processing. Data to be displayed on these devices is sent to the terminal in a single block of 24 lines of 80 characters. ◆

Communications Device Management

Initially, most businesses did all of their batch data processing and interactive terminal functions at their corporate offices. In this scenario, card readers, line printers, and terminals were just attached directly to a mainframe channel. Eventually, however, these companies developed a need to locate these types of devices at remote branch offices. To meet this need, IBM developed special versions of its interactive terminals that could work over telephone lines. IBM also developed *Remote Job Entry* (RJE) workstations that allowed a device consisting of a card reader and a line printer to be supported the same way.

Mainframe channels and operating system access methods had originally been developed only to support locally attached devices. To support remote devices adequately, special hardware and software access methods had to be developed. The new hardware took the form of communications controllers (such as the IBM 3745) that were locally attached to a mainframe channel on one side and a communications network on the other. These communications devices offload communications processing overhead from the mainframe CPU and channels. Like the mainframe channels discussed later in Chapter 6, these communications controllers are also special-purposes computers designed for communications processing. These devices even run a special dedicated operating system of their own, called the *Network Control Program* (NCP).

To manage these devices at the CPU, IBM developed specialized access methods. The most recent access method that IBM provides for this purpose is the *Virtual Telecommunications Access Method* (VTAM). Chapter 14, "Networking," discusses the communications capabilities of OS/390 and Windows 2000.

Transaction Processing

TSO and SPF were fine for program development and batch job scheduling. However, early attempts to implement highly interactive transaction-processing applications proved that the mainframe operating system was inadequate for this type of processing. To support these types of applications, IBM subsequently added the CICS subsystem in the 1970s. Chapter 15, "Transaction, Database, and Message Processing," will explore Windows 2000 considerations related to CICS.

Teleprocessing Monitors

The fact that early mainframe operating systems could not adequately handle transaction processing was so obvious that many companies, IBM included, developed quite a few software packages to augment the operating system in this area. IBM did a study at one point and determined that they had at least 26 different packages in this category that had been developed for various IBM projects. After completing this study, IBM selected one package as its flagship transaction-processing product. This package was CICS. CICS had originally been developed for an electric power utility Customer Information File project. It allegedly got its somewhat obscure name from that project.

Additional products that originally competed with CICS in this area were Intercomm from Programming Methods Incorporated, and Taskmaster from Turnkey Systems. ◆

To support, store, and forward message processing, IBM also implemented the MQSeries Message-Oriented Middleware (discussed later in Chapter 15). Chapter 15 also discusses the relationship between IBM's MQSeries to the *Microsoft Message Queuing System* (MSMQ) in that chapter.

Database Management

Early file access methods provided simple record access to disk data, based on position of the record in the file or a symbolic key. To add more sophisticated data-management capabilities, IBM and others developed *Database Management Systems* (DBMSs). One of the first DBMSs that IBM produced was the hierarchical *Information Management System* (IMS). Because most business data can be structured in an organizational hierarchy, this was quite useful. IMS databases are still in use in use in many mainframe shops today. A company called Cullinet subsequently implemented a database (IDMS) built according to a different model. Although IMS was good for modeling hierarchical processes and data, real business data is only approximately hierarchical in nature. The network model (on which IDMS was built) allowed data elements to be organized according to a network structure. This was thought to be more flexible and powerful. This DBMS, now owned by Computer Associates, was chosen by many as an alternative to IMS and is also still in use in many mainframe shops today. Based on pioneering work done in its research labs, IBM developed a new database based not on the hierarchical or network models, but on a new relational model. In a Relational database, data is treated as related tables without considering any hierarchical or network relationships. This database, DB/2, is currently the most popular database in use by mainframe shops today. An additional Relational database, sold by Oracle, is also used in some mainframe shops.

Windows 2000

OS/390, in one form or another, has existed for over 30 years. Windows 2000, like Windows NT before it, is a much newer operating system. In recent years, operating system researchers have been promoting the construction of operating systems with a layered object-oriented approach. In this approach, the single monolithic kernel is replaced with a smaller microkernel that provides basic operating system services to higher operating system layers. Windows 2000 is based, at least in part, on this research. Although it is not an object-oriented operating system, it is built with object-oriented techniques and a layered approach.

Windows 2000 Design Objectives

This section looks at some of the design objectives of Windows 2000. As you examine the architecture of Widows 2000, you will begin to understand how well it meets these objectives.

These objectives are as follows:

- Portability
- Extensibility
- Reliability
- Compatibility
- Security
- High performance
- Effective networking

Portability

IBM, SUN, and other operating system vendors sell hardware. Microsoft does not. To maximize the sale of the operating system, Microsoft wanted to make it run on as many hardware platforms as possible. In addition, one of the key selling points of the UNIX operating system is that it has been ported to multiple hardware platforms. It runs on nearly everything from the Intel x86 all the way up to large IBM mainframes. Although it originally ran on MIPS and Power PC hardware as well, it is the currently available only for the Intel x86 and DEC Alpha architectures.

You will see later in this chapter how the internal design of Windows 2000—with its *Hardware Abstraction Layer* (HAL), kernel, and object-oriented approach—lends itself well to porting the operating system to additional platforms. All these considerations led Microsoft to consider portability a major design objective, giving users of Windows 2000 more flexibility in the choice of hardware vendor and platforms.

Until Windows 2000, there were different versions of the operating system for different countries. To reduce the cost of maintenance, Microsoft wanted to have only one version of the operating system for all countries. To accommodate this portability objective, Windows 2000 uses an expanded dual-byte character code internally called Unicode.

Extensibility

Early operating systems were built on a monolithic design. Over time, changes in CPU, bus, and peripheral-device architectures required major operating system changes. Early IBM mainframes, for example, were designed for batch processing. They did not lend themselves well to handling remote terminals and interactive transaction processing (see Chapter 14). For an operating system to be extensible in these areas, Microsoft wanted to make it modular with an architecture that isolated the basic kernel from peripheral devices. Microsoft also wanted to make the operating system extensible in the face of new device types and protocols such as the *Universal Serial Bus* (USB) and the *Intelligent Input/Output* device standard (I2O). Later in this chapter, you will see how Windows 2000 uses a kernel, device drives, and the HAL architecture to accomplish this objective.

Microsoft also had an objective to make the operating system capable of sensing installed hardware and automatically loading the software necessary to support it. A workstation, for instance, should be able to sense whether it is docked or undocked from a docking station. It also should be possible for a server to sense that a new disk or backup device has been installed so that it can make use of it immediately without requiring a reboot. This support is called Plug and Play and is an enhanced version of similar support provided by Windows 95 and Windows 98. It is a very useful feature, but using it is not without its risks. (See the comments in the next section, titled "Reliability.")

Extensibility in Windows 2000 also extends to being able to mimic the behavior of other operating systems. You will see later how Windows 2000 includes support for additional operating system personalities such as Posix, OS/2, and Win16.

Reliability

The predecessors of Windows 2000 were often accused of being unreliable. Experience has shown, however, that most cases of Windows NT operating system unreliability can be traced to either hardware failures or the installation of buggy device drivers. The plug-and-play support in Windows 2000, discussed earlier, is a terrific feature when it works correctly. Because device drivers operate in Kernel mode, a bug in a device driver can easily crash the entire operating system. In an ideal world you could, indeed, upgrade a server while it was serving real users. In practice, however, you risk a system crash by doing this. So, although this is a nice feature, you should probably still perform the upgrade while the server is idle.

The operating system should also protect applications from each other and protect the operating system and hardware from contamination by applications and subsystems. The file system should be reliable even in the face of failures. This should include fault tolerance in the file system and hardware redundancy through clustering.

Another aspect of reliability is the operating system's capability to keep operating, or at least shut down gracefully, in the face of a power failure. Windows 2000 works with the *Advanced Power Management* (APM) features of newer hardware and *Universal Power Supplies* (UPS) to provide this capability.

Compatibility

Microsoft wanted the new operating system to continue to support the large number of 16-bit Windows 3.1 and DOS applications. They also wanted it to continue to be compatible with early OS/2 and Console mode UNIX (Posix) programs. The actual UNIX support in Windows 2000, by itself, is all but useless. Why this is so is discussed later in this chapter, along with a few pointers about what to do if you really need UNIX support. The OS/2 situation, unfortunately, is hopeless.

Security

Any new operating system should provide a secure computing experience. It is important to protect operating system–managed resources such as programs, directories, and files from misuse within the organization. In addition, the possibility of outside access to networks from places like the Internet makes this even more important. To protect these resources, security blocks should protect access to all hardware and operating system resources. All access to system resources should be authenticated by the operating system and only valid accesses allowed. Chapter 13 explains how the security features of Windows 2000 can be used to protect these resources.

High Performance

Microsoft also wanted the new operating system to take full advantage of the 32-bit Intel, 64-bit Alpha, and other future 64-bit architectures. It should also be scalable from the small desktop workstations, up to data-center–sized servers. To support this, it should be capable of multitasking, multiway SMP, and clustering. Chapter 19, "Scalability," covers these issues in detail.

Effective Networking

Most prior operating systems, including Windows, had networking support built in as an afterthought. As with Windows NT before it, Windows 2000 should have networking built in to the operating system and not just added on. It should support all protocols including NetBIOS, TCP/IP, SPX/IPX, and so on, as well as new protocols as they are developed.

The Architecture of Windows 2000

Previous sections discussed the overall objectives that Windows 2000 needed to satisfy. The following sections, discuss the architecture of Windows 2000 and how well it satisfies each of these objectives.

Windows NT is built on a layered client/server model. Operating system components communicate with each other by passing messages that request service and respond to service requests. This holds true for the User-mode subsystems as well as for routines within the operating system executive. To implement this, Windows 2000 supports a highly optimized *Local Procedure Call* (LPC) facility. Much of Windows 2000 is written using *dynamic link libraries* (DLLs). DLLs make it possible to load parts of the operating system on demand instead of having them statically linked and resident in memory all the time. Some parts of Windows 2000 are loaded at startup and kept resident in memory. Other parts can be paged out of memory when not needed.

Just as the bulk of OS/390 is written in a high-level language, the bulk of Windows 2000 is written in C and C++. In addition, Microsoft uses the same code base for all four versions of Windows 2000. These versions differ mainly by the addition of advanced subsystems, utility programs, and advanced features activated by key values in the Windows 2000 Registry.

Figure 2.2 shows the architecture of Windows 2000. This figure shows the relationship of Windows 2000 components to each other and to the hardware on which it runs.

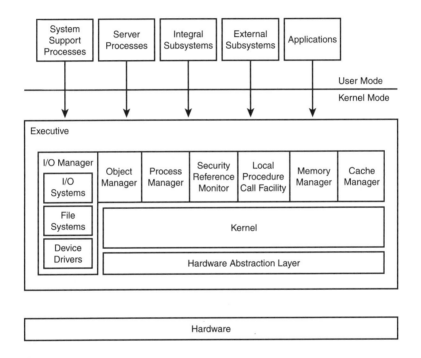

Figure 2.2 *Windows 2000 kernel, executive, and subsystems.*

The remainder of this chapter explains how the components in Figure 2.2 function and interact in Windows 2000.

The Windows 2000 Registry

In previous versions of the operating system, the operating parameters used by applications and various parts of the operating system were stored in initialization files with an .INI extension. When Microsoft developed Windows NT and Windows 95, they changed this to store all these initialization parameters in a common hierarchical database called the Registry. The Registry gathered all the relevant parameters in one place and reduced the number of .INI files scattered around the system disk.

Processes Threads and Jobs

In Windows 2000, units of work are grouped logically into entities called *processes* and *threads*.

A process is the code and data of an executable program together with any resources assigned to it—such as a private address space in which to run, open files, and at least one thread of execution.

A thread is defined by the following:

- A set of instructions that can be executed
- The contents of machine registers that define the context or state of the processor when the thread is running
- Two stacks: one for use in User mode and one for use in Kernel mode

When a process is created, one thread (called the primary thread) is created. As the primary thread executes in the process, it can create additional threads.

All the threads in a process run in the same address space and share the same resources as all threads. Using multiple threads in an application is very efficient because the application can use the multitasking provided by the operating system to do work when one or more of its other threads are blocked. If the application does not make use of multiple threads, the application will give up control to another application when the primary thread blocks.

Because of the efficient nature of creating threads, it was not necessary to resort to developing aids such as teleprocessing monitors for Windows 2000. (You will remember from the earlier OS/390 discussion that the lack of an efficient task-creation mechanism led to the need for products [such as CICS] that did their own internal multitasking.) Chapter 15 examines other reasons for developing this type of software for Windows 2000. Independent processes normally have no relationship to each other. The new Job object, first implemented in Windows 2000, provides a way to group multiple processes together for the purpose of controlling their lifetime and use of system resources, such as disk space and CPU time (see Chapter 9).

Application Programs

All application programs run under the control of one of the Windows 2000 external subsystems discussed later in this chapter. When a program running under Windows 2000 needs a service from the operating system, it issues an *Application Program Interface* (API) request. The types of requests that a given program can issue are based on the type of program. As discussed in the following sections, Windows 2000 supports many different types of APIs. When a program issues an API call, the underlying subsystem converts the API call to an LPC message to request the appropriate service from other subsystems and the executive. If the API call is to access resources on a remote computer, the API call is translated to a *Remote Procedure Call* (RPC) and executed on the remote computer.

Subsystems

As shown in Figure 2.2, Windows 2000 has two types of subsystems: external subsystems and integral subsystems. External subsystems are those subsystems that give the operating system an apparent "personality." They modify the logical view of the operating system to make it appear to support a particular API and to respond as if the program were running in that particular environment. The Win32, Posix, and OS/2 subsystems, for example, all present different views of the operating system to application programs run under those subsystems.

In addition to the external subsystems discussed earlier, Windows 2000 supports several integral subsystems. Integral subsystems provide system-wide services for other subsystems. These subsystems include the Security subsystem, the Secure Logon Process, the Session Manager, and the Networking subsystem.

All subsystems run in User mode, unlike the executive, which runs in Kernel mode. They also run in their own address spaces, just like user applications.

The Win32 Subsystem

The "dominant" personality of Windows NT is the Win32 API provided by the Win32 subsystem. In addition, the Win32 subsystem is responsible for managing all screen, keyboard, and mouse interaction for all the external subsystems. This includes supporting the Windows 2000 desktop. The Windows 2000 desktop is the primary user interface shell that users interact with when operating Windows 2000.

When a request is received to start up a new program, the Win32 subsystem determines the type of program that will be run. If it is a Win32 program, the Win32 subsystem initiates its execution by making the appropriate requests to the executive. This causes the program to be run in a new address space. If it is a 16-bit Windows or DOS program, the Win32 subsystem requests its execution in one of two special virtual machine environments, either the *Windows on Windows* (WOW) environment or the *NT Virtual DOS Machine* (NTVDM) environment.

> ### No OS/390 GUI
>
> GUIs were never implemented in OS/390 because OS/390 predated all but the research lab versions of GUIs. As a result, everything in OS/390 is command-line oriented. Multiple console support and TSO/SPF provide the only non–command-line user interfaces. Even these products still provide only a character-based pseudo–full-screen display interface where commands still have to be entered on a command line. Some third-party add-ons for OS/390, provided by companies such as IBM's Tivoli subsidiary, do provide GUI front ends that can be run on a PC and used to manage OS/390. ◆

16-Bit Windows Applications

The WOW subsystem supports 16-bit Windows applications. Under this subsystem, all 16-bit Windows applications run together in the same address space, just as they did in native 16-bit Windows. In this environment, they do not benefit from the address separation that protects 32-bit Windows applications from each other.

DOS Applications

When a DOS application is run, the operating system sets up a separate address space for each DOS application. Windows 2000 does its best to set up an execution environment that mimics the native DOS environment as closely as possible. Bear in mind, however, that native DOS applications often manipulate the hardware directly. This is not permitted in a secure, reliable operating system environment. Consequently, not all DOS programs will run under Windows 2000. This is a necessary side effect of the desire to make the operating system more reliable, but it does have the effect of limiting compatibility somewhat. This restriction is generally not a problem. Most 16-bit Windows and DOS programs seem to run well under Windows NT and Windows 2000 (except perhaps some games).

OS/2 and Posix Subsystems

Windows 2000 provides two additional subsystems that support an OS/2 and a Posix (UNIX) personality. Unfortunately neither interface is much use as it is. The OS/2 subsystem is only compatible with OS/2 1.2 Character-mode applications. The Posix interface is only compatible with simple Character-mode (non-GUI) UNIX applications. In the case of the OS/2 support provided by Windows 2000, not much can be done to improve its lack of capabilities. Too many versions of OS/2 have gone by since OS/2 1.2.

The story with respect to the Posix subsystem is better. Several vendors, such as Softway Systems, provide third-party products, such as Interix, that can be added to the Posix interface of Windows 2000 to make the Posix subsystem useful if you also have UNIX as part of your operating system mix.

The Security Subsystem

The Windows 2000 Security subsystem, like the ones provided by RACF and ACF under OS/390, is responsible for protecting system resources. The Security subsystem maintains a database of user and group account information. It services requests from the Secure Logon Process and authenticates all entities requesting access (see Figure 2.3). It also assigns a SID to each user or process. This SID is included in an access token, which is used to authenticate the user or process when accessing protected resources. Components of the Security subsystem include the Local Security Authority, the Security Accounts Manager, and the Logon Process. (For more information, see Chapter 13.)

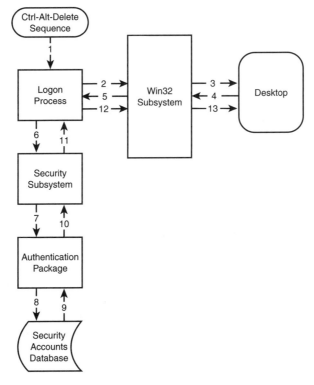

Figure 2.3 *Windows 2000 security processing flow.*

Directory Service Subsystem

The Active Directory service is new in Windows 2000. In previous versions of the operating system, no global directory of resources could be used to locate system-wide resources such as printers, directories, and files. In a widely distributed network with multiple domains, this lack made locating resources and administering users difficult. Also, other vendors such as Novell and Banyan already supported global directories. This made Windows NT look bad by comparison. (Chapter 10, "Catalogs and Directories," examines the Active Directory in detail.)

Note that OS/390 as a centralized mainframe operating system has limited support for distributed resources and therefore no need for a global Directory service.

Networking Subsystem

The Windows 2000 networking architecture implements a layered protocol design. In this design, high-level protocol modules call lower-level modules, which, in turn, interface with the hardware in the form of the *network interface cards* (NICs) installed in the computer. This design makes it possible for Windows 2000 to support many popular networking protocols such as TCP/IP, NetBUI, IPX/SPX, and so on. It also provides *Distributed File System* (DFS) support. In DFS, an application program's view of the file system is extended to directories and files located on remote computers.

In addition, Windows 2000 networking supports the capability of a program or operating system component to call another component running on a different computer. This RPC facility is a distributed version of the LPC facility used internally within Windows 2000.

Contrast this design with the VTAM/NCP design of OS/390 described in Chapter 14. VTAM provides the underlying layers of protocol that higher-level subsystems and applications call for service. The NCP, however, runs on an outboard processor all its own to improve performance and offload work from the mainframe. In Windows 2000 workstations, all these functions normally run directly on the workstation itself. Some intelligent NICs do have local processing capability, however.

The Executive

All the subsystems already discussed run in User mode in their own address spaces. The part of the operating system that runs in Kernel mode is called the Executive. Conceptually it is very much like the OS/390 nucleus. The Executive includes the following components:

- Local Procedure Call facility
- Object Manager
- Security Reference Monitor
- Memory Manager
- Process and Thread Manager
- Input/Output Manager, file system drivers, and device drivers
- Cache Manager

The Local Procedure Call Facility

As mentioned earlier, the architecture of Windows 2000 depends heavily on message passing between subsystems, threads, executive components, and Kernel service routines. The LPC facility provides this capability. The LPC facility is based on an industry-standard RPC facility used to internetwork computers running many other operating systems. It is highly optimized for local communications between components on the same computer. (To my knowledge no other commercial operating systems has extended this technique to internal operating system component intercommunication.)

OS/390, for instance, relies on passing pointers to parameter data to called modules. It implements module calls by a branch instruction and passes parameters to them by passing a parameter address in a register.

OS/390 and Windows 2000 RPCs

Windows 2000 uses its RPC facility to call a program located on another computer. There is an analogous feature in the OS/390 CICS subsystem. The CICS Distributed Transaction Processing (DTP) feature also allows a CICS application program to link to a subprogram located on another CICS system. This feature has existed at least since the late 1980s (see Chapter 15). ◆

Object Manager

Because everything in Windows 2000 is treated like an object, the Object Manager is another key executive component. The Object Manager is responsible for allocating objects, assigning names to them so that they can be referenced by other objects, and protecting them from corruption by multiple users. Objects managed by the Object Manager include Process objects, Thread objects, File objects, File System objects, File Mapping objects, Memory objects, Pipe objects, and Synchronization objects such as semaphores, mutexes, and events.

The Security Reference Monitor

The *Security Reference Monitor* (SRM) works with the Logon Process and the LSA. Its job is to ensure that no object is accessed without the proper authority. It also implements local audit and security policy.

The SRM processes a user logon request. It generates the access token, which includes a user's SID. The SID is used to determine a user's right to access other objects in the system. In this respect, it functions much like RACF and ACF do in OS/390.

Chapter 13 discusses the subject of security more fully.

The Memory Manager
As in OS/390, managing real and virtual memory is the job of the Memory
Manager. The Memory Manager is responsible for translating virtual
addresses into real addresses in memory and translating pages to and
from system page files. (See Chapter 4 for more details.)

Process and Thread Manager
In Windows 2000, units of work are grouped logically into entities called
processes and threads. It is the job of the Process Manager to request the
creation of Process and Thread objects. Every process must have at least
one thread. After their creation, the Process Manager manages the execution of the processes and threads in an orderly fashion based on priority.
The Process Manager has no concept of the hierarchical relationships
of processes. That is left up to the invoking subsystem and could be
implemented differently, for example, by the Win32 and Posix subsystems.

A process is the code and data of an executable program together with
any resources assigned to it such as a private address space in which to run,
open files, and at least one thread of execution. All threads in a process
run in the same address space and share the same resources as the primary
thread.

No Need for Teleprocessing Monitors

*This isn't to say that Teleprocessing Monitors don't exist for Windows 2000. They
do. Teleprocessing, or Transaction Monitors, in the OS/390 world also serve other
purposes. In addition to efficient tasking, they also ensure database integrity by
journaling updates to the databases and by rolling back the updates if all the
updates are not completed successfully. This feature is called* Dynamic Transaction
Coordination (DTC) *and it is part of the reason for the* Microsoft Transaction
Server (MTS). *Chapter 18, "Structuring a Mainframe-like Development
Environment," explains how ports of mainframe teleprocessing packages such as
CICS make it possible to integrate Windows 2000 and OS/390 applications and
development environments together.* ◆

Processes in Windows 2000 have no hierarchical relationship to each other
as they do in OS/390 and UNIX. The Job object, new to Windows 2000,
adds a type of process grouping that can be used to assign some resources
(such as disk quotas and maximum execution time) to a group of processes.
Chapter 9 covers process and thread management.

Note that the concept of Jobs, Job Steps, and Job Control in the OS/390
context is almost completely missing in Windows 2000. Prior versions of
Windows 2000 had only a primitive batch file programming language

inherited from DOS. Windows 2000 does have the *Windows Scripting Host* (WSH), which allows tasks to be scripted in a higher-level language such as VBScript (a dialect of Visual Basic) or JavaScript. Third-party add-ons can also be used to extend this capability.

Input/Output Manager, File System Drivers, and Device Drivers
The Input/Output Manager, as its name implies, supports input/output. The input/output architecture in Windows 2000 is a layered architecture, as illustrated in Figure 2.4.

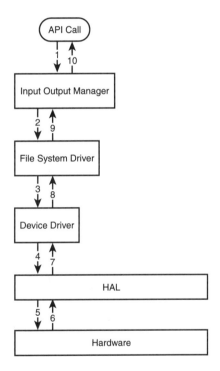

Figure 2.4 *Windows 2000 input/output request processing.*

Applications and subsystems make input/output requests to a file system driver. The file system driver in turn passes the request on to a device driver, which manages the actual device. This provides a set of logical I/O capabilities and presents a simplified interface to applications and subsystems.

The architecture here is somewhat simpler than in the case of OS/390. OS/390 has external I/O channels, device controllers, and devices to manage. It is interesting to note that the System/390 channel architecture, with minor modifications, is the basis for the *Small Computer Systems Interface* (SCSI) design used in servers and other high-performance workstations.

Cache Manager
The Cache Manager works with the Virtual Memory Manager and the I/O Manager to keep recently used application data and program pages in real memory as long as possible. Windows 2000 allocates most of virtual memory for caching and only gives back what other subsystems and applications need. Caching data in memory improves application program I/O performance by satisfying I/O read and write requests from the cache. This reduces program delays due to the number of physical disk I/O operations.

The Kernel
The kernel of Windows 2000 is based on a microkernel design. The kernel provides a small core of essential services to higher-level routines. Upper layers of the operating system then build on these services.

In Windows 2000, the kernel includes basic thread scheduling, multiprocessor scheduling, exception handling, interrupt handling, power-failure handling, and recovery-handling primitives of the operating system.

The Hardware Abstraction Layer
The Windows 2000 HAL sits below the executive and above the hardware. It presents a virtual hardware interface to higher-level modules of the operating system. This isolation makes it possible to implement the same operating system on widely different computer architectures such as those provided by Intel and the Digital Alpha. It also isolates the upper layers of the operating system from most hardware dependencies. It does this by providing a common set of services available on all supported hardware platforms. It also offers a standard mechanism for all kernel code to access the hardware. *Original equipment manufacturers* (OEMs) customize their own HALs to expose the special functionality of their hardware.

Terminal Server
Initially Windows 2000 was developed as a single-user system. Microsoft was eventually faced with the threat of thin workstations in the form of a "Network Computer" design that Oracle and others were pushing. To combat this, Microsoft added support for multiple thin "network workstations" to Windows 2000. In the Windows 200 Terminal Server architecture, these workstations are usually older machines not capable of running Windows 2000 or they are special hardware that run a smaller operating system (Windows CE) in memory or in firmware.

This implementation was based on earlier work done by Citrix in developing a product called WinFrame. Citrix still sells enhancement software to improve and extend the capabilities of Terminal Server.

The Death of the Network Computer?

At press time, the threat of the "network computer" seems to have pretty much evaporated. Terminal Server, however, is still finding use as a replacement for dumb terminals in applications where thin clients are cost effective. In general, Terminal Server and thin terminals will find only limited use in selected applications and environments. ♦

Windows 2000 Boot Process

Just as in the case of OS/390, the Windows 2000 operating system has to get started somehow. Windows 2000 starts when the computer is started. The following assumes an Intel x86–based architecture computer. The Alpha system's boot process is slightly different.

First, the computer performs a standard hardware *Power On Systems Self Test* (POST). Then the master boot record and partition table are read from the device identified as the boot device. The master boot record executes the boot loader program (NTLDR).

NTLDR displays the operating system selection menu. The list of operating systems that can be started is maintained in a file called BOOT.INI. This file may also include an option to boot other operating systems such as Windows 98, OS/2, or Linux. This menu is displayed for a fixed time that can be set by the user via the GUI. During this time period, the user can select an operating system or allow the timeout period to expire. This will select the default operating system, which is normally Windows 2000.

Following operating system selection, the Windows 2000 hardware-detection process (NTDETECT.COM) is run. NTDETECT.COM determines the hardware device drivers to load for that execution of Windows 2000.

After that, the user is given the option to select a startup configuration. If the user has just made a change to a critical component of the operating system, such as the Video or Disk subsystems, the operating system can be rendered unbootable. If this is the case, the user can reboot the system and select execution of a previously saved configuration; called the "Last Known Good" configuration in the Windows 2000 documentation.

Following configuration selection, the executive, kernel, and HAL are loaded and initialized.

Finally, the Windows 2000 Logon Process presents the Secure Logon screen so that the user can log on and begin using the system. Note that while this latter process is going on, the system is also starting up services and subsystems that support the operating system processes.

This chapter discussed how the architectures of OS/390 and Windows 2000 are similar and how they are different. The rest of the chapters in this book explain how these components work together and how they relate to familiar components of OS/390. The next chapter discusses the role that the CPU plays in these two operating systems.

3

Central Processing Units

As discussed in Chapter 1, "Origins and Evolution of OS/390 and Windows 2000," OS/390 is a mature operating system that has been evolving over the last 30+ years. It is a monolithic operating system with a nucleus that interacts directly with the hardware.

In contrast, Windows 2000 is a relatively new operating system, which is based on a layered client/server and microkernel design.

To understand the features of the OS/390 and Windows 2000 operating systems, it's important to understand a bit about the underlying hardware platforms on which they live. This will not be an in depth discussion of the hardware. For that, you can refer to IBM's Enterprise Systems Architecture 390 Principles of Operation (SA22-7201) or the Intel Architecture Software Developers Manual. Although Windows 2000 runs on other architectures, such as the Digital Alpha line of processors, most installed systems run on Intel processors. This book concentrates on Windows 2000 running on the Intel platform, referred to here as the x86 architecture.

OS/390 Processors

OS/390 runs on the System/390 family of processors. The architecture of the IBM System 360/370/390 family has remained remarkably consistent over the years in terms of word sizes and instruction formats. The architecture of the System/390 is comprised of one or more CPUs, external memory, and an outboard I/O subsystem consisting of external channels, device controllers, and devices. The CPU interfaces with each of these components. Figure 3.1 symbolically shows the System/390 CPU architecture.

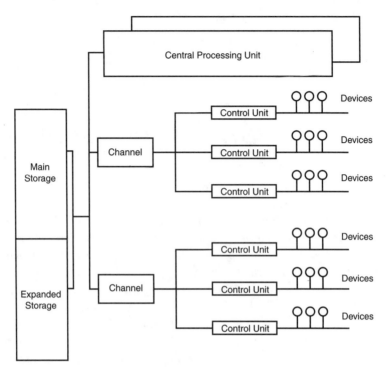

Figure 3.1 *System 390 CPU architecture.*

The remainder of this section addresses considerations such as: how data is represented in the CPU, the types of instructions executed by the CPU, and how it performs arithmetic on these data types. In addition, this section covers how the CPU handles interrupts, how the internal registers of the CPU are used to support arithmetic as well as program context switching, procedure calling, I/O operations, and multiprocessing.

Data Representation

The CPU accesses external memory to retrieve instructions and data and to store the results of calculations.

Memory is represented in units of 8-bit bytes. Data is encoded using the *Extended Binary Coded Decimal Interchange Code* (EBCDIC). Although memory is byte addressable in System/390, it is also word oriented, thanks to the size of CPU registers and the lengths of instructions. The natural word size of System/390 is 32 bits.

The bits in a byte and the bytes in a word are numbered from left to right. The sign, if present, is in the leftmost bit (see Figure 3.2).

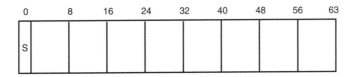

Figure 3.2 *System/390 byte ordering.*

Code of the System/390

Note that the internal code of the System/390 is EBCDIC and not the American Standard Code for Information Interchange *(ASCII) or the Unicode character set used internally by Windows 2000.* ◆

Arithmetic Data

Arithmetic data units are made up of bytes. The types of arithmetic data units include the following:

- *Binary short*—Integers consisting of a sign bit and a 31-bit value
- *Binary long*—Integers consisting of a sign bit and a 63-bit value
- *Packed decimal*—Numbers appearing as strings of digits that encode two 4-digit decimal numbers in each byte using the *Binary Coded Decimal* Interchange Code (BCD)
- *Zoned (unpacked) decimal*—Numbers that hold a string of BCD-encoded digits where the upper half-byte holds a zone character and the lower half-byte holds a BCD digit
- *Short floating point*—Numbers that contain a sign bit, a 7-bit exponent, and a 24-bit fractional value
- *Long floating point*—Numbers that are the same as short floating-point numbers, except that the fraction also takes up the following 32-bits for greater precision

Instruction Execution

Instructions, like data, are stored in external memory. They are brought into the memory execution unit of the CPU to be executed together with the necessary operands and data. The consequence of this execution may result in data being stored back into memory. An Add Register instruction, for example, takes two operands. The first operand is the name of a register holding the first number. The second operand is the memory address of the second number to be added to the first.

Each instruction contains an operation code and up to three operands that refer to internal registers or memory locations. Instruction execution proceeds sequentially from one instruction to the next in memory unless the program explicitly modifies this sequence.

CPU Registers

To perform its function efficiently, the System/390 CPU uses a limited amount of high-speed internal register storage. These registers are used for arithmetic, memory addressing, loop control, string moves, and procedure calls.

System/390 has 16, 32-bit general registers. There are also four, 64-bit floating-point registers used to perform floating-point arithmetic. In addition, there are a number of control registers.

Procedure Calling

Normally, OS/390 uses general registers 1, 13, 14, and 15 for program linkage. The address of a parameter list is usually passed in register 1. Register 15 is normally loaded with the entry point of the routine to be called. A *Branch and Link Register* (BALR 14,15) instruction is then issued to pass control to the called program. This instruction stores the return address in register 14. When the called program is complete, it can return to the caller by branching back to the address in register 14. Because a called program may reuse some of the registers, their contents must be saved before a program is called. To do this, the OS/390 calling convention defines register 13 as a pointer to a register save area. Called programs, in turn, set up save areas following the same convention. These save areas are all chained together in memory so that a memory dump can be used to reconstruct the calling history of the program.

Memory Addressing

As discussed in the preceding section, CPU registers are implemented in high-speed memory. Because high-speed memory is expensive, the number of CPU registers is limited. Less expensive, more plentiful memory is used to store larger amounts of data. Instructions and data have to be loaded into the CPU registers from memory.

Memory is addressed by location starting from low memory addresses and proceeding to higher addresses. Memory addressing is done in one of two modes: Real mode or Virtual mode.

In Real mode, an address in an instruction maps directly to a specific address in the external memory unit. This was the only method supported by early versions of this hardware and software. (For more information, see Chapter 1, "The Origins and Evolution of OS/390 and Windows 2000.")

In Virtual mode, the address in an instruction is translated to a real memory address through the use of page tables and a special hardware *Dynamic Address Translation* (DAT) unit. Thus, it is possible to map the same logical address to different physical addresses. This feature is used to protect applications from each other by giving each application its own address space separate and distinct from other applications in the system. A bug in one program can abort that program, for example, and can even cause an entire batch job to fail. It will not, however, affect any other jobs or interactive tasks in the system.

The mode in which the CPU is executing is determined by the setting of a bit in the Program Status Word of the CPU. Application programs generally operate in Problem Program state using addresses that they think are real. These addresses are really virtualized by the operating system and the architecture hardware.

Memory Addressing and Backward Compatibility

Initially, System/360 and 370 used the low-order 24 bits of an address to represent a storage location, and the high-order byte as a flag byte. This allowed addressing a maximum of 16MB of memory. To provide a larger address space for programs, this was eventually changed to allow 31 out of 32 bits to be used for addressing. This allows addressing up to 2GB of memory.

Because CPU architecture of earlier applications could not address above 16MB, the design of the operating system had to be backward compatible with these programs. The second half of this chapter explains how the x86 architecture has its own backward-compatibility requirements.

This explains why there are duplicate areas above and below the 16MB line for both the operating system and the application (see Figure 3.3). ◆

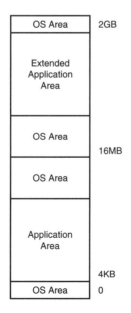

Figure 3.3 *OS/390 address space layout.*

Processor Context

In any multitasking operating system, the state of the CPU must be saved and restored as different processes receive and lose control. This state is called the processor context. The processor context is defined in a special register called the *Program Status Word* (PSW).

Although this discussion doesn't examine the PSW in detail, the PSW does contain some interesting elements. One of these is the address of the next instruction to be executed. Another field in the PSW indicates whether this address is a real or a virtual address.

To prevent applications from executing privileged instructions that should only be executed by the operating system, the PSW has a flag, which indicates whether the CPU is executing instructions in supervisor or problem program state. In problem program state, the CPU is prohibited from executing certain protected instructions. In supervisor state, all instructions are valid. The PSW also specifies whether interruption of the processor is allowed during the current instruction.

Allowing an application program to modify the control registers that specify the location of the OS/390 page tables, for example, could defeat the memory protection provided by the operating system. Likewise, allowing an application program to change the PSW directly would put the application program in supervisor state where it would then be free to execute any instruction, whether privileged or nonprivileged.

Interrupt Handling

As discussed earlier, in a multiprogramming operating system, the processor context must be saved and restored rapidly. Interrupts are used to signal the processor that a change is required. In addition, the processor must respond to interrupts from external I/O devices as well as internally generated interrupts, whether due to program errors or other conditions requiring immediate attention.

The CPU has to respond to interrupts. Interrupts can occur for a number of reasons. They can be due to the completion of an I/O operation, a Supervisor Call request, an external interrupt, or a hardware error. They can also be used to report programming problems, such as a memory protection exception or the use of invalid data for the current instruction. When an interrupt occurs, the interrupt code is stored in the PSW. Based on this code, the operating system and/or application program can determine the cause of the interrupt.

Some (but not all) interrupts can be masked off by bits in the System Mask field of the PSW. When an interrupt occurs, the CPU must service the interrupt. Interrupts are handled in a predefined priory order.

Input/Output

One type of interrupt is generated by an external I/O device when it requires servicing. Fields in the PSW indicate whether the CPU can be interrupted at any point in time.

As previously discussed, System/390 offloads I/O processing to special-purpose outboard computers called channels. These channels can receive an I/O program (called a *channel program*) from the host when the application issues a Start-IO instruction. The channel executes the channel program independently and only interrupts the host when it needs additional channel programs to execute or when the I/O operation is complete.

Multiprocessing

The System/390 Parallel Sysplex architecture supports both tightly coupled and loosely coupled multiprocessing.

Tightly coupled multiprocessors share the execution of a single copy of an operating system. Tightly coupled multiprocessing normally comes in two flavors: Asymmetric Multiprocessing and *Symmetric Multiprocessing* (SMP).

In SMP, the operating system treats processors as equal resources. The operating system can use any free processor to execute the next instruction to be executed.

In Asymmetric Multiprocessing, some of the processors specialize in executing specific classes of instructions. An I/O processor, for example, can only execute I/O instructions.

In a loosely coupled multiprocessing system, each processor runs its own copy of an operating system. These operating systems cooperate on performing parts of a job, usually sharing memory or external I/O devices. This type of multiprocessing is normally called clustering.

System/390 supports both SMP and clustering, as does Windows 2000. Windows 2000, as discussed later, supports only tightly coupled SMP. Chapter 19, "Scalability," compares the Parallel Sysplex multiprocessing architecture of OS/390 with Windows 2000 SMP and Wolfpack clustering.

Windows 2000 and the Intel x86 Architecture

Just as the preceding section examined the features of the System/390 CPU, this section looks at the equivalent features of the Intel x86 CPU. You will notice a lot of similarities and a few major differences.

As discussed in the introduction to this chapter, Windows 2000 runs on multiple architectures such as the Intel x86 family and the Digital Alpha line of processors. Most of the installed base, however, is running on the Intel x86 family of processors. Windows 2000 runs on all members of this family from the 80486 up to the latest Pentium II and Pentium III processors. In practice, however, you should not even think of running the workstation version of Windows 2000 (Professional) on a system with less than a 233MHz Pentium processor. You should also have at least a 300MHz Pentium processor to run the entry-level server version of Windows 2000.

Hardware Requirements

Microsoft publishes a Hardware Compatibility List (HCL) to identify systems and components that are compatible with Windows 2000. You should check this list before installing Windows 2000 on any system. If you do use a system that is not on this list, you may not be able to get support from Microsoft when problems occur. ◆

Architecture

The Intel x86 architecture, like the System/390 architecture, has remained fairly constant over the years.

As discussed in Chapter 2, "Operating System Architecture," Windows 2000 makes use of a HAL to present a virtual computer interface to upper layers of the operating system. This makes it possible to implement the same operating system on widely different computer architectures such as the Intel x86 and the DEC Alpha. It will be useful to understand the relationship of Windows 2000 to the Intel x86 architecture. As in the case of System/390, this chapter covers the essential aspects of this hardware, thereby providing a basis for discussing the upper layers and services provided by Windows 2000.

Figure 3.4 shows the hardware architecture of a computer system based on the Intel x86 architecture.

This architecture consists of one or more CPUs, external memory, memory caches, I/O controllers, and devices. The CPU interfaces with each of these components via a common bus. This architecture mimics the design of its bigger brother, the mainframe, except that the I/O subsystem has very little intelligence of its own. Therefore, the low-level I/O processing handled by Sytem/390 channels has to be taken care of by the CPUs themselves. An exception to this is the SCSI controller and device architecture preferred on Windows 2000 servers. The SCSI architecture was pattered after the IBM System/360 channel architecture. SCSI controllers and devices mimic the channels of mainframe systems, although they are not nearly as fast or complete.

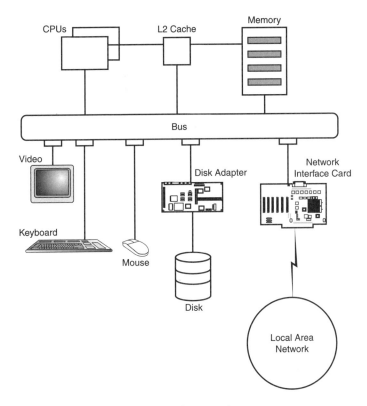

Figure 3.4 *Intel x86 architecture.*

Data Representation

The x86 memory is organized into units based on an 8-bit byte, just like System/390. Bit positions, however, are numbered from right to left.

The x86 also has a word size based on the size of the registers and instructions that are used to process data. The natural word size of the x86 processor is 32 bits.

An x86 word has the high- and low-order bytes reversed so that the low-order byte of the word precedes the high-order byte. Note that this is the opposite of System/390 byte ordering, as illustrated in Figure 3.5.

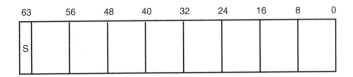

Figure 3.5 *x86 byte ordering.*

An 8-bit byte can contain one character. In the case of this architecture, however, a character is encoded with the ASCII character code used internally by Windows 2000. The EBCDIC character set is not used. (Internally, Windows 2000 uses the double-byte Unicode character set to represent most data strings. This supports foreign languages that require more than 8 bits to represent a character.)

The x86 supports arithmetic with signed and unsigned values and both long and short integers. It also supports arithmetic with long and short floating-point numbers.

Instructions

As in the case of System/390, data and instructions are brought into the memory execution unit of the computer to be executed together with the necessary operands and data. Also like the System/390, an instruction can have up to three operands. Instruction execution proceeds sequentially unless the order of execution is modified by branch instructions.

Registers

Like the System/390, the x86 processor uses a set of high-speed internal registers. Although they can be used as general registers, they also have special purposes. Some registers are accumulators for performing arithmetic, for instance; other registers are for handling addressing, loop control, and string move operations. Still others are used to manage the two-processor stacks used by Windows 2000 to support User-mode and Kernel-mode processing.

The Blue Screen of Death

Unless you are a developer, you probably don't need to concern yourself with registers. There is, however, one case where you might need to understand them. OS/390 can present you with a memory dump when a serious error occurs. In like fashion, Windows 2000 will present you with the infamous Blue Screen of Death! This is, of course, nothing more than a register dump together with some additional information. It can be used to troubleshoot a problem just as an OS/390 dump can be used. ◆

Procedure Calling

The OS/390 architecture discussed in the preceding section used the general registers of the System/390 to affect procedure calls. The Intel x86 architecture has special hardware to support a hardware/software stack mechanism.

The stack architecture of the x86 represents a fundamental difference between it and the System/390 architecture, because System/390 has no hardware support for stacks.

In the x86 architecture, the stack is used to pass parameters and return addresses to a called subroutine. It is also used to allocate local storage when in a called module. This makes releasing local storage and temporary parameters fast. This feature is an improvement over the support for local memory allocation and procedure calling provided by System/390.

Windows 2000 uses two stacks for each process. One stack is used when the process is operating in User mode. The other is used when the process is operating in Kernel mode. The *stack* is an area of memory used in descending order. The "base" of the stack is pointed to by the *stack base pointer* (SBP) register. It points to the highest memory location occupied by the stack. As entries are added to the stack, it grows downward toward lower memory locations. Note that this is just the opposite of normal memory, which is allocated in an upward direction.

The PUSH and POP instructions are used to push new values onto the stack and pop them off again. The stack's current *location pointer* (ESP) register points to the last allocated entry in the stack. To add an entry, the PUSH instruction only has to increment the current stack pointer and then use that address as the target of a move instruction to add the data to the stack. To pop a value off the stack after it is no longer needed, the POP instruction just has to decrement the pointer (see Figure 3.6).

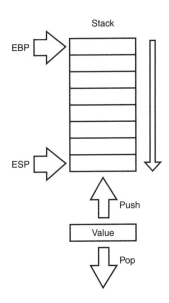

Figure 3.6 *Stacks.*

Memory Addressing

Like System/390, x86 processors address memory from low to higher locations. Memory addresses can be either real or virtual. Windows 2000 processes normally execute in Virtual Memory mode.

Earlier Microsoft operating systems based on the x86 architecture used a 16-bit register size and had to address memory with a segment pointer, plus an offset from the address pointed to by the segment pointer. This required different registers to be set up to point to code, data, and stack segments. The net effect of this architecture was that it required roughly twice the number of instructions to perform a task. Current models of the x86 processor provide the flat 32-bit memory model. The flat 32-bit memory model is the one used by Windows 2000.

Address Space

Windows 2000 makes use of virtual memory management techniques to provide a private address space for each process, very much like OS/390.

In the x86 architecture, a 32-bit address is used to define a 4GB address space. Of this address, 31 bits define a user address space of up to 2GB. The high-order (32nd) bit allows the definition of a 2GB system address space as well. (Note that in the Enterprise Edition of Windows 2000, this can be adjusted to allow a 3GB user address space for large applications such as SQL Server that run best with a lot of memory allocated. In this case, the operating system is restricted to a 1GB address space.) Figure 3.7 shows how Windows 2000 allocates this address space.

Virtual memory addresses are resolved to real addresses through the use of page tables. These page tables are used to define a separate address space for each process. This protects the processes in the system from each other and protects the operating system from wayward processes. The next chapter discusses this in more detail.

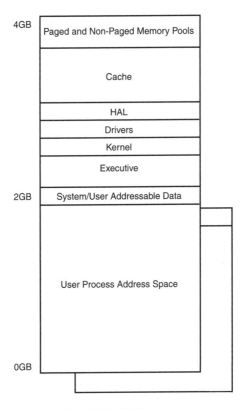

Figure 3.7 *Address space.*

Processor Context

As in the case of OS/390, the state of an x86 CPU hosting Windows 2000 must be saved and restored as different processes receive and relinquish control. This state is called the processor context.

Windows 2000 uses the hardware-protection capabilities of the x86 processor to define two operating levels: User mode and Kernel mode. In Kernel mode, all instructions and the addressing of all memory locations and I/O ports are valid. In User mode application, code can address only the address space of its own process and it cannot address I/O ports directly. This requires, for instance, that all I/O go through the operating system. Thus, the operating system can synchronize I/O requests from multiple applications running at the same time. The x86 processor has a status register that controls the operating mode.

Interrupt Handling

As in the case of OS/390, the context of each user process must be saved and restored rapidly. Also like the System/390 processor, interrupts are used to signal that a change is required. In addition, the x86 processor must respond to interrupts from external I/O devices as well as internally generated interrupts due to program errors or other conditions requiring immediate attention.

Interrupts can occur for a number of reasons. These reasons can be the completion of an I/O operation, a program error, a deliberate interrupt by a program, or a hardware error.

Like OS/390 running on a System/390 processor, Windows 2000 also makes use of interrupts on the x86 processor. There are two types of interrupts: hardware and software. Interrupts on OS/390 are controlled by mask bits in the PSW. Interrupts in the x86 architecture are controlled by an interrupt priority scheme. Each CPU executes instructions at an *interrupt request level* (IRQL).

When an interrupt occurs from a source with an IRQL higher than the current IRQL, the executing thread is interrupted and the interrupt is handled. The IRQLs used by Windows 2000 running on the x86 processor are shown in the following table. This is a fairly complex subject and one addressed only briefly in this book. For a more detailed treatment of the subject, refer to *Windows NT Device Driver Development* (Viscarola & Mason, Macmillan Technical Publishing, 1999, ISBN 1-57870-058-2). The following table is taken from page 122 of the "Interrupt Request Levels and DPCs" chapter of that publication.

Table 3.1   Windows NT IRQL Names

IRQL Mnemonic	Numeric Value	Example of Usage
HIGH_LEVEL	31	NMI, machine check
POWER_LEVEL	30	Power-failure handling
SYNCH_LEVEL	30	Synchronization level
IPI_LEVEL	29	Interprocessor interrupts
CLOCK2_LEVEL	28	Clock handing
PROFILE_LEVEL	27	Profile timer
	12–27	Device IRQs on some x86 systems
DISPATCH_LEVEL	2	Dispatcher and DPCs
APC_LEVEL	1	Kernel APC handling; paging
PASSIVE_LEVEL	0	Ordinary thread execution in both Kernel and User modes

User threads normally execute while the processor is running at IRQL PAS-SIVE_LEVEL. Any device or condition assigned a higher interrupt level can interrupt this process and preempt the CPU. Interrupts at the same level or a lower level cannot interrupt the CPU. An ordinary clock tick, which occurs at IRQL 28, for example, will interrupt the current thread briefly so that the system timer can be updated. While servicing an interrupt, the IRQL of the processor is raised to the level of the interrupt. This means that interrupts from devices and other sources with a lower IRQL cannot interrupt the processor until the processor interrupt level drops back below the level of the new interrupt. This ensures that high-priority interrupts, such as a power-failure interrupt, get serviced before any lower-priority interrupts.

Note in the table that some interrupts are hardware related (HIGH_LEVEL, POWER_LEVEL, and so on) and some interrupts are software related (DISPATCH_LEVEL, APC_LEVEL, and so forth). As an example, Windows 2000 raises the IRQL to DISPATCH_LEVEL when the operating system thread dispatcher is determining the next thread to run. Any lower-level interrupts that occur will not be serviced until the processor level is lowered.

HIGH_LEVEL is used to mask off all other interrupts. One of the things that can signal this level interrupt is when a virtual memory reference maps to a page that is not yet in memory. This interrupt, also called a page fault, causes the operating system to attempt to load the required page into memory. If it is a valid reference, the page will be loaded and the interrupted thread resumed. If it is not a valid reference, the thread will be aborted with an error. (For more information, see Chapter 4, "Memory Management.")

Some errors are more important than others, and some are considered so serious that the operating system cannot be allowed to continue operation. IRQL_LESS_THAN_OR_EQUAL is a dreaded error message that pops up when Windows 2000 halts after displaying the Blue Screen of Death discussed in a previous sidebar. This just means that an interrupt occurred at an invalid level. It is normally caused by a hardware error or a buggy device driver.

I/O Instructions

As in the case of OS/390, the CPU has instructions used to perform I/O. Unlike OS/390, however, the x86 processor must handle most of the I/O processing itself. Chapter 6, "Input/Output Device Management," discusses the Windows NT Input/Output subsystem and how it fits into the architecture of Windows 2000.

I²O

The Intelligent Input/Output Architecture (I²O) standard for intelligent peripherals is supported by Windows 2000. This standard supports intelligent I/O devices, which can offload I/O processing to special dedicated processors. Sounds a lot like an OS/390 channel, doesn't it? ◆

The x86 architecture connects the CPUs and memory units with a high-speed bus. Adapter cards plug in to the bus and are used to control attached devices. These devices can be used to control a disk. They can also be used to control an external tape drive, or the interface to a local area network.

Note that under Windows 2000, programs cannot access I/O device ports directly. They must perform their I/O via the operating system. This protection has a negative side. It also prevents some 16-bit DOS and Windows applications from executing correctly under Windows 2000.

DOS applications normally have the entire computer at their disposal when they execute. Windows 2000 runs multiple programs at the same time, and must protect them from each other. This limitation is a necessary side effect of the protected operating system environment. Most applications, with the exception of games, have already been converted to Windows 95, 98, NT, or Windows 2000. Windows 2000 also supports the Direct-X graphics API, primarily to support future game development so that even this limitation can be eliminated.

Multiprocessing

As in the case of OS/390, Windows 2000 can run on a system with multiple processors. You will recall that the OS/390 section defined tightly and loosely coupled multiprocessing architectures, and also distinguished between SMP and Asymmetric Multiprocessing. Windows 2000 supports only tightly coupled SMP. It does not support any form of Asymmetric Multiprocessing. It also supports loosely coupled multiprocessing in the form of computer clusters through the Wolfpack clustering architecture.

The Windows 2000 operating system treats each processor in a tightly coupled SMP configuration as a resource to be dispatched to execute instructions. Only one copy of the operating system is run on all the processors. The instructions of a running process may run on one processor in one time-slice and on another processor during the next time-slice. It is also possible for a program to be written to favor one processor. This feature is called *Processor Affinity*. High-performance applications, such as SQL Server, have been written to take advantage of this feature.

This chapter discussed the role of the CPUs in a modern computer system running either OS/390 or Windows 2000. The next chapter explains how memory management is handled in OS/390 and Windows 2000.

4

Memory Management

This chapter examines the use of memory in OS/390 and Windows 2000. Memory, next to peripheral storage, is the most important resource in any computer system. In fact, memory performance is a function of the speed of memory plus the performance of the I/O subsystem, as this chapter explains.

OS/390 Memory Management

OS/390, like Windows 2000, is a demand-paged virtual memory operating system. Although they differ a little in the details of implementation, they both do pretty much the same thing. This discussion begins with a review of virtual memory management in OS/390—including topics such as program memory requests, page management, swap files, and mapped I/O—and then compares these to the same types of features appearing in Windows 2000.

Program Memory Requests

The preceding chapter discussed how the System/390 CPU accesses memory. This chapter focuses in more detail on how this memory is used by the operating system.

Initially when a region is allocated for the execution of a job step, all the memory in the region is unallocated. The initiator allocates some of this memory as it loads the program and control blocks associated with the job step. The memory remaining free in the region, when the program begins to execute, is available for allocation by the program.

OS/390 programs request and free memory via the memory management APIs provided by the operating system. Direct access to these APIs is provided to assembly language programs. These APIs are defined in the IBM publication "OS/390 MVS Assembler Services Reference" (IBM publication number GC28-1910-03). The most commonly used APIs are Getmain and Freemain, as illustrated in the following code excerpt:

```
GETMAIN RC,LV=1000
FREEMAIN  RC,LV=1000,ADDRESS=(1)
```

Getmain

The Getmain API request is used to allocate a block of data from one of several storage pools maintained by the operating system. In OS/390 a virtual memory address uses 31 bits, which can address up to 2GB. Getmain requests allocate memory in multiples of 8 bytes up to this limit. Some Getmain parameters can be used to specify the size of the area requested and the storage pool from which to allocate it.

Storage requests can be conditional or unconditional. A conditional request will return an error code to the program and allow the program to continue execution even if the request cannot be satisfied. An unconditional request must be satisfied or the program will be terminated.

Typically, a program requests memory to support its processing, does its processing, and then releases the memory back to the operating system. If there is not enough memory in the storage pool to satisfy the request and the request is unconditional, the operating system program will abort the program. This can be caused by a buggy program that allocates memory but does not free it when it should. This condition is called a *memory leak* and can affect Windows 2000 programs as well.

Freemain

The Freemain API request is used to release the memory allocated by Getmain. When the memory is freed, it becomes available for reallocation. Free memory blocks in the region are chained together and consolidated whenever possible to minimize fragmentation. Fragmentation is bad because there may not be a large enough block of contiguous memory to satisfy a new request even when there is enough total free memory to satisfy the request.

High-level languages, such as COBOL and C, encapsulate these APIs in higher-level language constructs. COBOL programs cannot allocate memory dynamically, for example. All memory is allocated statically at the time that the program is loaded. C programs, on the other hand, provide the malloc and free memory management library functions to allocate and free memory.

Page Management

As discussed in Chapter 2, "Operating System Architecture," OS/390 is a virtual memory operating system. Memory references use virtual addresses. These addresses must be mapped into real addresses by the operating system and hardware. This mapping is performed by the page management component of the operating system.

A virtual address is converted to a real address by the operating system assisted by the *Dynamic Address Translation* (DAT) feature of the hardware. This feature is used to map virtual addresses to real addresses. To do this, OS/390 uses a page table to keep track of page locations and references. If the target page is present in memory, execution continues. If a referenced target page is not present in memory, a page fault interrupt occurs. This signals the operating system that the page containing the referenced data must be brought into memory. (For more information, see the discussion of interrupts in Chapter 3, "Central Processing Units.")

OS/390 uses both demand paging and segmentation to manage memory. Demand paging is used to simulate a larger address space than the one that actually exists. Segmentation is used to roll out whole applications when they become idle for a long period of time.

OS/390 uses a 4KB page size and a 1MB segment size. OS/390 can manage up to 2,048 memory segments. Each memory segment can contain to up to 256 pages.

In the event that a page has to be replaced in memory, OS/390 uses a *Least Recently Used* (LRU) replacement strategy to decide which page to replace. OS/390 looks at each frame periodically. If the frame's reference bit is set, the reference bit is cleared and the time since last reference is cleared. This indicates that the frame has been referenced recently and that it is not a good candidate to be replaced.

If, on the other hand, the reference bit is clear, that indicates that the frame has not been referenced recently. In this case, OS/390 increments the time to show how long the frame has been unreferenced. The frame eventually chosen will be the one with the longest time since the last reference or the LRU page.

In general, this works out well, because programs normally execute one instruction after another proceeding through ascending memory locations in a page. If a program's page reference pattern is more random, this algorithm can cause poor performance by causing pages to be moved in and out of memory frequently. This contributes to a high paging rate and could result in a condition known as *thrashing*—that is, the system is spending most of its time performing paging operations and not doing useful work.

Page and Swap Files

To provide storage for pages that cannot be in memory at any point in time, OS/390 uses page-backing files located on one or more disk volumes. Normally these are dedicated devices allocated for this purpose at the time that the operating system is configured. As the next section shows, Windows 2000 also uses paging files.

In addition to paging files, OS/390 uses swap files. Swap files are used to hold whole program segments that have been rolled out of memory. A program waiting for an operator to reply to a tape mount message may be swapped completely out of memory, for example, to free up resources for program execution. Figure 4.1 shows an example of OS/390 paging. In Figure 4.1, pages F and J have been paged out to disk. In order to page them into memory, some other pages must be replaced.

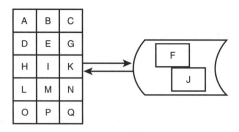

Figure 4.1 *OS/390 paging.*

Unless you are a programmer the only control you have over the amount of OS/390 memory allocated to a job or step is the job or Execute JCL statement region-size parameters. Chapter 9, "Job and Task Management," discusses the JCL of OS/390 and its relationship to Windows 2000.

Memory-Mapped I/O

Although this is a chapter on memory, it is necessary to mention I/O here because of the close relationship between memory and I/O as implemented in OS/390 dataspaces and hiperspaces.

In early versions of the mainframe operating system, memory was relatively scarce compared to disk space. More recent versions of the operating system can support larger real and virtual memory sizes. OS/390 supports the mapping of data files into up to 15 private address spaces. This reduces the address space requirements of any process that needs to access this data. This use of *Hiperspaces* and *Dataspaces* in OS/390 is implemented using the paging mechanism of the operating system. This paging mechanism is used to memory-map a file into memory so that all the file need not be in memory at the same time.

This technique is often used for temporary work files such as Sort Work files. The use of the paging mechanism works out well because data access, like program access, is normally sequential. Access normally starts at the beginning of a file and proceeds through successive records until the program reaches the end of the file.

The use of Hiperspaces and Dataspaces in OS/390 closely parallels the use of memory-mapped files in Windows 2000.

Windows 2000 Memory Management

Windows 2000, like OS/390, is a demand-paged virtual memory operating system. Just as in the case of OS/390, system performance is a function of memory performance and disk performance.

Program Memory Requests

Windows 2000 programs ultimately request memory using the Win32. API VirtualAlloc and VirtualFree are the most often used API calls. See the following code excerpt for an example.

```
pMem=VirtualAlloc(nBytes, MEM_RESERVE MEM_COMMIT, PAGE_READWRITE);
VirtualFree(pMem, nBytes, FreeType);
```

VirtualAlloc is used to allocate a range of pages in the virtual address space of the calling process. Parameters can be used to specify whether memory is completely committed or whether the pages are just reserved for the processes' use (as discussed later). VirtualAlloc can also specify additional parameters such as whether the allocated memory is read-write or read-only and whether writes to it are cached.

VirtualFree is used to release a range of pages in the virtual address space of the calling process. It has parameters that can be used to specify the starting address and size of the page region to be freed. It can also be used to decommit a range of pages without freeing them (as discussed later).

Objects in memory are allocated from one of two memory pools. The *paged pool* is used for objects that can be paged into and out of memory. The *non-paged pool* is used for system objects that cannot be paged out of memory.

Just as in the case of COBOL programs under OS/390, high-level language Windows 2000 programs are provided with libraries of access routines that shield them from the intricacies of dealing with the Win32 API directly. C programs, for instance, have the standard *malloc* and *free* functions used to allocate and free memory.

Memory is allocated and used in several stages. A range of memory addresses can be reserved by a process, but not physically allocated in a paging file. The advantage of this type of operation is speed, because it involves updating in-memory page tables only. Prior to using a memory range, the application must *commit* the memory. This actually allocates backup storage in a paging file.

After the program has finished with the memory, it can (and should) free it. By doing so, the program releases the pages in the paging file and the page frames in memory for reuse.

Note that memory is a precious commodity. A well-behaved program should allocate only the memory that it needs when it needs it. It should also free the memory when it is through using it. Memory requests should be matched with memory releases. A program that runs for a long time and continues to allocate memory without freeing it is said to have a *memory leak*. A severe memory leak will lead to a system failure and the need to reboot Windows 2000. Tracking down memory leaks in applications, or in operating system components, is a difficult process.

Additional efficiency techniques used by Windows 2000 are Lazy Write and Copy-on-Write.

With Lazy Write, the Windows 2000 OS defers the writing of updated (dirty) pages out to the paging file until the system is relatively idle. The program can, of course, override this using a Write-Through flag when it opens the file. It can also flush the pages to disk using the API. This Lazy Write feature improves program performance by returning immediately to the program when a write request is issued.

Lazy Write is not without its dangers, however. If the system crashes, or if the computer is turned off before the data is actually written to disk, file corruption can occur. Therefore, it is extremely important to perform a controlled shutdown of a Windows 2000 system. The normal Windows 2000 shutdown process will flush unwritten data to disk before halting the operating system.

Windows 2000 also defines read/write pages initially as Copy-on-Write. A Copy-on-Write page is shared as long as all processes perform read-only access to the page. A soon as a process attempts to modify the page, it gets its own private copy. This is efficient because it maximizes sharing and defers the creation of a private copy of the page until the first update reference is made to it. This feature minimizes the total number of memory pages in use at any one point in time, and thereby allows more processes to run simultaneously.

Page Management

Pages that are not in memory exist in one of two places. Writable data pages are assigned a location in one of the paging files. Executable code and non-writable data do not take up space in the paging files because they can be loaded from the original executable program image.

As in the case of OS/390, Windows 2000 uses page tables to translate virtual to real addresses. In the case of Windows 2000, a 32-bit address is used to locate a page table entry. The page table entry contains the address of the appropriate page frame and the byte offset into that page. Figure 4.2 illustrates this.

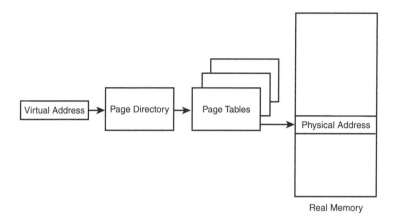

Figure 4.2 *Windows 2000 page tables.*

Windows 2000 maintains pages on one of several lists: Free, In Use, Modified, or Standby.

- *Free*—A free page is one whose page frame can be stolen to load another page.
- *In Use*—An in use page is owned by an active thread.
- *Modified*—A modified page is in use and has been modified by an active thread. In this case, the page would have to be rewritten to be preempted.
- *Standby*—A page marked as standby has already been saved to disk so that it can be reused if necessary.

When the number of available frames goes below a threshold value, Windows 2000 converts some of active page frames to free frames. By examining the reference bit and the change bit in the page table entry for that page, Windows 2000 can tell whether the page has been "used" recently. When it is necessary for Windows 2000 to take pages to increase the number of free pages, it takes pages based on an LRU algorithm.

Each page table entry includes bit indicators that indicate the state of the page. Some of these bits and their functions are as follows:

- Page Present bit—This bit indicates whether the page is present in memory. If a reference is made to a page that is not in memory, a page fault interrupt occurs. This signals the operating system to suspend that process until the page can be brought into memory.
- Accessed bit—This bit indicates whether the page has been accessed since it was brought into memory.

- Available bit—This bit indicates whether the operating system can reuse the page frame without paging its contents out to the paging files.

- Read/Write bit—This bit indicates whether the page can be written to, or whether it is read-only.

- Dirty bit—This bit identifies whether the data in the page has been modified since it was last written to the paging file. If it has been modified, the operating system will have to page it out before the page frame can be preempted.

- User/Supervisor—This bit, like the Problem Program/Supervisor state bits in the OS/390 PSW, indicates whether the page is accessible by the process operating in User mode. If not, an attempt to access this page will result in a protection exception.

Paging Files

Because disk I/O is relatively slow compared to memory speeds, it is a good idea to limit the amount of paging that takes place. As mentioned earlier, when a system is spending a lot of its time paging data into and out of memory, it is said to be thrashing. In this state, the disk light is on constantly and little useful work is being done. Just as in OS/390, a high paging rate is a bad idea, because it impacts both program execution speed and I/O performance.

Improving Paging Speed

High-performance disk subsystems often come with their own memory cache. This can further improve paging speed by caching the most recently used pages in its own memory. This can speed up paging speed tremendously. ◆

Several factors affect the paging rate. These factors include the number of active processes running at the same time and the Working Set of those processes. The *Working Set* is the number of page frames that Windows 2000 assigns to a process. This Working Set will be reserved for the life of the process.

Another factor is the location and speed of I/O devices that host the paging files. Obviously it is a bad idea to place the paging files on a busy disk drive. Windows 2000 installation places a single paging file on the same drive and disk partition that Windows 2000 is located on. (This is the System Volume, or SYSVOL). A common performance-optimization option is to use multiple paging files and move them off of the SYSVOL and onto a less used disk. This is normally done on a server because the chance of having multiple disks on a server is higher than on a workstation.

Microsoft recommends that the total of your page space equal the size of the real memory installed in a machine plus 11MB. A better way to determine the size of paging files is to run a sample workload and measure the performance of the system under load. The Task Manager and the Performance Monitor can be used to do this. The Task Manager has a page that shows a quick summary of system performance. You can open it by right-clicking on the taskbar and selecting the Task Manager from the pop-up menu. The Performance Monitor is located in the Administrative Tools group. It is another one of the great free utility programs that come bundled with Windows 2000.

To make changes to the paging file configuration of a system, you can use the Control Panel System object by following these steps:

1. Single-click on the *Start* button on the taskbar located at the bottom of your desktop.

2. Move your mouse pointer to the *Settings* entry on the pop-up menu that appears next.

3. Then move your mouse pointer to the *Control Panel* from the cascade menu that slides out when your mouse pointer is over Settings.

4. Single-click on the *Control Panel* menu entry. This opens the Control Panel Windows. In this windows you will see many system control and configuration objects.

5. Double-click on the *System* object. A configuration notebook will appear. This notebook has several tabs across the top. On one of these tabs, you can select to change the page displayed in the notebook.

6. Select the *Advanced* tab of the notebook.

7. Single-click on the *Performance Options* button on the page.

8. Then select the *Change* button in the Virtual Memory group on the page. This presents you with the dialog box shown in Figure 4.3. From this page, you can change the number, location, and size of the paging file(s). From here, you can also change the amount of disk space allocated to the Registry.

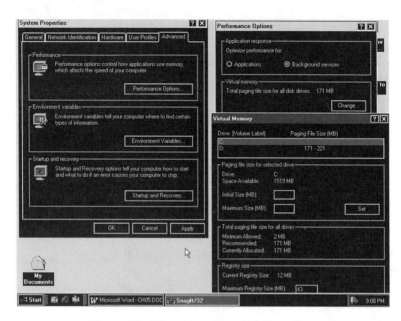

Figure 4.3 *Changing paging file allocations.*

Note that, as discussed earlier, you can specify multiple paging files. Specifying multiple paging files on different physical disks can improve performance by allowing Windows 2000 to perform I/O to one disk while another is busy.

Also note that when you install Windows 2000, the default paging file is automatically allocated on the SYSVOL. Because this is often located on a busy disk, moving it to a less active disk can also improve performance.

Memory-Mapped Files

To maximize I/O performance, Windows 2000 allocates most of its free memory as a file system cache. When an application needs memory, the operating system releases it back to the requesting process. This feature improves I/O performance by satisfying most I/O requests immediately from memory instead of waiting for the data to be brought in from relatively slow disks.

In addition, Windows 2000 supports the sharing of memory between processes by the use of *memory-mapped* files. Remember that different processes are normally prohibited from accessing the memory owned by other processes. By treating an address range as an in-memory file, the file can be mapped into the address space of more than one process at a time. This allows a program to treat a file like a directly updateable in-memory data array. This allows the program to ignore the dirty details of reading and writing the data to disk.

A memory-mapped file can represent an actual file on disk, in which case the file itself acts as the backing store of pages. For a temporary file, the system can use the system paging file for a backing store.

This chapter discussed how OS/390 and Windows 2000 manage memory. If an operating system had only to run a single program at a given time, it would not be necessary for the operating system to manage the memory in use at any point in time. It could just let a running program use all available memory for its own purposes as it saw fit. In fact, single-tasking operating systems, such as MS/DOS, frequently used this method. The next chapter discusses how simultaneously executing programs and tasks are managed via multiprogramming. The need to allocate and share memory among multiple programs, tasks, and subtasks makes memory management a necessity.

5
Multiprogramming

Multiprogramming is defined as having multiple programs resident and runnable in memory at the same time on the same computer system. Note that this is different from multiprocessing. Multiprogramming involves the sharing of a single CPU on a time-slice or time-quantum basis. As discussed in this chapter, multiprocessing takes this one step further by using multiple CPUs to perform this multiprogramming.

This chapter explains how both OS/390 and Windows 2000 support multiprogramming, and discusses OS/390 jobs and the new Windows 2000 job object. This chapter also covers the similarities and differences of program handling in OS/390 and Windows 2000. And finally, this chapter discusses OS/390 tasks and Windows 2000 processes and threads, focusing on their similarities and differences.

OS/390 Multiprogramming

Early mainframe computers were much slower than they are now. They were often purchased to do a single job at a time, such as tabulating the U.S. census or calculating ballistic missile trajectories. As computers became faster, the gap between CPU speed and I/O device performance began to widen. Eventually computer designers realized that the CPU of the computer was spending most of its time idle waiting for something external such as I/O completion to happen. To make use of this idle time, multiprogramming was introduced. OS/390's capability to multiprogram exists at three levels: jobs, steps, and tasks (see Figure 5.1).

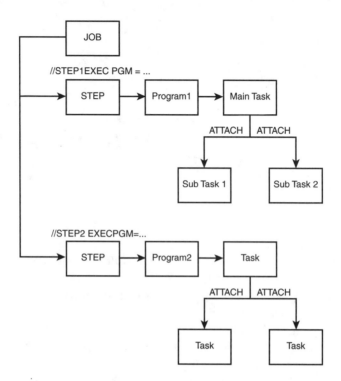

Figure 5.1 *OS/390 Multiprogramming.*

Jobs

An OS/390 job is defined as the execution of a dependent series of
programs. An OS/390 system can run multiple jobs at the same time using
the Job Management component of the operating system.

Jobs are defined to the operating system through the use of a *Job Control
Language* (JCL). When the operating system runs a job, it does so by executing programs as part of the individual job steps specified by JCL statements. These steps are run by the operating system in separate address
spaces or regions. Because of this, individual jobs and job steps are protected from each other, as discussed in Chapter 9, "Job and Task
Management."

Jobs, the JCL of OS/390, and Windows 2000 equivalents are discussed
more fully in Chapter 9. For now, it is only important to know that a job
consists of an overall definition of resources specified by some leading
control statements, followed by a definition of the programs and other
resources to be used to execute each job step.

A job's significance to the execution-time environment of OS/390 is
that it can be used to define limits on the use of resources, such as total

execution time, memory address space, and printed output. This is in addition to its primary function of grouping together a related series of program-execution steps.

A job is also used to account for the use of mainframe resources. Mainframes are expensive. It was an early requirement to be able to keep track of the resources used by jobs run on behalf of individual departments and users. Resources, such as memory, execution time, and I/O, can be tracked and recorded on a job and job step basis. This record can be used to bill-back the cost of the computer system to its users.

PCs, on the other hand, started out small and inexpensive. Until recently there has been no need to allocate usage costs. This is changing as Windows 2000-based servers become more of an expensive corporate resource.

Job Steps

As stated earlier, a job consists of job steps. Each job stepefines the datasets (files) and other resources to be used by the, job together with the name of a program to execute.

In addition, a job step is also used to define limits on resources used by the individual steps—such as total execution time, memory address space, and printed output. This is in addition to the limits specified at the job level. A job step involves the execution of one or more programs. A program involves the execution of one or more tasks.

Tasks

An OS/390 task is the fundamental execution entity in OS/390. It has some of the attributes of a Windows 2000 process and some of the attributes of a Windows 2000 thread. Like a Windows 2000 process, it owns resources. Like a thread, it is the primary scheduling and execution object.

When a program is executed, the operating system creates at least one task to manage the resources of the executing program. Running programs can also create additional tasks (called *subtasks*) by issuing a Data Management ATTACH macro request (refer back to Figure 5.1).

The operating system executes tasks that are defined and ready to run by allocating an available CPU to them on a priority basis. During its execution, a task owns resources in the form of allocated memory, open datasets, I/O request areas, and synchronization-control objects.

A task is represented to the operating system by a *Task Control Block* (TCB). The TCB is used by the operating system to manage the resources used by the execution of the current program in the current job step. As each step finishes, these resources are totaled up to the job level and contribute to the overall job limits and job accounting information.

The Trouble with *Tasks*

The operating system overhead required to start a new task originally required a fairly high degree of CPU overhead. This overhead was acceptable when the computer was dedicated to running relatively long jobs and job steps. With the advent of the need to support activities such as time-sharing and transaction processing, however, the task creation mechanism originally designed for batch processing was not good enough. Taking one or two seconds to start a new task may not be noticeable in a batch job because batch programs normally run for a relatively long time and no one normally sits there waiting for them to complete. Interactive transactions, however, normally require a total response time of one or two seconds, including task creation time and database access time. The same delay would be intolerable, for instance, to a customer service representative with an irate customer on the phone!

To provide an alternative to this task creation mechanism, and to tailor other batch-oriented system resource allocation mechanisms to this environment, IBM and others developed add-on software called *teleprocessing (TP) monitors,* such as the CICS.

CICS was originally developed to run as a single operating system task. Internally, CICS manages its own list of tasks executed on behalf of interactive terminals making resource requests. As far as the operating system is concerned, this all appears as a single operating system task under a single TCB. (You will find a lot more information about CICS, mainframes, and Windows 2000 in Chapter 15, "Transaction, Database, and Message Processing.")

System Resource Blocks

In more recent versions of OS/390, a lower-level of multitasking was added to allow the operating system to overlap internal functions for a job with lower overhead than the task. The SRB is a streamlined task mechanism that can only be used by operating system tasks. It is not usable at the application program level. ◆

Displaying Job Status

The OS/390 operator has a number of operator commands available to display the status of jobs running in the system. Many of these commands are also available through the TSO/SPF interface to allow non-operators to keep track of the jobs that they submit. For instance, a computer operator can issue the Display Active (D A,LIST) command to display the active jobs in the system. A TSO/SPF user can issue the DA command from the SPF *System Display and Search Facility* (SDSF) panel.

Windows 2000 Multiprogramming

When the first PCs were developed, history again repeated itself. Early PCs, like the early mainframes, were relatively slow. Because of this, they were usually relegated to performing one job at a time, such as calculating spreadsheets or handling word processing. As these computers became faster, operating system developers began to apply techniques such as spooling and multitasking to them as they had previously done to mainframe computers. Several operating systems were developed for PCs, but DOS was the most popular; as a result, it is the direct ancestor of Windows 2000.

Early Multiprogramming Attempts

DOS, as originally written, was a simple operating system. It was never architected for multiprogramming. In spite of this, Microsoft, IBM, and others attempted to force DOS to support multiprogramming with only limited success.

The Terminate and Stay Resident Program

One early attempt to force DOS to support multiprogramming was the TSR. TSRs allow the creation of an environment in which the CPU can be shared between a foreground and a background program. Although this sounds like a good idea in theory, in practice it led to operating system instability as discussed later.

TSRs were programs that could execute and end, but remain in memory. Prior to ending, these programs would often arrange to be awakened by a specific hotkey sequence or an external event. The program would then do some work for a time and relinquish the CPU back to the interrupted program.

An early use of TSR techniques for multitasking was the addition of rudimentary print spooling to DOS as implemented by the DOS PRINT command. The PRINT command is a DOS TSR that resides in memory and intercepts printer output. It then sends the output to the printer during the time that the CPU would otherwise be idle.

Memory Managers and *Task* Switchers

TSR techniques, in turn, led to the advent of memory managers and task switchers such as Quarterdeck's DeskView, IBM's TopView, and the original Microsoft Windows. These approaches met with only limited success because the underlying operating system (DOS) was never designed to support multitasking.

In addition, the operating system features to support TSRs were largely undocumented and unsupported. Use of this feature often led to the infamous Windows GPF or a machine lockup.

Microsoft eventually decided that an entirely new Windows-compatible operating system designed from the ground up to support multitasking was the answer. This resulted in the development of Windows NT, the predecessor of Windows 2000, which was released in 1983.

"Other" Operating Systems

DOS, of course, was not the only operating system developed for the x86 architecture. Chapter 1, "The Origins and Evolution of OS/390 and Windows 2000," mentioned how of Microsoft and IBM originally collaborated on the development of OS/2. In addition, there were (and still are) several flavors of UNIX for the x86 architecture as well as Microsoft's legacy desktop operating system, Windows 98. ◆

Single and Multiuser Support

OS/390 was originally designed to be operated by a single operator who fed it jobs to run and mounted tapes and disks as required. As explained in Chapter 16, "Communicating with OS/390," only after multiuser features, such as TSO and SPF, were added did OS/390 support more than one "operator." Windows 2000 and its predecessors, like early mainframe operating systems, were designed from the start to be single-user systems even though they were designed to run multiple programs simultaneously on behalf of a user.

Most of the Windows NT and Windows 2000 systems deployed today are still single-user systems running on individual workstations. (Servers can also be considered to be single-user systems because they have a single-operator interface, even though they do support multiple remote workstations that can access their resources.)

The only true multiuser support in Windows 2000 is the support for the Terminal Server features of Windows 2000.

Processes

As discussed earlier, multiprogramming requires that the operating system keep track of multiple unrelated programs and their resources. The fundamental unit of resource ownership in Windows 2000 is the process object. (There is a higher-level grouping unit, the Windows 2000 job object. It is new to Windows 2000 and not yet fully developed. The job object is discussed at the end of this section.)

What Is a Process?

A Windows 2000 process is defined as an instance of an executing application. A process owns resources in the form of a virtual address space containing its code and data, allocated memory, open files, semaphores, and I/O control blocks (see Figure 5.2). A process is identified to the operating system by a process ID (PID).

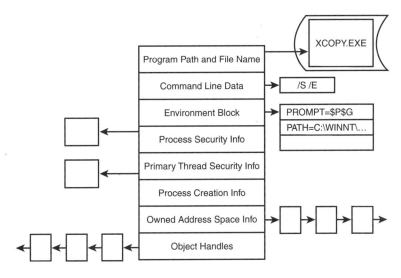

Figure 5.2 *Processes.*

A process by itself is inert. A process requires at least one thread of execution in order to perform work (see the section titled "Threads," later in this chapter).

How Processes Are Started

Processes need to get started somehow. The primary method for starting new processes is the Windows 2000 GUI desktop. The desktop is managed by an interface shell program called the Windows 2000 *Explorer*. Icons on the desktop represent objects such as data files and programs. Programs can be started in several ways.

You can activate a program directly by double-clicking the icon that represents the program. You can activate it by dragging a data file to the icon that represents the program. You can even activate it by double-clicking a data-file icon of the appropriate type if that type has been associated with the appropriate program.

The Windows 2000 Explorer and the Active Desktop

In writing this section, I was faced with a problem. Windows 2000 provides two ways to control the desktop: the Windows Explorer interface inherited from its predecessors, and the newer Active Desktop interface. In the Explorer interface, you double-click on an icon to activate it. The Active Desktop interface acts more like a Web browser. The desktop appears like a browser window and the titles under Icons act like browser links. To activate an object in this environment, you single-click it. Because some actions still require you to double-click, this can be confusing to the user. (One of the attributes of a good user interface is consistency.) In any case, this interface is optional and users can select which way they want to operate. Because most of us are more comfortable with the "old" Explorer way, that is the one that I use in this book. ♦

Program files normally end with an .EXE or .COM file extension. In addition to executing programs directly or indirectly by the previously discussed methods, you can also execute DOS-style batch files that end in .BAT or .CMD. You can also execute higher-level script programs written in languages such as VBScript and JScript using the new Windows Scripting Host (see Chapter 9).

Another way to start a process is from a desktop Console window. The Console window presents a DOS-style command-prompt interface (see Figure 5.3). From this command line, you can also execute programs of any type. An additional command-line capability is available from the Start menu Run option.

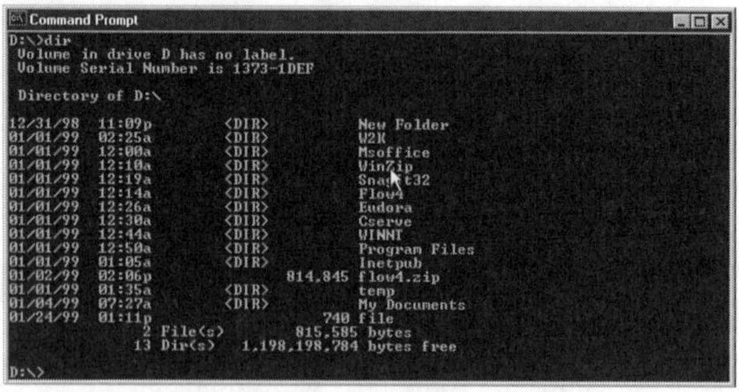

Figure 5.3 *The Console window.*

Finally, each Environmental subsystem supports program-callable APIs for process creation. A process can create another process of the same type, subject to the rules enforced by the Environmental subsystem for that process type.

As you will recall from Chapter 2, "Operating System Architecture," Windows 2000 supports five different types of processes. These process types are as follows:

- Win32
- DOS16
- Win16
- Posix
- OS/2

When a request is made to start a new process, the operating system determines the type of process. The process is then handed off to the appropriate Environmental subsystem, which runs it. This allows the Environmental subsystem to set up an execution environment unique to that type of process.

Processes in Posix have a parent/child relationship with the processes that they spawn, for instance. Win32 processes have a somewhat looser relationship between processes. After a process is started, it is normally not attached to a parent process.

The Win32 Process

The Win32 process fulfils a dual role in Windows 2000. In addition to providing an execution environment for native Windows 2000 (Win32) processes, it also acts as a part of the operating system (see Figure 5.4).

This subsystem is crucial to desktop management and the Windows 2000 security scheme. Because of this important role, it is the only Environmental subsystem that must be operating for Windows 2000 to function. If for any reason it fails, Windows 2000 will halt. (Other subsystems, such as the Posix subsystem, can fail and the operating system will still be able to run other types of programs.) Combining the control of overall system management with the control of Win32 processes instead of separating them into two subsystems seems to be a performance decision. It makes Win32 the most important and optimized personality supported by Windows 2000.

In addition to hosting its own native process type, it can also host a special runtime environment for 16-bit DOS and 16-bit Windows applications using a special Virtual x86 mode provided by the x86 processor. From the discussion of Windows 2000 in Chapter 2, you should remember that the Win32 subsystem is responsible for determining the type of program to be run and for either running it itself (if it is a native Win32 process), or passing it off to the proper Environmental subsystems to be started.

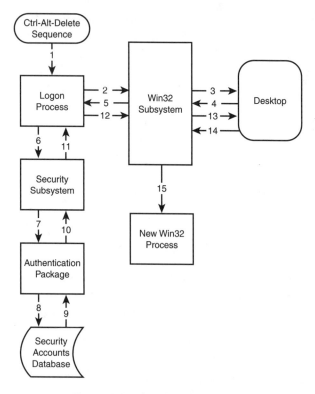

Figure 5.4 *The Win32 subsystem.*

DOS 16-Bit Processes

Most legacy DOS applications were written to assume that they would be run alone in the computer. Based on this, DOS applications normally assume that they can access all installed memory and directly control all the hardware in the computer. In a multitasking operating system such as Windows 2000, this cannot be allowed because it might interfere with other applications being run at the same time. Therefore Windows 2000 must set up a protected environment in which to run these applications. This protected environment must simulate the dedicated environment that the program was originally written for. At the same time, it must keep the legacy DOS application from interfering with the operating system and other active programs.

To achieve this simulation and protection, all DOS 16-bit programs are run in separate virtual memory environments called Windows 2000 *Virtual DOS Machines* (VDMs). Note that you may see this referred to as NTVDM because it was originally developed as part of Windows NT. The VDM simulates the execution environment of a DOS-based computer system. (This VDM together with the normal Windows 2000 protection mechanisms provide the protection for the operating system and the other applications.) A DOS VDM runs the DOS application under a single execution thread. Note that not all functions available to a DOS application are simulated by the VDM. Therefore, not all DOS application programs can be run under Windows 2000.

Win16 Processes

All 16-bit Windows applications run by default in a common VDM using the *Windows 16 on Windows 32 subsystem* (WOW). The WOW uses the VDM to simulate the 16-bit Windows execution environment. Each application in the WOW VDM is managed with a separate thread.

Although the default is to run all Win16 programs in a common VDM, you can also run selected Win16 programs in a separate VDM. To run a Win16 application in its own VDM, follow these steps:

1. Right-click on the icon of the Win16 program.
2. Select *Properties*.
3. Select the *Shortcut* tab of the Properties notebook.
4. Select the Run in separate memory space check box.

This starts a new VDM when the program is executed.

Posix Processes

The Posix Environmental subsystem provides a very limited UNIX execution environment. As discussed in Chapter 2, "Operating System Architecture," this subsystem is not very useful unless you add third-party software such as Interix from Softway Systems. For more information on UNIX and NT integration, you can consult one of the books dedicated to this topic such as *Windows NT and UNIX Integration*, (Gene Henriksen, Macmillan Technical Publishing, 1998).

OS/2 Processes

As also indicated in Chapter 2, the OS/2 capabilities of Windows 2000 are nearly useless. Because it is unlikely that this capability will be enhanced in the future, no space is wasted here discussing it further.

Displaying Process Information

The Windows 2000 *Task* Manager can be used to display all the active processes in the system. To display this list, follow these steps:

1. Right-click on the taskbar at the bottom of the desktop.

2. Select the *Task Manager* menu entry.

3. Select the *Process* tab in the resulting Task Manager notebook.

This displays all the active processes in the system (see Figure 5.5).

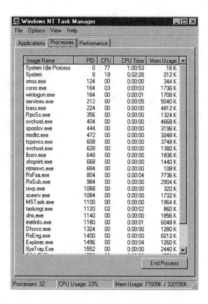

Figure 5.5   *Displaying processes.*

Note that one process, the System Idle process, seems to be taking up most of the CPU time. This is not really an active process at all. It just represents the amount of available CPU.

While you are in the Task Manager, you should also take a look at the Applications and Performance pages. The Application page displays all the executing applications in your system. The Performance page shows a really nice summary of CPU and memory usage.

Threads

The thread is the atomic execution unit of Windows 2000. Every process must contain at least one thread. It is the thread that is scheduled by the operating system and given CPU resources as required.

A Windows 2000 thread owns the contents of the CPU registers that define the execution state or context of the system when the thread is running and the Kernel- and User mode stacks used by the thread during execution. A thread is implemented by a program function passed to the *CreateThread* function in the creating thread. Threads are identified to the operating system by a thread ID (TID).

The Windows 2000 Resource Kit contains a large number of useful systems analysis tools and utilities. It is a must for anyone who is serious about Windows 2000. One of these tools is the PSTAT utility, which is used here to show the active threads in CRSS.EXE, the Win32 Environmental subsystem.

```
pid: a4 pri:13 Hnd:  460 Pf:   1127 Ws:   1872K csrss.exe
tid pri Ctx Swtch StrtAddr   User Time  Kernel Time  State
  a8  14         2 5ffa4711  0:00:00.000 0:00:00.000 Wait:UserRequest
  ac  14      1287 5ff83617  0:00:00.030 0:00:01.742 Wait:LpcReceive
  b0  13         1 77fb6543  0:00:00.000 0:00:00.000 Wait:LpcReceive
  b4  14         3 5ff8302f  0:00:00.000 0:00:00.000 Wait:LpcReceive
  bc  14      1281 5ff83617  0:00:00.040 0:00:01.271 Wait:LpcReceive
  c0  19      8107 a0011981  0:00:00.000 0:00:02.553 Wait:UserRequest
  c4  16       226 a000fb50  0:00:00.000 0:00:00.050 Wait:UserRequest
  e8  16         3 a000fb50  0:00:00.000 0:00:00.000 Wait:UserRequest
 694  15        84 5ffa3485  0:00:00.010 0:00:00.020 Wait:UserRequest
```

Note, in this example, the number of threads active even when there are no user applications running. Most system processes have multiple threads standing by ready to act on behalf of applications when they need them.

Windows 2000 Fibers

Because of the comparatively high performance of process creation, most applications that want to do internal multitasking use threads. To enable developers to create even faster applications, Microsoft implemented a streamlined thread mechanism called fibers in a service pack to Windows NT 3.51. This is somewhat analogous to the creation of the SMB in OS/390. Unlike SMBs, however, the fiber is accessible to developers. A fiber is a lightweight thread that is manually scheduled by an application. It is used primarily to support the development of applications that do their own thread scheduling and management such as Windows 2000 ports of applications like CICS. Because this is not a book on programming per se, this feature is not discussed in this book. For more information, refer to the documentation on this feature located at http://msdn.microsoft.com/library/sdkdoc/winbase/prothred_5mur.htm. ◆

The Job Object

A Windows 2000 job is a group of processes that can be managed as a unit. Processes can be grouped into jobs so that the operating system can enforce limits (quotas) on their use of per-process and group CPU time, disk space, Working Set size, and the number of active processes in a job. This grouping allows security and scheduling parameters to be applied to processes as a group. It also allows the definition of CPU affinity on a multiple-process basis. Figure 5.6 illustrates the capabilities of the job object.

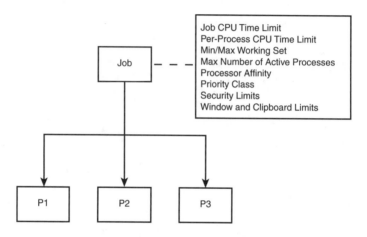

Figure 5.6   *The Windows 2000 job object.*

Windows NT, the predecessor of Windows 2000, did not include the concept of a job as the execution of a dependent series of program executions. It only featured processes and threads. The job object is new to Windows 2000 and as such it does not yet have many capabilities. It is easy to see, however, that it provides the underpinnings for the evolution of more extensive job management capabilities such as the ones provided by mainframes. Third-party packages—such as AutoSys from Platinum Technologies and Queue Manager from Argent Software—can be used to provide more sophisticated batch-processing and program-scheduling capabilities for Windows 2000.

Windows NT did not have a Job Control Language as sophisticated as the one provided by OS/390 JCL. Its capability to execute programs in sequence was limited to the very primitive Batch File language inherited from DOS. Starting with Windows 2000, however, Microsoft provided a sophisticated scripting language, the *Windows Script Host* (WSH). This provides more advanced system control capabilities. (This is the WSH mentioned in passing earlier in the chapter and which is covered more fully in Chapter 9.) The WSH provides built-in supportfor scripting the execution of programs in VBScript and JavaScript. It also supports additional third-party add-in scripting engines such as PerlScript.

Several third-party scripting tools can also be used for this purpose. WinBatch is a scripting package that has had a long and successful history with different versions of Windows.

One of the important features of an OS/390 job is that it can be used to charge-back the cost of computing resources to users. Windows 2000 has no such accounting capability built in. Third-party packages for Windows NT—such as CIMS from Platinum Technologies—can be used to add charge-back capabilities. It is easy to see that the job object provides the "hooks" for adding this capability in the future. In addition, Windows 2000 maintains a large number of performance counters internally. Although these counters are currently used only by the Windows 2000 Performance Monitor, they could also be used to collect job accounting information. Chapter 9 discusses OS/390 and Windows 2000 job management in more detail.

This chapter covered OS/390 and Windows 2000 multiprogramming and how these operating systems manage jobs, processes, tasks, and threads. The whole point of multiprogramming is to maximize the amount of useful work that a given computer system can perform. Useful work normally involves doing some kind of I/O processing. The next chapter examines how these two operating systems manage all I/O operations performed on behalf of applications.

6

Input/Output Device Management

The I/O devices managed by OS/390 and Windows 2000 are close cousins. In fact, the model for the SCSI disk architecture was based on the channel and control-unit architecture of early IBM mainframes. This chapter looks more closely at the I/O architecture of OS/390 and Windows 2000.

OS/390 Input/Output Device Management

In OS/390, I/O devices are identified by a three-digit hexadecimal number. The first digit identifies a channel. The second digit identifies a control unit. The third digit identifies a specific device. Device numbers are in hexadecimal, which allows for a possibility of 16 choices (0–15) in each position. For instance, a line printer address might be 00E. This specifies that the printer is located on channel 0, control unit 0, and device E (15).

Device Addressing Enhancements

OS/390 originally used a three-digit address with one digit each for channel, device, and unit. Recently, a fourth digit has been added to increase the addressing alternatives. ◆

Channels and Channel Programs

Chapter 3, "Central Processing Units," discussed how the CPU shares the responsibility for managing I/O operations with the channels. The CPU initiates an I/O operation by passing data and control instructions to the channel. The CPU then responds to interrupts from the channel as it requires service.

The reason for dedicating processors to perform I/O is, of course, performance. By relieving the CPU of the need to handle the details of I/O processing, the CPU can be released to perform other work. Having several channels, the modern mainframe can overlap calculation with I/O processing and thus achieve a higher level of multiprogramming.

Control Units

The channel-attached control units handle device commands that are unique to a particular device type, such as a particular model of magnetic disk. Control units can perform low-level device operations on their attached devices without involving the channel. For instance, a control unit can instruct the disk drives attached to it to seek to a particular location and notify the control unit when they have completed the requested seek operation. Refer back to Figure 3.1 for further information.

The major mainframe device types are as follows:

- DASD (Disk)
- Tapes
- Unit-Record
- Communications controllers
- Consoles

DASD

DASD stands for *direct access storage device*. This is another fancy name for a hard disk. In the early days of System/390 (back when it was System/360), disks were small and expensive. Disks were originally removable. They had to be physically mounted on a disk drive and logically "mounted" with the MOUNT command before data could be read or written to the device. More recent members of the DASD family are permanently mounted in place, as are most PC disks. Windows 2000 also supports removable disks. The following section discusses this feature.

The architecture of mainframe disks is quite different from that of the PC on which Windows 2000 runs (see Figure 6.1).

PC disks normally consist of a single platter with data recorded on both sides. Mainframe disks, on the other hand, typically consist of stacks of multiple platters. These platters usually are read from and written to by comb-like read/write heads that move back and forth from the rim of the disk to its center.

Each platter has data tracks arranged around its circumference. The read/write heads sit over the same track on each platter at the same time. The tracks in the same location on each platter form a cylinder of data that can be accessed without moving the read/write heads. Moving the heads is a physical operation that takes a relatively long time compared to the time it takes to transfer data from the disk to or from memory.

Side View

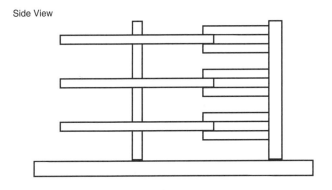

Track View

Figure 6.1 *Mainframe disk architecture.*

Unlike PC disks, mainframe disk tracks are not split into sectors. Instead, data is recorded in a three-part format:

1. A count of the number of bytes in the record
2. A symbolic key that uniquely identifies the record
3. The record data

Each of these three entities is delimited by a bit of wasted space called an inter-record gap. Records are often small. Because there is wasted space between records, small records are often combined into larger blocks of data to store the data more efficiently. The size of these data blocks, which is usually a multiple of the record size, is specified by the program or in JCL when the dataset is created. The architecture of the PC disks used by Windows 2000 is discussed later in this chapter.

Blurring the Line Between PCs and Mainframe Disks

Until recently, mainframe disks and PC disk were built using the two different architectures described in this chapter. Recently, however, IBM and other mainframe manufacturers have begun to offer disk storage built using techniques pioneered in the PC world. For instance, the IBM RAMAC DASD is actually made up of many small PC-type disks configured into a RAID array in a large box together with cache memory. ◆

Tapes

In the mainframe world, magnetic tape is used for four purposes:

1. Backup/Recovery
2. Primary data storage
3. Work files
4. Hierarchical storage management

In early mainframe days, magnetic tape was used for backup and recovery, primary data storage, and work files. As disks have gotten larger and cheaper over the years, the use of tape files for primary data storage and work files has decreased. OS/390 backup/recovery and hierarchical storage management are discussed later in this section.

Unit-Record

In the early days of automated record keeping, the data owned by a company business unit was punched into cardboard cards using devices called keypunches. Output from computers and other tabulating devices was in the form of either more punched cards or printed output. Because a business unit owned this data, it was called Unit-Record data. Card readers, card punches, and line printers were called Unit-Record devices.

Card Input

As previously mentioned, the primary input medium in early mainframe days was the punched card. This has given way to card images stored on disks created and edited by a text editor such as the SPF text editor (see Chapter 18, "Structuring a Mainframe-like Development Environment"). The original punched card could hold 80 characters of data. Because of its punched card heritage, it is usual to see 80 character records in these data files.

Printer Output

Mainframe shops generate large quantities of output on paper in the form of printed reports. IBM 3900 class printers chew up huge rolls of paper and spew out reams of output on a daily basis, and the volume of output is constantly growing. Recently the trend has been toward minimizing this output of paper through the use of report files managed by report distribution and display packages. Hopefully this trend will continue and at least slow down growth in the volume of printed output. In large shops where there are a lot of printers, there may even be dedicated printer pool operators responsible for managing the printers.

OS/390 spooling is quite sophisticated. JCL Data Definition and JES Output Control statements are used to specify the destination of printed output by output class (see Chapter 11, "Printer Management"). These classes are used to route the output to a specific output queue. When the job is run, the *Job Entry System* (JES) intercepts output directed to printer devices. The output is then saved on disk in one of several printer queues by class of output. Components of JES called Output Writers scan these queues looking for jobs to print. When a printer is available and a job of the proper class is ready to print, JES sends the output to the printer.

Mainframe Printing

The original mainframe printers were called line printers because they were mechanical devices that printed a line of data at a time before advancing the page to print the next line. These mechanical devices were fairly slow. For instance, assuming 50 lines per page, a 1,200 line per minute line printer would only print 20 pages a minute.

Recent mainframe printers are more like PC page printers such as the Hewlett-Packard LaserJet. Page printing in OS/390 is supported by a page-printing architecture called Advance Function Printing (AFP). AFP uses a page-definition language to define structured documents and control printing in a fashion similar to the page-composition language (PCL) and PostScript languages used in the PC world. To contrast these with the line printers, a modern IBM 3900 printer can print up to 229 pages a minute. ◆

Communications Controllers

Mainframes traditionally have supported both local and remote workstations. These workstations have included interactive terminals such as the IBM 3270 and batch *Remote Job Entry* (RJE) workstations such as the IBM 3780.

Initially, local devices were connected by coaxial cables to cluster controllers, which in turn were connected to mainframe channels. Terminal clusters and RJE devices at remote locations were connected vial leased telephone lines. Recently, LAN connections have replaced coaxial cable as the primary means of connecting local terminals to a mainframe.

In a modern mainframe system, special communications controllers are used to relieve the CPU of the need to handle low-level network processing operations. This frees up the mainframe to perform other work. Communications controllers, such as the IBM 3745, are specialized boxes that are optimized for this task. They even have their own operating system, called the *Network Control Program* (NCP). OS/390 supports a special access method, the *Virtual Telecommunications Access Method* (VTAM), which is used to manage communications devices. VTAM and Windows 2000 alternatives are further discussed in Chapter 14, "Networking."

Consoles

The work performed by each type of mainframe operator can be highly specialized. OS/390 supports multiple operator consoles as I/O devices. The OS/390 *Multiple Console Support* (MCS) is used to route the messages needed to perform a particular job to the appropriate operator console.

Before closing this analysis of OS/390 I/O management, it is important to examine three topics that involve multiple device types: removable storage management, backup/recovery, and hierarchical storage management.

Removable Storage Management

Early in the history of OS/390, the operating system provided support for removable disks and tapes.

Disks

Thanks to OS/390's heavy reliance on magnetic tapes, it has always had excellent support for removable devices. In the early days of the mainframe operating system, DASD devices were all removable. Disk storage was provided in the form of multiplatter removable disk packs. These disk packs were inserted into disk drives to read data from and write data to them. Any disk could be mounted on any disk drive. Every disk drive was encoded with a volume label that uniquely identified the disk. The *Automatic Volume Recognition* (AVR) feature of the operating system could determine the exact disk volume mounted on the drive by reading the electronic label on the disk.

Although disks were originally removable, the need to make disks faster and denser in storage capacity has led manufacturers to build nonremovable, sealed disk drives with integrated disk assemblies. As a result, most mainframe disks are currently nonremovable.

Tapes

Because the original mainframe disks were small and expensive, most mainframe shops relied heavily on the use of reel-to-reel magnetic tapes for storing large data files and keeping backup copies of disk volumes.

Magnetic tape reels were mounted on tape drives, which were used to read data from and write data to the tape media. Tape volumes were usually initialized with a serial number. When mounted on a drive, the AVR feature of the operating system would then determine the serial number of the mounted tape. When a program attempted to open a file on the tape, AVR would verify that the right tape was mounted on the drive.

Although the operating system does provide basic support for managing manually mounted tapes, it was left to third-party vendors to develop hardware and software to support tape libraries. One such third-party company is *Storage Technology Corporation* (STC). Recent models of their Tape Silo product can store, catalog, and retrieve up to 6,000 20MB cartridge tapes with a retrieval time of approximately 11 seconds.

Backup/Recovery

As stated previously, one of the primary uses for removable tape media was (and is) for backup and recovery. Backup and recovery is extremely important to OS/390 (and, for that matter, to Windows 2000 as well).

OS/390 has, over time, provided many utilities such as IEBGENER, IEBCOPY, DITTO, and IDCAMS to back up and restore specific types of datasets and whole disk volumes. Most of these utilities have by now been incorporated into the *Data Facility*, *Systems Managed Storage* (DFSMS) utilities package of OS/390. (For more information on OS/390 Systems Managed Storage, look at www.storage.ibm.com/software/sms/sysmngd.htm.) Many OS/390 shops also use a third-party backup product, *Fast Dump Restore* (FDR), from Innovation Software.

OS/390 SMS and Windows 2000 SMS

Unfortunately, there are only so many three-letter acronyms available. Don't confuse OS/390 SMS (Systems Managed Storage) with Windows 2000 SMS (Systems Management Server). The former is a set of services for managing storage. The latter is a Microsoft product used to deploy software and manage Windows systems in a network. ♦

As part of a backup strategy, an installation will often create a minimal runnable copy of the operating system similar to the starter system that comes with an operating system distribution. This is normally located on a separate volume from the production copy of the operating system. If the volume containing the production version of the operating system is rendered unusable for any reason, the operating system can be rebooted from the backup copy and used to restore the full production version of the operating system. (As discussed later in this chapter, this technique can be used in a Windows 2000 recovery strategy as well.) This improves the speed of recovery. Recovering quickly is important because most mainframe installations maintain a 24-hour, 7-day-a-week operating schedule. Mainframe shops normally have as an objective a 99.999% uptime to downtime ratio. This amounts to only a few minutes a year of downtime. (See the discussion comparing Windows NT and Windows 2000 reliability to mainframe reliability in the Windows 2000 section of this chapter.)

Hierarchical Storage Management

Hierarchical storage management (HSM) allows a systems programmer to specify rules that the operating system will use to migrate infrequently accessed disk data to magnetic tape. The HSM software will then recall the data automatically when it is needed.

Recent versions of OS/390 have implemented a form of HSM called *System Managed Storage* (SMS). SMS allows the automatic migration of datasets from fast but expensive online disks to slower, less expensive nearly online (near-line) devices such as optical disks and tape libraries; to completely archival (offline) media such as racks of magnetic tape. The operating system can be instructed to perform this function so that the most inactive datasets are the ones to be migrated to lower-speed, cheaper storage devices.

With SMS, the operating system keeps track of the exact location of the data. When a program attempts to open a dataset that has been migrated, the operating system can either bring the data back to online storage or notify the programmer that a delay will be required before that data can be made available.

As discussed later in this chapter, HSM is finding its way gradually into the Windows 2000 world as Windows 2000 penetrates into the mainframe environment.

Now that you understand how OS/390 handles the management of I/O devices, it's time to take a look at Windows 2000.

Windows 2000 Input/Output Device Management

The Windows 2000 I/O architecture has some similarity to the I/O architecture of OS/390. The biggest difference between the two is that the Windows 2000 I/O architecture has no channels to offload processing from the CPU. Windows 2000 does support the I²O standard for intelligent devices, which will provide this capability. Currently, however, few devices take advantage of this capability.

The preceding chapter discussed how the Windows 2000 CPU is responsible for initiating I/O operations and responding to interrupts from device adapters that are installed in slots on the PC bus. The following part of this chapter discusses this architecture in more detail.

Processor Bus

Device addressing in the x86 architecture is done by referencing physical buss addresses of the installed adapters. You can look back at Figure 3.4 for more information.

This bus connects all the components together. Typically this is a *Peripheral Interconnect* (PCI) bus, although other bus types do exist. The PCI bus is currently the most popular bus type because it works well with the *Plug and Play* (PnP) feature of Windows operating systems (see Chapter 2, "Operating System Architecture"). When used in conjunction with these operating systems, it can automatically sense the interrupt level and I/O port addresses used by an adapter installed in a PCI slot. Although Windows 2000 does support automatic configuration of newer devices through its PnP feature, the continued use of older non-PnP devices makes configuring these adapters a continuing challenge.

Note that many workstation-class PCs currently come with a combination of buses installed. For instance, you may have slots in your PC for both PCI and ISA adapters. In actuality, what you have is a PC with two interconnected buses.

Device Adapters

Device adapters fulfill part of the role filled by OS/390 channels. A device adapter provides the interface between the CPU bus and the control logic of a specific device type or class. Each adapter is plugged into a slot on the PC bus. The device adapter is responsible for controlling the low-level operations of the device. When a program issues a read operation to a disk adapter, for instance, the disk handles all the details of actually reading the data and transferring it into memory.

Windows 2000 supports a rich set of device types. It supports both fixed and removable disks, tape drives, disk drives, and scanners. In particular, removable devices such as Iomega JAZ and Zip drives benefit from the new support for removable devices that premiered with Windows 2000.

Some device types require a specific type of adapter. A video display will be plugged into a video adapter, for example, which, in turn, is plugged into a slot on the bus. Other device types can plug into other types of adapters. For instance, a SCSI device plugs into a SCSI adapter. The SCSI adapter can be used to control any device type that has been built to the SCSI standard. Such devices include a wide range of disk drives, tape drives, sound cards, CD-ROM drives, and scanners. Still other device types have their adapter logic built right in to the device. For instance, an *IDE* (Integrated Data Electronics) or Extended IDE disk drive will be plugged into a simple connector that plugs right into the PC bus.

Not all devices have device adapters. Some devices have their control logic built right in to the motherboard. Mouse and keyboard logic is often built in to the motherboard, for instance. It is all but impossible to find a motherboard today without serial, parallel, IDE disk, *universal serial bus*

(USB) connector, and *infrared* (IR) printer port, a keyboard controller, and a BUS (PS/2)-style mouse built in. In fact, the new ATX standard from Intel requires a motherboard to have all these features.

IDE versus SCSI

IDE disks are normally used in workstations because they are cheaper than SCSI disks because they do not require a separate disk controller. SCSI disks are normally higher in cost but provide superior performance. SCSI is the preferred disk type in servers where the improved performance is needed and the cost can be spread across multiple users. ◆

Devices

Windows 2000 supports a wide range of I/O devices. Microsoft provides a large number of device drivers in the Windows 2000 box. In addition third-party hardware vendors provide additional drivers to have their devices supported under Windows 2000. (This number will grow even larger as Windows 2000 Professional continues to replace Windows 95 and Windows 98 on corporate desktops.)

Devices are identified by names in the Windows 2000 name space. Disk devices are identified by single letters, A: through Z:. Other devices use multiletter combinations such as LPT:, CON:, and PRT:. The following sections cover the major device types supported by Windows 2000.

Disks

Disk storage under Windows 2000 is managed in units of allocation called *volumes*. Originally a volume was synonymous with a physical disk drive. This has been generalized in Windows 2000 to support logical volumes that span physical disks.

Windows 2000 supports two types of storage volumes: basic and dynamic. Basic storage volumes are a holdover from Windows NT and its predecessors. Only dynamic storage volumes support most of the advanced features of Windows 2000 Disk Management. As time goes on, basic storage will probably be used to an increasingly lesser degree. Therefore, the focus of this discussion is dynamic storage.

Storage volumes are managed by Disk Manager. Figure 6.2 shows the Disk Manager snap-in. This MMC snap-in tool replaces Disk Administrator of Windows NT. Unlike Windows NT Disk Administrator, Windows 2000 Disk Manager can manage storage on remote systems as well as on local systems.

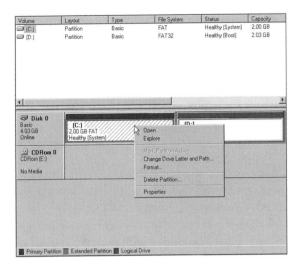

Figure 6.2 *The Disk Manager.*

As mentioned earlier, disk identifiers are automatically allocated from the set of letters A: through Z: during system installation. Disk Manager can be used to change disk IDs after installation. (Contrast this with OS/390, where disk volumes are given names such as SYSRES and TMPVOL.)

One of the major improvements of Windows 2000 Disk Manager over Windows NT Disk Administrator is that changes can be made to disk space allocations without rebooting the computer. Another key improvement is that Disk Manager can be used to manage storage on remote systems.

Basic Storage

As stated previously, basic disk volumes are a holdover from earlier versions of the operating system. Most changes to basic storage volumes require that the operating system be rebooted for the change to take effect. This reduces system availability because the system must be taken completely out of service for the time it takes to reboot it.

A basic storage volume is defined by a master boot record, which contains information on the partition structure of the disk. This is followed by up to four *primary partitions*. A primary partition can contain directories and files. One primary partition can be defined as an *extended partition*. An extended partition can be divided up, in turn, into multiple logical partitions. One of the primary partitions can also be marked as the active, or bootable partition. This is the partition that will be searched for an operating system when you turn on the computer.

The physical drive letter (A: through Z:) serves as the high-level partition name. Directories and files are defined as relative to the device. The following chapter discusses Windows 2000 file systems, directories, and files.

Basic disks have data describing them stored in the Windows NT Registry. This ties the disk to a particular system and makes it difficult to move disks from one system to another.

As indicated earlier, most of the advanced volume management features of Windows 2000 are supported only by dynamic storage volumes.

Dynamic Storage

Dynamic storage is volume-oriented, unlike basic storage, which is partition-oriented. Changes to dynamic volumes do not, in general, require a reboot for the changes to take effect. Dynamic disks can also be in use at the time that they are being changed without affecting the users. Unlike basic disks, dynamic disks are self-defining. They do not depend on Registry data. This makes it possible to move a drive to another system and use it directly, if necessary.

In Windows 2000 dynamic storage, the operating system supports the creation of logical volumes that can consist of space on one or more physical disks. This allows changes such as extending the size of a volume without resorting to backing up and re-allocating the partitions on a disk, which basic storage requires.

Dynamic volume management supports the following four volume types:

- Simple volumes
- Mirrored volumes
- Striped volumes
- Spanned volumes

Some of these volume types can be used to implement fault-tolerant disk configurations using one or more RAID (*redundant array of inexpensive disk*) architectures. As discuss later in this chapter, you can implement some of these architectures in software using Windows 2000. You can also choose a hardware implementation as well. (For more detail on all the RAID levels, refer to the Web page at www.adaptec.com/products/guide/abcriaf.html.

Simple Volumes

This volume organization most closely resembles a basic storage volume. It exists on a single disk and does not make use of any of the more advanced volume organization features discussed here. A simple volume acts a lot like a primary or logical partition of a basic storage volume.

Mirrored Volumes

Disk mirroring, also called RAID-1, uses two disk extents of the same or different sizes to duplicate the data written to and read from disks. When a disk is mirrored, the data is written to both sides of the mirror at the same time. If either side of a mirrored set fails, data can still be read from or written to the other disk. This provides a high degree of fault tolerance. It also improves performance over a single disk volume, because data can be read from either extent (see Figure 6.3).

Mirroring can also be used to duplicate a disk that is going to be dismounted for backup or moved to another system. When a mirror is added to a mirror set, the operating system will synchronize its contents with the original. For a large disk, this can take a while. It will also degrade overall I/O performance while it is being done. (This degradation is a small price to pay because the alternative would be total loss of the data on the disk.)

Disk mirroring normally refers to duplicate disks on the same storage controller. Adding a second controller so that there is a totally separate hardware path to the data is called disk duplexing and represents an added degree of fault tolerance (see Figure 6.3).

Hardware or Software RAID-1?

Software RAID-1 (disk mirroring) is useful for building an inexpensive fault-tolerant system out of inexpensive disks. (RAID, after all, does stand for redundant array of inexpensive disks.) For more industrial-strength servers, you will probably want to invest in a hardware RAID solution. ◆

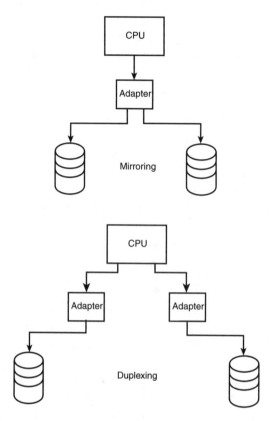

Figure 6.3 *Disk mirroring and duplexing.*

Striped Volumes

Striped volumes come in two variations: with and without redundancy. Striped volumes with redundancy are also called RAID-5.

All striped volumes are constructed from noncontiguous blocks of storage on one or more physical disks. Data is written to a striped volume in alternating blocks to improve performance.

Striped volumes without redundancy do not provide any degree of fault tolerance. During operation, data blocks are written to alternating stripes. If these stripes are on different physical disks, this can improve performance. Striping with redundancy does add fault tolerance to a disk configuration.

A striped volume set with redundancy uses areas on at least three separate physical disks. Data is striped across all but one of the available disks as in striping without redundancy. In this case, however, the remaining disk is used to store parity data for the records on the other disk. If one of the disks fails, this parity information can be used to reconstruct the data on the lost disk. As in the case of a mirrored disk, this can take some time and will degrade I/O performance while the operating system performs this operation.

An advantage of striping with redundancy over mirroring is that striping takes less storage than complete mirroring. Mirroring requires twice the storage that the un-mirrored data would take. RAID-5 adds only a percentage of that value. If three disks are used, for example, the overhead is only 30% and not the 50% that disk mirroring would require. This percentage goes down as the number of disks used goes up.

Hardware or Software RAID-5?

As with RAID-1 (mirroring), Software RAID-5 (striping with redundancy) is useful for building an inexpensive fault-tolerant system out of inexpensive disks. As in the case of RAID-1, for more industrial-strength servers you will probably want to invest in a hardware RAID solution. ◆

Spanned Volumes

A spanned volume is made up of disk allocations that exist on two or more physical disks. This appears to applications as a single volume. Unlike striped volumes, the data in a spanned volume is written sequentially until each extent is filled.

A spanned volume does not add any fault tolerance. Its only advantage is that it can be used to make one logical device out of multiple physical devices or partitions. This is handy when all the space on a physical device is used up. Prior to the availability of this feature, the only way to solve this problem was to find space on another device or partition, create a larger partition, and then relocate the data to it. During this process, the files and directories in that partition would not be available to users.

As with other dynamic volumes, a disk can be extended while it is in use. The computer does not have to be rebooted for the change to take effect.

Tapes

Magnetic tape devices have not traditionally played a major part in the Windows 2000 storage scheme. Their use was primarily relegated to providing storage for disk backups. (As discussed earlier in this chapter, tapes were also used for data files and work files in early mainframe installations.) As you will see later in this chapter, hierarchical storage management systems meld disk and tape storage into a virtual disk environment that can appear to be much larger than installed disk storage.

Printers

Because Windows 2000 is a newer operating system than OS/390, there are no Unit-Record card-image devices defined in Windows 2000. There are, however, printers. Unlike the original line printers of OS/390, most popular PC printers are laser-based printers founded on copier technology such as the popular Hewlett-Packard LaserJet line of printers. These printers normally print whole pages based on either the proprietary Hewlett-Packard PCL or Adobe PostScript. This capability to print a page at a time rather than line by line contributes to the higher speed of modern printers. Note that the page definition language used by more modern mainframe printers is actually patterned after this printing system.

In the enterprise where mainframes and Windows 2000 systems coexist, third-party printing solutions can also be used to integrate printing systems. Several vendors, such as Barr Systems, make products that can be used to print mainframe data on Windows 2000 printers and vice versa.

When a printer is installed in Windows 2000, it is given a name that is loosely analogous to the OS/390 printer device name. Printers can be associated with several queues, and multiple queues can also be associated with the same printer. In this way, the administrator can set up printer pools similar to the printer pools that can be set up in OS/390.

As in the case of mainframes, Windows 2000 printing uses spooling to overlap printing with other processing. This spooling, although similar to mainframe spooling, is not as sophisticated.

When a file is printed by a Windows 2000 application, the Windows 2000 spooler intercepts the output. Next, it partially processes the output and writes it to one of several printer queues. When an associated printer is free, Windows 2000 reads the print data from the print queue, performs final page rendering, and then sends the output to the printer.

Third-party solutions from companies such as Barr Systems and Network Imaging Corporation allow mainframe data to be downloaded to Windows 2000 servers and printers on network printers. Some of these solutions also support attaching Windows NT systems directly to a mainframe channel for high-speed output. In addition, the *Line Printer Request* (LPR) protocol that originated with UNIX can be used to print from the mainframe to Windows 2000–attached printers if you have TCP/IP installed on your mainframe. (In my experience, however, most mainframe shops do not yet have TCP/IP installed.)

Communications Devices

Windows 2000 also supports several types of devices that allow it to be connected to a network.

To connect Windows 2000 to a *wide area network* (WAN), a modem or data service adapter is normally used. This connects locations via the public telephone network or dedicated lines leased for this purpose. A modem is normally plugged into a serial port located on a serial/parallel adapter plugged into the bus. (In some cases, the serial-port adapter is integrated directly with the motherboard.)

The serial port is responsible for handling the low-level operations such as receiving bits one at a time from the sender, assembling these bits into characters, and interrupting the CPU when a character is ready to transfer to memory. Some serial ports also buffer multiple characters and transfer the data to the CPU in whole blocks. These "high-speed" serial ports are really the only ones that you should use for WAN communications.

Windows 2000 systems can also be connected to Ethernet and Token Ring *local area networks* (LANs) using a *network interface card* (NIC). The typical NIC plugs into the PC bus on one side and connects to the LAN on the other. The LAN connections can be used to allow workstations to connect to one or more Windows 2000 servers for the purpose of running remote applications or sharing files located on a server. A LAN connection can also be used to connect a workstation to an OS/390 system.

To describe communications protocols, the *Open Systems Interconnect* (OSI) standards body has defined a seven-layer communications model. Windows 2000 supports communications with a layered architecture that is close to, but not exactly the same as, the OSI communications layers. Figure 6.4 shows this layered architecture. (In the interest of brevity, the figure shows only TCP/IP and LAN Manager protocols. Another popular set of protocols, IPX/SPX, used to support Novell NetWare servers and/or clients is not shown here.)

This diagram compares the OSI networking model with the communications layering of two popular networking protocol stacks, TCP/IP and LAN Manager (NetBIOS). Note that these two protocol stacks do not map perfectly to the OSI model layers.

You should also note that both of these protocol layers sit on top of a common data link layer supported by the NDIS driver architecture. This makes it possible to support multiple protocols simultaneously over the same network connection. With a multiprotocol stack, multiple endpoints can be connected at the same time. This multiprotocol stack implementation is shown at the bottom of Figure 6.4.

For instance, on my system at work I have access to several disk directories located on various file servers. I also have Attachmate Extra! (a 3270 emulator package) installed so that I can access an OS/390 system using TSO/SPF. I can also transfer files from my workstation to OS/390 using the file-transfer capabilities of the 3270 emulator. At the same time, I have a modem connection to the Internet, which I am using to check my email at my Internet service provider. 3270 emulation and Windows 2000–to–mainframe file transfer are discussed in Chapters 16 and 18.

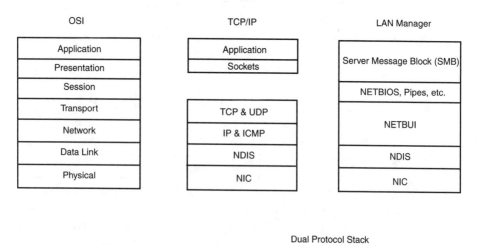

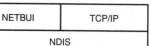

Figure 6.4   *Windows 2000 network layers.*

Telnet 3270

Currently, very few IBM mainframes support TCP/IP. If your mainframe does support TCP/IP, however, the Telnet 3270 (TN3270) feature that originated with UNIX can be used to access mainframe TSO and SPF sessions. Windows 2000 comes with a basic TN3270 client applet. If you use this applet a lot, however, you will probably want to invest in a more robust third-party version. ◆

Consoles and the User Interface

The Windows NT systems that preceded Windows 2000 did not generally require more than a single operator. Even in Windows NT, however, you could define user accounts' backup operator or printer operator privileges. This enabled the administrator to delegate responsibilities to other users without giving them full administrative privileges. This capability has been extended in Windows 2000.

The operator (user) interface of Windows 2000 is covered adequately in many other books on Windows 2000, so it is not discussed here.

As in the case of OS/390, it is important to review three topics that involve multiple device types: removable storage management, backup/recovery, and hierarchical storage management.

Removable Storage Management

The Windows 2000 *Removable Storage Manager* (RSM) is responsible for managing local and remote removable storage media and devices. This supports magnetic tape stackers, libraries, and optical disk libraries. It also includes individual removable disks such as Zip and JAZ drives. This support is comparable to the support provided by vendors of mainframe products. For instance, the same *Storage Technology Corporation* (STC) Tape Silo system mentioned in the OS/390 section of this chapter can be connected to a Windows 2000 system and managed by RSM.

RSM provides the capability to do the following:

- Manage removable storage resources using a GUI interface
- Track online and offline media
- Mount, dismount, allocate, deallocate, and decommission media
- Control media inventories

Using the MMC snap-in Remote Services Manager, a computer operator can control devices and media located on different local or remote library systems (see Figure 6.5).

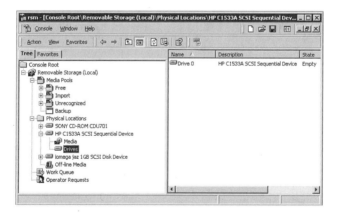

Figure 6.5   *The Removable Storage Manager.*

Figure 6.5 shows removable media and devices in several logical views using the MMC Explorer design. This shows a tree organization on the left side of the GUI window and a details panel on the right side of the window. The following views are available:

- *Media Pools view* shows logical groups of media. These groups can be unassigned (free, import, unrecognized), or they may be assigned to an application. For instance, Figure 6.5 shows a media pool assigned to the Windows 2000 backup application Backup. Other applications can have assigned media pools as well. For instance, an accounts receivable application may have its own dedicated set of backup media used to perform cyclic backups of key files.

- *Physical Locations view* shows the devices that are available and the media identifiers of all the media currently mounted in the devices.

- *Work Queue view* shows any requested but not yet complete storage management operations. For instance, a request may be pending to mount a tape volume for backup. The specific volume may be in the process of being cleaned (assuming the tape library system has a built-in tape cleaner). The mount request will go into this queue and be satisfied automatically when the cleaning operation is complete.

- *Operator Request view* shows all outstanding requests to the computer operator. For instance, the operator may be requested to retrieve and mount tapes from offline storage, such as from the shelves of a manual tape library. The operator or administrator will perform the requested operation and then enter a response so that the system will know that it can proceed to use the requested media.

The Removable Storage Management service was originally developed for Microsoft by HighGround Systems, Inc. As delivered with Windows 2000, it supports only management of media and removable media devices on a single Windows 2000 system. HighGround Systems' main product, Storage Resource Manager, provides enterprise-wide storage monitoring, reporting, planning, and analysis for Windows 2000 disks and RAID systems, and extends the basic Removable Storage Management functions in Windows 2000 with network-wide capabilities. For more details, refer to www.highground.com.

Backup/Recovery

The Removable Storage Manager works in conjunction with the Windows NT backup program NTBackup. As with OS/390, backup and recovery is extremely important to Windows 2000.

As indicated in the preceding section, mainframe shops have as an objective a 99.999% uptime to downtime ratio. This amounts to only a few minutes a year of downtime. Windows 2000's predecessors could not claim to support this type of uptime. Although clustering is normally required to achieve this level of reliability, a good backup and recovery strategy can go a long way toward maximizing system uptime.

Windows 2000 comes with a simple backup and recovery application. This application can be used to back up the data on a local workstation or server. It supports backup to magnetic tapes cartridges, stackers, and tape libraries. It also supports backup to disks and other hard drives for disk-to-disk backup.

The Windows 2000 backup and recovery program integrates system recovery features that were previously separate in Windows NT. This is embodied in a feature called Automatic System Recovery. In earlier versions of the operating system, a separate utility (Rdisk) was used to prepare a system for eventual recovery.

The Windows 2000 version of NTBackup contains the following three wizards to simplify taking a backup, preparing for an emergency recovery, and performing system recovery:

- *The Backup Wizard* helps you select what to back up on your computer. (For a server, this could also include key system files such as the Registry and Active Directory.) You can also specify that NTBackup is to perform full, incremental, differential, or daily back-ups. You can also specify that any data migrated offline by HSM be backed up as well. (See the following discussion on HSM.) The backup can be done immediately or scheduled to be done at a future time.

- *The Disaster Recovery Preparation Wizard* can be used to create a backup of key system files in a recovery directory on your hard drive. It can also create an *emergency repair disk* (ERD) that can be used to recover key system files if they become corrupted.

- *The Recovery Wizard* is used to recover a damaged Windows 2000 system. It will assist you in specifying the Windows 2000 components to recover.

NTBackup works only to back up local resources. Add-on products from other vendors add features such as the capability to back up multiple servers and workstations over a network via a dedicated backup server. One such product is provided by Seagate Software, the original developer of the NTBackup program included in Windows 2000.

Comparing Mainframe and Windows 2000 Reliability

Reliability is a slippery term to define. IBM mainframes and some clustered fault-tolerant VMS and UNIX systems claim to achieve a five nines (99.999%) uptime rating. This equates to only about five to six minutes of downtime a year! Recently IBM, Unisys, Data General, Compaq, and Hewlett-Packard published a joint commitment to provide Windows NT– and Windows 2000–based systems with a "three nines" (99.9%) uptime rating. This equates to less than nine hours of downtime a year. Although not in the same league with mainframes' 99.999% rating, this is still pretty impressive. Prior to this, Windows NT was generally thought to provide only 99.5% uptime, which corresponds to about 44 hours of downtime a year. This new commitment on the part of these major vendors is an indication that Windows NT and Windows 2000 systems will continue to be made more and more reliable. As in the mainframe and UNIX world, however, this quoted figure is only an approximation. Your mileage may vary based on what you are actually doing and how you do it. Chapter 19, "Scalability," discusses this issue in more detail. ◆

As in the case of OS/390, it is also advantageous to have a small starter system for recovery purposes. This starter system should be built on a different device from the device that holds your production operating system. If the volume containing the production version of the operating system is rendered unusable for any reason, the operating system can be rebooted from the backup copy and used to restore the full production version of the operating system. (This technique is useful on a server where rapid recovery is a must. It can also be used for a critical workstation as well.)

Hierarchical Storage Management

Empirical studies have shown that only 20% of the data on a hard drive is used roughly 80% of the time. HSM systems migrate less frequently used data files automatically from disk to less expensive offline or near-line storage such as tapes and optical disks. Support is built in to the Windows NT file system to allow files to be migrated while appearing to be present on disk until actually accessed.

Windows 2000 HSM is supported with a built-in service and an MMC snap-in, the Remote Storage Manager. This snap-in provides basic two-level data migration between disk and magnetic tape. It also provides an API for third-party vendors to implement more advanced HSM support. For instance, some vendors support a three-tier HSM architecture migrating data from expensive (online) disk to less expensive (near-line) optical disk to still less expensive (offline) magnetic tape (see Figure 6.6).

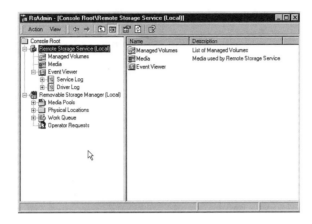

Figure 6.6 *Hierarchical storage management.*

In the next chapter, we will delve into Data Management and see how OS/390 and Windows 2000 actually uses the data stored on these devices.

7

Data Management

Data management is the process of creating, using, and deleting data in datasets. The preceding chapter explained how OS/390 and Windows 2000 support I/O devices at a low level. This chapter covers the higher-level I/O interface that OS/390 and Windows 2000 present.

OS/390 Data Management

This section of the chapter reviews the I/O features of OS/390 used the most by mainframe operators and programmers. This will set the stage for the comparison of OS/390 features to the equivalent features in Windows 2000. Although OS/390 does support datasets on tape, the discussion in this chapter concentrates primarily on disk datasets. Topics covered here include dataset naming conventions, dataset allocation, location and disposition considerations, file contents and structure, file organization and access, operating system access methods, memory-mapped files, the distributed file system, and several assorted topics related to the efficient use of disk space.

Posix Support in OS/390

OS/390 also provides supports for the Posix file system when accessed by Posix applications run under OS/390. It does this by mapping the Posix file system view into the OS/390 file system. This book does not cover this OS/390 feature. ◆

Dataset Naming Conventions

A named collection of data on disk is called a *dataset* in the OS/390 literature. COBOL programs, on the other hand, call the same entity a *file*. This book uses these terms somewhat interchangeably; however, the term dataset is normally used when talking about the physical characteristics of the collection, such as where it is physically allocated and how it is referred to by JCL. When referred to in this book as a file, the focus is on how it is processed by a program.

Dataset names in OS/390 consist of up to 44 alphanumeric characters. This dataset name can consist of multiple 1–8 character identifiers separated by periods. This name space is *mildly* hierarchical in that the first level or two of the dotted representation of the dataset name can be used to locate the catalog that describes the location of the dataset. This is analogous to the use of the backslash character (\) in the Windows 2000 Directory structure.

Each identifier in a dataset name consists of letters and numbers plus these special characters: the at sign (@); the pound sign (#); the dollar sign ($);the hyphen (-); and the period (.). Note, however, that neither a period (.) nor a hyphen (-) can appear at the beginning of the name.

For example, the following are typical dataset names:

```
SYS1.PROCLIB
CICS.TEST.RPLLIB
ZACK.ARPROJEC.COB
```

In the preceding example, SYS1.PROCLIB is the system procedure library used to store JCL-cataloged procedures. CICS.TEST.RPLLIB is the CICS online program library, and ZACK.ARPROJEC.COB is a TSO library that holds COBOL source code for an Accounts Receivable project.

Note that dataset names are not case sensitive; they are, however, usually written and entered in uppercase. MYFILE means the same dataset as MyFile, for example. The SPF editor has an option to shift the entered text to uppercase even if it is entered in lowercase.

Although the structure of dataset name components is not rigidly enforced by OS/390, some products, such as the SPF editor, do attempt to enforce a three-level hierarchical structure on this namespace. SPF entry panels encourage the specification of datasets in the structure: Project, Dataset, and Data type. A file containing a COBOL program could be named ZACK.ARPROJEC.COB, for example.

In addition, the part of the dataset name following the last period (.) is used by many applications as a data type indicator. Some applications (such as the SPF editor) use this data type to default parameters such as editing margins and line-numbering specifications. You will see toward the end of this chapter how this is similar to the way that Windows 2000 uses the part of the filename after the last period (.) as a file type. In Windows 2000, there is an even stronger operating system level association of the last qualifier after the period (called the file extension) to a specific program to be used to handle that file type.

Dataset Allocation

Datasets normally must be allocated space on disk. (The exception to this rule, the In-Memory dataset, is discussed later in this section.) Datasets are normally allocated space on a volume. (We covered the physical aspects of disk volumes in Chapter 6, "Input/Output Device Management.") You will remember that OS/390 disk volumes have 1 to 6 character identifiers, such as the SYSRES volume shown in Figure 7.1.

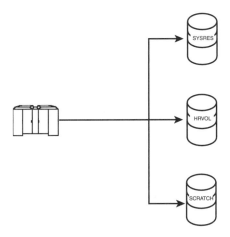

Figure 7.1 *OS/390 disk volumes.*

In a typical OS/390 installation, separate volumes are often reserved for production datasets while others are used for temporary files and work areas. Originally, disk volumes were relatively small, in the neighborhood of 10 to 20 megabytes. Currently they are tens to hundreds of Gigabytes in size.

As discussed in Chapter 6, every OS/390 disk volume contains a Volume Table of Contents (VTOC), which describes and manages the space on the volume. The disk VTOC contains a header record for each dataset. This header record is used to specify the location of data on the disk, as shown in Figure 7.2.

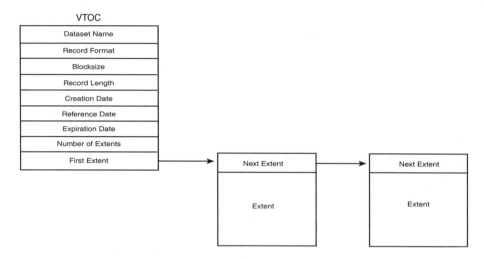

Figure 7.2 *OS/390 disk space allocation.*

Space is allocated to a dataset in one or more units of allocation called *Extents*. When a dataset is created, it is given an initial extent of data on disk. As the extent fills up, additional extents are allocated up to a fixed limit. When this limit is exceeded, or when there is no more space left on the volume, the program will abnormally terminate.

This limit on maximum space allocation reflects the concern of the early operating system developers that a runaway program could easily consume all the space on a disk. OS/390 and its predecessors were designed to support the simultaneous execution of multiple applications running at the same time under control of the operating system. No single application can be allowed to consume all the available space on a disk volume at the expense of other applications. Windows 2000's predecessors, on the other hand, were predominantly running a single program at a time. It was assumed that the program could take up as much disk space as it needed. Later in this chapter, you will see how Windows 2000 disk quotas can be used to limit the unconstrained growth of disk files

An initial space allocation is first assigned to a dataset when a JCL Data Definition (DD) statement is processed with space allocation and dataset disposition parameters specified. For example:

```
//INFILE DD DSN=MYFILE,SPACE=(TRK,(20,10)),
// DISP=(NEW,KEEP),DCB=BLKSIZE=80
```

In this example, the dataset MYFILE is allocated an initial 20 tracks and a secondary allocation of 10 tracks. The DISP parameter indicates that the dataset is to be created in this job and kept after the job completes (see "Dataset Disposition"). Chapter 9, "Job and Task Management," discusses this and the other JCL statements in more detail.

Finding Datasets

After a dataset is created, future jobs can refer to the dataset. Without the use of the OS/390 catalog, every job that uses a particular dataset must refer to it using its specific volume location. To allow a more location-independent method of keeping track of datasets, OS/390 introduced the concept of catalogs. A catalog makes it possible for a dataset to be located by name without reference to the physical volume that the dataset is on. (Chapter 10, "Catalogs and Directories," discusses catalogs in more detail.)

Dataset Disposition

By specifying a dataset disposition (DISP) parameter of CATLG when creating a dataset, the programmer can rely on OS/390 to keep track of the location of the dataset. (You can, of course, continue to specify a disposition of KEEP if you want to continue to specify the location of the dataset yourself.) In practice, heavy use is made of the CATLG option because it relieves the programmer of the chore of remembering where the dataset is located. Chapter 10 deals with the subject of OS/390 catalogs and Windows 2000 directories.

File Contents and Structure

A file is a named collection of data structured into records (and blocks) on disk. Each data record is, in turn, made up of data fields.

Records

The data in OS/390 files is stored in the form of records with a program-defined structure. This is quite different from Windows 2000 files, which consider the data in a file as a continuous stream of bytes.

The data in the record is encoded in the EBCDIC character set. Each EBCDIC character takes up one 8-bit byte of memory. The letter *A*, for example, is represented in hexadecimal by the value C1 and in binary by the value 1100. Some programmer with a sense of humor long ago defined 4 bits as a nibble (half a byte). You can represent 256 different characters in 1 byte. (Windows 2000 files, on the other hand, use the ASCII character set rather than EBCDIC.)

Records come in three record formats as defined by the JCL DD statement RECFM parameter. These formats are fixed, variable, and undefined.

- Fixed-length records in a file (RECFM=F) are all the same size. There is no length information contained in the record because the programs that process the data in the file are expected to know the exact length of the record (its RECLEN).

- Variable-length records in a file (RECFM=V) can be of different lengths. Therefore, the record itself must contain an operating system–defined length field at the start of the record. Programs must use this length information to determine the extent of the data in the record.

- Undefined records (RECFM=U) can be of variable size, but do not contain a length field at the start of the record. To process the data in these records, a program must be able to determine the length of the record dynamically from the data in the record. Because this is difficult to do, application programs rarely use this format. It is used mostly by operating system utilities.

Blocks

You will recall from Chapter 6 that mainframe disks use a count-key-data architecture rather than the sector-oriented architecture used by PC disks. As discussed in that chapter, an inter-record gap separates each data block on disk. Because these gaps waste space, the programmer will normally combine multiple logical records into larger physical data blocks so that they can be written efficiently to disk. The DD statement LRECL (record length) and BLKSIZE (block size) parameters are used to specify this blocking factor. These parameters can also be specified in the creating program.

Data Fields

Data in a record is grouped logically into one or more data fields. In the case of a file holding text lines, such as program code, the data in a record can consist of one or more logical text lines separated by delimiter characters such as carriage-return and new-line characters. In the case of non-text line data records, the content of the record may contain multiple data fields of predefined length. These fields may represent any of the character or arithmetic data types discussed in Chapter 3, "Central Processing Units." The following example shows a COBOL record description for a small data record:

```
01    INPUT-RECORD.
   05 CUSTOMER-NUMBER    PIC X(25).
   05 ACCOUNT-NUMBER     PIC 9(12).
   05 ACCOUNT BALANCE    PIC S9(5)V99.
```

In this COBOL example, the record is defined with three fields. The CUSTOMER-NUMBER field contains 25 characters. The ACCOUNT-NUMBER field contains 12 numeric digits. The ACCOUNT BALANCE field contains a signed numeric quantity with five digits before an assumed decimal point and two digits after the decimal point.

How File Data Is Organized and Accessed

Programs that need to access data in a file must specify two important characteristics of the file: its *organization* and its *access*. The following discussion adopts the COBOL program view of files because COBOL is the most popular OS/390 programming language.

File Organization

Organization defines how records are physically placed in a file. COBOL supports the following types of file organization:

- *Sequential* —Files are written to the file in sequence, starting with the first byte of the file. These records must be read from the file in the same order. Normally all the records in the file are read from beginning to end by a program. Although records can be added to the end of a sequential file, they cannot be inserted or deleted. To insert records into a sequential file, the old file must be merged with update records and a new sequential file created.

- *Relative*—Files can be considered to consist of a fixed number of slots that can each contain one data record. Records can be written into the file randomly at any position. Records can also be inserted, deleted, and updated randomly. To determine the record to access, a program must know the relative record number of the record in the file.

- *Indexed*—Files combine the best features of sequential and relative files. An indexed file consist of two parts. The data area is organized like a relatively organized file. It holds the data records of the file. In addition, there is a second part used as an index to the records in the data area. The index enables data records in the file to be accessed by a symbolic key. Data records in an indexed file can be processed both randomly and sequentially. In addition, there can be more than one index to the file so that the file can be processed in different key sequences without sorting the data records.

File Access

Access defines how a program accesses the records in a file. COBOL supports the following file access types:

- *Sequential*— This means that the program will process the file sequentially from beginning to end. A program first opens a file, which positions it at the beginning. Then it either writes records to the file or reads records from the file. Note that the file can have any of the previously discussed organizations and still be accessed sequentially. A sequential file, a relative file, and an indexed file can all be read by asking for the next record in the file, for instance. (Processing of a sequential file must start at the beginning. Processing of a relative file can start at a specific record position. Processing of an indexed file can start at the beginning of the file, or at a particular symbolic key.)

- *Random*—This is used to access records based on either a record number (in the case of a relative file) or a symbolic key (in the case of an indexed file). Sequential files can only be accessed sequentially.

- *Dynamic*—This combines sequential and random access. A file opened for dynamic access can be positioned to an arbitrary record position, and then subsequent records can be processed sequentially from that point in the file.

Operating System Access Methods

As discussed earlier, programs specify organization and access to define how they will logically process the record in a file. The operating system supports this logical organization and access with operating system modules called *access methods*. OS/390 supports the following access methods:

- *Basic sequential access method*—BSAM is used to read and write data sequentially. It does not buffer the data.

- *Queued sequential access methods*—QSAM is used to read and write data sequentially. It does buffer the data in memory.

- *Basic direct access method*—BDAM is left over from earlier versions of the operating system and has largely fallen out of use due to the introduction of the virtual sequential access method (VSAM), discussed later (although there are probably legacy systems in your shop that still have applications using it!).

- *Partitioned access method*—PAM is used primarily to organize and hold source and executable programs and small amounts of textual data. Other dataset organizations contain data for a single file. PAM datasets, on the other hand, are datasets that contain multiple subdivisions in the form of members which can be accessed sequentially as if they are small independent files.

- *Indexed sequential access method*—ISAM is also an obsolete access method which once existed to support the storage and retrieval of keyed files. It has been replaced with the virtual sequential access method (VSAM), which is more powerful and flexible.

- *Virtual sequential access method*—VSAM supports the storage and retrieval of both keyed and non-keyed data records in datasets. *VSAM key-sequenced datasets* can be used to store and retrieve records from a VSAM file sequentially or randomly based on a symbolic key. VSAM *entry-sequenced datasets* are used to store and retrieve non-keyed data. Although VSAM files originally had to be created using a special utility program called *Access Method Services* (IDCAMS), it is currently possible to create VSAM files with normal JCL.

Memory-Mapped Files

The "Allocation" section of this chapter mentioned that there is one exception to the rule that dataset must be allocated physical space on disk. This exception is the memory-mapped file. To understand how memory-mapped files work, it's important to understand a little about the different types of memory that can be installed in a System/390 complex.

System/390 can be configured with two types of memory:

- *Central storage*—This is fast, but expensive and limited in size.

- *Expanded memory*—This is cheaper and larger.

Programs and data can both be loaded into central storage. Programs can be run from central storage, and they can refer to data located in central storage. Although data can also reside in expanded storage, programs cannot be run from expanded storage. This makes expanded storage mainly useful for keeping large segments of highly used data files resident in memory. These files can also be "mapped" into the address space of multiple jobs or users to share access to them.

OS/390 has two types of memory-mapped files, Dataspaces, and Hiperspaces. They perform essentially the same data caching and sharing function discussed earlier. Through the use of these facilities, OS/390 supports the use of files that reside completely or partially in memory. It does this by using the paging facilities provided by the operating system to these map these files into memory locations without actually paging them out to disk.

OS/390 JCL statements can be used to instruct the operating system to use memory-mapped files regardless of whether the program was originally written to use them. Later in this section, you will see how Windows 2000 also supports memory-mapped files.

DOS Expanded memory

For those of you who grew up with DOS, you will undoubtedly remember that DOS also supported different types of memory (conventional memory, expanded memory, and extended memory). DOS expanded memory performed essentially the same function as expanded memory does in OS/390. ◆

Distributed File Systems

The networking support in OS/390 is mainly dedicated to managing interactive terminals. There is support for remote job entry and output distribution through the operating system and the virtual telecommunications access method (VTAM). Until recently, however, there was no support for any type of distributed file system. The network file system (NFS) is supported on mainframes where TCP/IP is an installed protocol. Unfortunately, TCP/IP is not yet in use on many mainframes mainly due to security considerations. Chapter 14, "Networking," discusses networking in more detail.

Effective Use of Space

This section discusses several topics related to the efficient use of disk space for files. These topics are disk defragmentation, data compression, disk quotas, and hierarchical storage management.

Disk Defragmentation

When an OS/390 disk volume is brand new, space is allocated to new datasets in a primary extent and (possibly) secondary extents. Normally, these extents are located close to each other on the disk. As datasets get deleted and new datasets get allocated, the free space on the disk gets fragmented into alternating free and allocated blocks.

This may require the operating system to write new data into widely separated extents. This effect is called fragmentation. This is bad because it causes the read-write heads to jump around while accessing the dataset. Moving the heads this way is an expensive operation and is bad for performance. In an extreme case, there may not be enough space on the volume to allocate all the required extents and the program may be abnormally terminated.

OS/390 has no utility to reorganize a disk volume. To remedy this, the systems programmer must manually reorganize the disk by backing it up to other media, such as magnetic tape. The programmer must then reinitialize the disk and restore it. As discussed later, Windows 2000 comes with a defragmentation utility, which can perform this operation in place without requiring the data to be backed up and restored.

Data Compression

Until recently, there was little support in OS/390 for data compression. Currently, OS/390 does support data compression on specific dataset types. This, however, requires the use of newer System/390 processors that have hardware support for this feature.

Several commercial data compression products can also be added to OS/390. There is even an OS/390 version of the popular PKZIP data compression utility that is a staple in the DOS/Windows world. This utility can be used to facilitate the transfer of compressed files between OS/390 and Windows 2000.

Disk Quotas

In OS/390, disk space allocations have to be predefined in JCL before a job is run. Because of this, OS/390 will not allow a rogue program to create files of unlimited size. When a program exceeds its maximum space allocation, the program will be abnormally terminated. Because this limit is on a dataset-by-dataset basis, it is not uncommon for a job to have to be rerun several times with increasing space allocations before it completes successfully. This can be quite frustrating for the operator or programmer submitting the job. It can also lead to overallocation of space just to be sure that the job does not fail. This can be quite wasteful of disk space.

Hierarchical Storage Management

Chapter 6 discussed the hierarchical storage-management capabilities of system-managed storage. It is mentioned here again because it interfaces with the OS/390 access methods to affect data migration and retrieval. When a dataset has been migrated, it looks to the access method as if the file still exists on disk. When the program attempts to open the file, however, the request is intercepted. If an online user opens the file and it can be retrieved quickly, the user may experience a minor delay but will be able to access the file. If the file is offline and cannot be retrieved quickly, the user will be notified and given the option of requesting that the file be retrieved while he waits, or that it be staged for retrieval at a later time. This would enable the user to perform other work and check back for the file at a later time.

What happens in the case of a batch program is similar, except that the program open-file request will wait for the file to be retrieved. If the operator cannot satisfy the request in a reasonable time frame, the operator may cancel the job and rerun it later.

Security

File security in OS/390 consist of access control placed on individual datasets and file data encryption.

File Access Controls

Chapter 13, "Security," covers the subject of overall security management in more detail. Dataset access is managed by the built-in security features of OS/390. In OS/390, datasets have access profiles stored in a security database. When a program attempts to access a dataset, the security subsystem determines whether it has the right to access the dataset in the access mode that it specified. If not, the request is denied. If the program is acting on behalf of an interactive TSO or CICS user, the user is sent an error message and can decide what to do next. In the case of a batch program, the program will be abnormally terminated.

File Data Encryption

OS/390 datasets can also be encrypted for increased security; however, this feature is somewhat limited, and not currently used in many mainframe shops.

As in the case of data compression, OS/390 did not support built-in encryption until recently. Like OS/390 data compression, the encryption support built in to OS/390 also requires special hardware built in to the latest System/390 processors.

Windows 2000 Data Management

Like OS/390, Windows 2000 supports two different file systems: the native Windows 2000 file system (NTFS) and the Posix file system. Again, because this is not a book on UNIX to mainframe integration, the discussion is restricted to the NTFS file system. Briefly, however, this discussion touches on the FAT and FAT32 file systems that preceded NTFS.

As indicated in the "OS/390" section, Windows 2000 is mainly a disk-oriented operating system. It does support tape devices, but usually only through the use of special utility programs used for backup and recovery. Normally, Windows 2000 applications process data only on disk. This may change in the future as Windows 2000 is used for more and more corporate applications that currently process large tape files.

Windows 2000–Supported File Systems

Data management in Windows 2000 is the province of the Windows 2000 I/O Manager, file systems, and device drivers. Windows 2000 supports multiple types of file systems, including the following:

- FAT
- FAT32
- OS/2 HPFS
- NTFS

In addition, the Posix and Macintosh file systems are also simulated by the NTFS file system for those subsystems. This book covers only the FAT, FAT32, and NTFS file systems, and devotes most of its coverage to the native Windows 2000 file system, NTFS.

The FAT and FAT32 File Systems

The Windows 2000 file system has its origins in the early days of the personal computer, which ran much simpler operating systems such as DOS. The *File Allocation Table* (FAT) file system was the file system used by those operating systems. The original FAT file system was developed when disks were relatively small (10–20MB). To support larger file and volume with greater efficiency, Microsoft subsequently developed the FAT32 file system, which was released in a service release of Windows 95 (OSR2) and also used as the primary file system of Windows 98. FAT32 used more bits to address dataset clusters and also reduced the size of a cluster. This enabled it to support larger disk volumes.

Although Windows 2000 does support the FAT file system, it does so for backward compatibility. Enterprise applications should use the NTFS file system instead.

FAT32 and Windows NT?

Although Windows NT versions prior to Windows 2000 do not support the FAT32 file system format, you can buy a third-party utility to add FAT32 support to Windows NT 4.0. This utility is named (aptly enough) FAT32. It is available from Winternals Software LLC. ◆

OS/2 HPFS

As indicated in several earlier chapters, the OS/2 support in Windows 2000 is not very useful. Therefore, it is not discussed further in this chapter.

The Windows NT File System

Although Windows 2000 still supports the FAT and FAT32 file systems of its predecessors, this chapter concentrates on the native Windows 2000 file system (NTFS). Only NTFS gives you the security, integrity, and reliability needed to support modern corporate applications.

It is the only file system that enables you to specify access permissions at the file level (see Chapter 13). The Posix support provided by NTFS does support UNIX-style access permissions, which are mapped to NTFS permissions.

In addition, the NTFS file system maintains recovery information in its data so that the file is always left in a consistent state after an attempted update.

Directory and File Naming Conventions

The NTFS file system in Windows 2000 is organized into directories and files in a hierarchical tree structure. In the GUI, this is represented as a tree of folders and documents (see Figure 7.3). The directories are shown as folder icons and the files within them are shown as document icons of the appropriate type based on the file association in effect for that type of file.

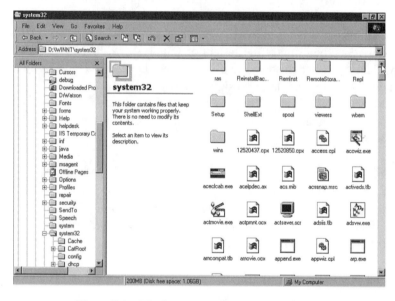

Figure 7.3 *Windows 2000 directories and files.*

Directory and filenames can consist of up to 255 alphanumeric and special characters. They cannot include these special characters: ?, ", / , \, <, >, *, |, and :. Windows 2000 is not case sensitive but it is case preserving. MyProgramFiles and MYPROGRAMFILES both refer to the same directory. A new file will be listed in this directory as MyFile if that is the case in which it was created.

Names can also contain embedded spaces; however, commands that manipulate them from a DOS window must enclose them in quotation marks to be understood. GUI operations are generally easier to perform on files and directories without embedded spaces because of this. Therefore, I recommend that you stay away from creating filenames with embedded spaces. Use names such as TestData rather than Test Data. Unfortunately,

Windows 2000 makes extensive use of directory- and filenames with embedded spaces. This really annoys command-line users such as myself!

You should also note that there are several system reserved filenames, such as LPT1, LPT2, CON, PRN, and so on, that cannot be used as program or directory names.

Command-line operations on files and directories can use "wildcard" characters such as the asterisk (*) and question mark (?). The asterisk stands for 0 or more characters that match the other characters in the filename For example: DEL PGM*.EXE will delete all files in the current directory that start with PGM followed by 0 or more characters and ending in with the file extension EXE. A question mark character is a stand-in for a single character in the specified position of the filename. For example: DEL FILE?.TXT will match File1.txt and File2.txt, but not File01.txt.

As in the case of OS/390, the last qualifier of the filename is normally used to associate a file with the program that handles it. In Windows 2000, however, this association is enforced by the operating system itself. If you double-click on a file in a directory folder in the GUI, for example, the appropriate program will be started and that file will be processed. (In the case of OS/390, you will recall that the program must decide what to do about the extension when it processes the file.) In the filename ARPROJECT.MDB, the MDB data type will tell Windows 2000 to associate Microsoft Access with the file. This association also works at the command line in a DOS window. If I type the filename **Memo.doc** in my Documents directory at a command prompt, Microsoft Word will start and load the document to be edited because the extension .doc is associated with Microsoft Word.

The Windows 2000 file system also supports the use of mount points. Mount points allow a directory to be grafted seamlessly on to another empty directory so that it appears to be part of the same physical path. This saves drive letters and simplifies accessing disparate directories and volumes in a single hierarchy. The Windows 2000 DFS takes advantage of this feature. (See the section titled "The Distributed File System" later in this chapter.)

File Location

As discussed in Chapter 6, a partition formatted with the NTFS file system contains a master file table, which describes data extents in a highly optimized fashion. Small files and directories may even be contained right in the MFT itself and not require any additional extents to be allocated. NTFS directories and files can be allocated on any Windows NT–supported volume subject to the user's access rights.

Where OS/390 has a system catalog to keep track of the location of datasets and other system objects, Windows 2000 has the Active Directory. The Active Directory is a distributed global repository of information on the location and key properties of all users, groups, printers, files, and other resources in an enterprise that employs multiple networked Windows 2000 systems. Through the Active Directory, any resource can be located anywhere in the network. This resource can then be allocated and used, subject to any access restrictions placed on the resource by the system administrator. (For more on the Active Directory, see Chapter 10, "Catalogs and Directories.")

One new feature that Windows 2000 inherited from its Internet Information Server component is its Content Indexing service. Content Indexing scans your entire hard disk during periods of low system activity. This results in an index that can be searched for files with specific properties or contents. The Content Indexing service uses the new Change Journal built in to the Windows 2000 version of NTFS.

File Disposition

Windows 2000 files must be explicitly deleted when they are no longer needed. There is nothing like the OS/390 JCL DISP parameter to control this process.

File Contents and Structure

Although the internal structure of data in files is not imposed by the operating system, most applications consider the data in a file to be in either binary fields or text format. In text format, the data consists of printable characters separated into editable lines with carriage-return and new-line characters at the end of each line and an end-of-file marker (Ctrl+Z) at the end of the file. Commands, such as COPY, that process files need to be told with an option which type of file they are copying, because copying of a binary file will end with the first Ctrl+Z found! Without the /B option, for example, the following COPY command would stop copying characters from FILE1 at the first Ctrl+Z character in the file.

```
(COPY /B FILE1 FILE2)
```

If the file is a binary file, the probability of hitting one of these characters before the actual end of the file is pretty high. In this case, FILE2 would not be an exact copy of FILE1.

As in the case of OS/390, programs normally open a data file, write data into the file during operation, and close the file when done. If a file is not properly closed by the program, it is normally unusable and has to be re-created.

PC-based operating systems prior to Windows 2000 stored file data in 8-bit ASCII characters. Internally Windows 2000 stores file data by default in an international format known as Unicode. Unicode characters take up 2 bytes (16 bits) per character to support languages whose individual characters cannot be represented in 8 bits. Windows 2000 does offer the programmer the option to override this and use ASCII when creating a file.

How a File Data Is Organized and Accessed

As with OS/390, a file is a named collection of data on disk. Unlike OS/390, a file is not assumed to have any internal structure. It is just treated as a continuous stream of bytes (see Chapter 18.)

Organization and access of Windows 2000 files is left completely up to the program that creates and/or processes the file.

As far as the operating system is concerned, a file is a sequential stream of characters. The file system maintains a file pointer to the current character in the file and is capable of determining when it is at the beginning or end of the file. Files can be created, deleted, overwritten, or extended by programs that specify the correct attributes when they open the file. You should note that the concept of a data record, central to OS/390 applications, does not exist in Windows 2000. If a record structure is necessary, it must be imposed by the program.

This can be a pain in the neck if you are editing a file of records created by a record-oriented program. Successively displayed lines will not line up correctly in the edit window of most editors. The UltraEdit-32 shareware text editor, from IDM Computer Solutions, has a feature to automatically insert new-line characters at the end of each logical record in this type of file. This will make the records line up in the edit window. (This is an excellent editor with many great features and is available at an extremely reasonable price.)

Even though the operating system imposes no record boundaries, commercial applications often impose an arbitrary record structure on each contiguous set of bytes. A programmer working in Microfocus COBOL under Windows 2000 can deal with logical records from an application perspective, for instance, as if the file system was actually structured that way. This aids in the conversion of mainframe applications to Windows 2000.

The Windows 2000 I/O Architecture

The I/O architecture of Windows 2000 is a layered architectures, as illustrated in Figure 7.4.

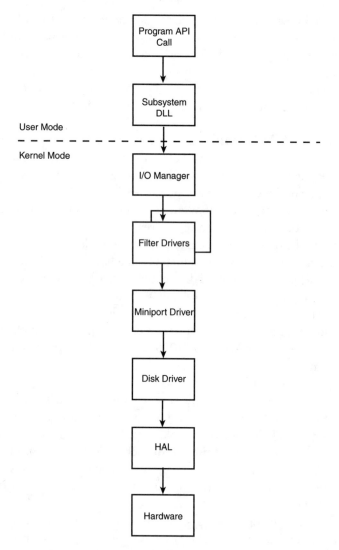

Figure 7.4 *Windows 2000 I/O architecture.*

Application programs make file system requests by issuing an API call to a DLL provided by a hosting subsystem such as the Win32 subsystem. The subsystem DLL in turn maps the subsystem-specific call to a native Windows 2000 call, which it passes to the I/O Manager in the executive.

The I/O Manager next passes the request by one or more filter drivers registered for the device. (The Windows 2000 filter driver is used to implement some of the advanced file system functions, such as HSM, discussed later in this chapter.)

After filter processing, the I/O Manager passes control to the miniport and port device drivers for the specific device type and device. These drivers interface with the actual hardware via the HAL, which provides hardware independence. (For more information, see Chapter 2.)

Memory-Mapped Files

Windows 2000, like OS/390, has support for memory-mapped files. As mentioned in Chapter 2, "Operating System Architecture," Windows 2000 uses nearly all free random access memory for file system caching. In addition, the operating system supports APIs that enable an application to map some or all of a file into memory. The program can then access data in the file as if it is a memory array. The same paging system that provides virtual memory page management takes care of all the I/O for the file. Because pages are managed in 4KB chunks, this makes most file operations quite efficient when dealing with memory-mapped files. Unlike OS/390, however, there is no JCL facility that can be used to introduce memory-mapped files to a program that has not been written specifically to use them.

Remote File Systems

Networking is an integral part of Windows 2000. Chapter 14 discusses networking in more detail. The various protocols and communication layers, which are discussed in Chapter 14, provide the basis for several methods of file sharing.

There are two ways to share a file or directory in Windows 2000:

1. Network drive assignment
2. The Distributed File System

Network Drive Assignment

You can assign a drive letter to a remote directory such that it appears to be a local device. To do this, you can map the drive to a drive letter by selecting *Tools* and then *Map network drive* from the menu bar in any folder window. This starts the Map Network Drive Wizard. Using this wizard you can specify an available drive letter and browse for a network drive to assign to that letter. You can also use the NET USE command-line command to associate the drive letter with a server directory. For instance, the command NET USE G: \\Billspc\Public could be used to effect the same result.

Note that a directory or file on a file server can also be referenced in programs and from the command line without a drive letter using the file's *Universal Naming Convention* (UNC) name. The command DEL \\Billspc\Public\Testfile could be used to delete the above file, for example, in addition to the command DEL G:\Testfile. UNC names have the format \\servername\sharename\filepath\filename, where servername is the name of the server hosting the file, sharename is the symbolic name assigned to the resource location on the server, filepath is a qualified file path to the directory or file to be accessed, and filename is the name of the file.

The Distributed File System

The second method of sharing a file requires the installation of the Windows 2000 Distributed File System (DFS).

DFS works like the Network File System (NFS) supported by most UNIX systems. It provides a single logical tree structure made up of multiple directory subtrees that can exist on multiple servers in a network. The actual location of the physical resource is hidden from the clients.

A DFS tree has one root volume. The root volume can have one level of leaf volume under it, which can be on different servers. Leaf volumes, in turn, can have multiple levels of directories in them. The same physical volume can exist in multiple DFS trees. This provides a degree of redundancy. (Leaf volumes can even be located on non-Windows 2000 systems, such as older versions of Windows NT, Windows 95/98, and even some non-Microsoft operating systems such as Novell NetWare.)

The advantage of this approach over the network drive assignment approach is that it saves drive letters, because the client needs only to allocate one drive letter for the entire tree even though it extends over multiple servers.

DFS also supports redundancy because multiple copies of a leaf volume can be mounted into different DFS trees. It also makes it possible to move file system resources from one server to another without having the change visible to clients. A physical directory can be moved from one server to another, for example, to improve performance without affecting existing client assignments.

DFS is not a feature in widespread use at this time. We do expect its use to grow over time, however, because it offers quite a few advantages over the network drive assignment method of file sharing.

Effective Use of Disk Storage

This section of the chapter is devoted to discussing several topics related to the efficient use of disk space. As in the case of OS/390, these topics include disk defragmentation, data compression, disk quotas, and hierarchical storage management. In addition, for Windows 2000, we also add a discussion of sparse files.

Defragmentation

Just as discussed in the OS/390 section, a disk can become fragmented over time. All disk file types suffer from fragmentation. Although NTFS files do not suffer from the effects of fragmentation as badly as FAT files do, they still need periodic defragmentation.

Windows 2000 defragmentation utilities can be used to reorganize a disk so that the files are allocated in contiguous locations. This improves performance. Windows 2000 itself comes with a simple defragmentation utility originally developed for Microsoft by Executive Software. This defragmentation utility can be used to defragment a single local disk at a time. Executive Software, the makers of the Windows 2000 defragmentation utility, also sell a more capable defragmentation utility called Diskkeeper. Diskkeeper can be used to defragment multiple local disks at the same time. It can be used to defragment the disks on other machines in the network. It even has its own priority-based scheduler built in so that disks can be defragmented in the middle of the night, or during the day, without degrading performance.

Disk Compression

Windows NT, the predecessor of Windows 2000, supported automatic compression of files and directories. Windows 2000 continues this tradition by allowing automatic compression of files, directories, and volumes. When you specify the *compressed* property for a file, it is compressed immediately. If you specify compression for a directory, files created or moved to that directory are automatically compressed. Existing files in the directory are not automatically compressed, however.

This sounds like a great feature; however, there are some caveats. Traditionally PC disks have not been as reliable as mainframe disks, and the risk of data loss was magnified by the use of data compression. That, plus the constantly decreasing cost of disk storage, makes me personally tend to recommend against using automatic data compression. In individual cases, data compression may be warranted. For instance, in the case of an extremely large file, where you have a large directory adequately backed up to other media, or for files that you need to transmit over slow communications lines, you may want to use compression.

Another type of compression, discussed in the OS/390 section earlier, is the manual use of PKZIP to compress selected files for storage or data transmission. (In that section, I recommended the use of PKZIP for MVS because of its compatibility with Windows versions of PKZIP.) One last point is that Windows 2000 compression and encryption are mutually exclusive; you cannot encrypt and compress the same directory or file.

Disk Quotas

In OS/390, limits on disk-space use are inherent in the requirement to predefine the disk-space allocation for a dataset. When an OS/390 dataset exceeds its limits, the program is abnormally terminated by the operating system.

Traditionally, PC operating systems have not placed any limits on the growth of files. A single rogue program could get stuck in a loop and fill up an entire disk with data. Windows 2000 improves on this situation by supporting disk quotas on a per-volume and per-user basis. (User, in this sense, could be either a local user or one logged on to the remote domain.)

In Windows 2000, disk quotas can be established on a user, group, or job basis. (You will remember that job is defined in Chapter 9, "Job and Task Management," as a related group of processes.) When a Windows 2000 program exceeds its quota, it receives an out-of-space error response just as if there really were no more space on the volume. It is then up to the program to handle the error condition. This feature is supported only by the NTFS file system. (This is another reason not to use the archaic FAT file system.)

Note that you can specify both a quota and a warning level. Note also that you can elect to track space usage without denying any user requests. This might be a friendlier way to manage storage initially.

Sparse files

Sparse files are a new capability of the Windows 2000 file system. To my knowledge, it has no parallel in OS/390. When a normal data file is created, the space for the file is allocated as records are written into it. As records are written to the file, it normally increases in size.

Some applications require the creation of a file with a large record address space. This file may not have a record present in every available record slot. To save space on disk, the address space can be allocated without actually committing the space on disk until it is needed. If the file is defined as a sparse file, space is not actually allocated for the records until they are written.

A file that can hold a whole year's worth of records may start out empty in January, for example, and get progressively larger. Periodically records from the front of the file may be deleted as they become obsolete. At the end of the year, the total amount of space actually consumed in a sparse file would be less than the total amount of space that would be necessary to hold a whole year's worth of data without this feature.

Hierarchical Storage Management

As discussed in the preceding chapter, Windows 2000 supports mainframe-style hierarchical storage management (HSM). This is similar to the support provided by OS/390. A file is opened by a call to the Windows 2000 file system. As in the case of OS/390, when a file has been migrated it looks to the file system as if the file still exists on disk. When the program attempts to open the file, however, the request is intercepted.

If the file has been migrated off of the disk, the appropriate file system filter driver will intercept the request. This filter driver can request that the operator restore the file. Windows 2000 provides basic two-level HSM support. Third-party vendors such as Eastman Software (the developer of the Remote Storage Manager in Windows 2000) sell more advanced multitier HSM systems.

Security

Throughout this and other chapters, the access rights that can be placed on a file or directory have been discussed. As explained, logged on users can access files and directories subject to their rights and privileges. An important file system consideration that bears mentioning here is that Windows 2000 also supports encrypted files through a special Encrypted File System (EFS).

Chapter 13 discusses security and encryption in more detail, including the subject of Windows 2000 security. Again, as mentioned earlier, encryption and compression cannot be used on the same directory or file.

This chapter has explored OS/390 and Windows 2000 features used to manage files located in disk storage. The following chapter discusses how OS/390 and Windows 2000 manage programs and how they support the APIs used by one program to invoke another.

8

Program Management

The von Neuman model of computers, on which almost all modern computers are based, uses the same data store for programs and data. OS/390 and Windows 2000 both store programs on disk and load them into memory as needed. This chapter covers how OS/390 and Windows 2000 handle program management, specifically looking at how programs communicate with each other, how the operating system stores and retrieves programs, and how programs are prepared for execution.

OS/390 Program Management

OS/390 programs are normally made up of a main executable program together with library functions and/or subroutines used by the program. Library functions are usually provided by the compiler vendor (normally IBM). Subroutines may be separately compiled routines purchased from a third party or developed by the programmer for use in more than one program. A programmer may develop a common date-calculation routine, for instance, for use in all applications.

Static and Dynamic Program Linkage

Functions and subroutines may be bound statically to the main executable at program preparation time. They can also be loaded and called dynamically at execution time. This dynamic call capability reduces the need to relink application programs when a common subroutine changes. Later in this section, you will see how Windows 2000 *dynamic load libraries* (DLLs) perform a similar function.

Program Libraries and Access Methods

The operating system uses a specialized software called access method to read programs from disk storage into memory. Programs are stored in program libraries called *partitioned datasets* (PDSs) and accessed by a special access method the *partitioned access method* (PAM).

Partitioned datasets are organized with an index at the start of the dataset and one or more internal subfiles called *members*. Each member is treated as a file within a file in the dataset. The index points to the start of the subfile and also contains the length of the subfile. These members can contain executable programs, source programs, or control statements for utility programs or the JCL processor. One of the major nuisances with the use of PDSs is that they do not reuse space when modules are updated. This often results in an *abnormal program end* (Abend) during the program preparation process. In this case, the library has to be compressed to recover wasted space. Recently a new PDS format, PDSE, was developed to reduce the need for PDS compression.

Examples of this are JCL libraries such as SYS1.PROCLIB used to store cataloged procedures, and program libraries such as CICS.TEST.RPLLIB, which is used to store executable CICS programs.

Source-Code Control Systems

Many installations use third-party source-code control systems such as Panvalet and Librarian from Computer Associates. These systems eliminate the PDS compression requirement by storing the source in a proprietary database. These products allow multiple versions of a program to be stored at the same time and support the rollback of program changes. They also keep a history of changes and who made them. ♦

The Program Development Process

Program development in OS/390 is a mixture of interactive and batch processes. The steps of program development are as follows:

1. Source program preparation
2. Compiling the program
3. Link editing the program

Figure 8.1 illustrates this process.

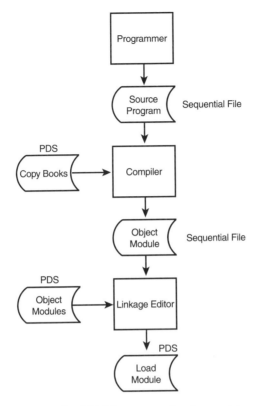

Figure 8.1 *The OS/390 program development process.*

Source Program Preparation

Initially the programmer uses a source-code editor such as the TSO/SPF editor to prepare a source program in a language such as COBOL, Assembly language, PL/1, or C. This program is created and maintained in a source PDS whose name normally ends in an extension specific to the compiler that will process the program. For instance, the library name could be ZACK.ARPROJ.COB. This of course assumes that they are not using one of the source-control systems previously listed. Some of these products have SPF interfaces so that programs can bypass the use of a PDS. The result of this process is a PDS member containing the source program. The dataset and PDS member could be defined as ZACK.ARPROJ.COB(ARPROGM), for example.

The remaining steps in this process can be performed interactively from SPF; however, they are normally done by submitting a batch job to be run at a later time. This frees up the programmer to do other work while the operating system is performing the compile process. If there are a lot of programmers, these jobs may take a while to run.

Compiling the Program

The next step in the preparation process is normally done using one of several multistep JCL cataloged procedures provided by IBM and customized by the local systems programmer. These procedures have names such as CB2CL (to compile and link a batch COBOL/2 program) or DCCB2CL (to compile and link a COBOL program that uses DB/2 and CICS). Figure 8.1 shows this compile and link procedure.

The compile step of the procedure is used to convert the source program into an object module that can be output to a sequential dataset to be used as input to the next processing step, as shown in Figure 8.1.

Link Editing the Program

In the next step of the procedure, the OS/390 *Linkage Editor* (LKED) is used to combine the object module together with any required subroutines from an object module library to create an executable program. During this step, the Linkage Editor combines the object module from the preceding step together with other object modules developed by the programmer or provided with the operating system. Also during this step, the Linkage Editor resolves references between modules.

The result of this process is either a complete executable program (Load module) or a subroutine module that can be dynamically loaded and called at runtime. Later you will see a direct parallel in how Windows 2000 supports calling functions in DLLs loaded at runtime.

The output of the link edit step is stored in a runtime program load library (PDS) with a name such as CICS.TEST.LOADLIB.

Object Modules and Object Libraries

An object module is a source program that has been converted to executable format; however, it has not yet been combined with the subroutines and other system functions necessary to make it an executable program.

Sometimes the output of the compile step is stored in an object library PDS rather than in a simple sequential file. This library is then used in a future processing step. A subroutine that will be linked with an executable program prepared in a later job can be saved in an object library (PDS), for instance. Then, that library can be used as input to a future Linkage Editor job.

ZACK.ARPROJ.OBJ could be the name of my object library, for example. If the member name of my program is ARPROGM, its full filename would be ZACK.ARPROJ.OBJ(ARPROGM). In JCL, you will sometimes see the SYSLMOD DD statement specify an output dataset and member name such as this. Often you will also see the Linkage Editor used to create this member in the library. When used this way, the NCAL parameter is used to tell the Linkage Editor not to combine other object modules with this one. To make it executable, it must be combined with other object modules in a subsequent Linkage Editor step. ◆

The next section explains how the Windows 2000 program preparation process compares with the OS/390 process. You will notice that they are quite similar, but that they do have some key differences.

Windows 2000 Program Management

Windows 2000 programs, like OS/390 programs, are normally made up of a main executable program together with library functions and/or subroutines used by the program. As in the case of OS/390, these components may be provided by the compiler vendor. For instance, the functions that implement string move and compare operations in Visual C/C++ come with the Microsoft compiler. Application-specific functions may also be purchased from a third party or developed by the programmer. This section covers Windows 2000 program linkage, how programs are stored and loaded by the operating system, and the program preparation process.

Static and Dynamic Program Linkage

As in the case of OS/390 programs, functions and subroutines may be bound statically to the main executable at program preparation time. They can also be bound into *dynamic link libraries* (DLLs) to be used at runtime. When a program needs to call a function in a DLL at execution time, the DLL can be loaded into memory dynamically. Then the desired function can be called.

Loading DLLs dynamically when they are needed reduces the need to relink application programs when a common subroutine or function changes. It also reduces the memory footprint of a running application.

In addition, it allows applications to share code. Applications such as Microsoft Word, Excel, and Access, for instance, all share common DLLs to save disk and memory space. It is interesting to note that most of the Win32 APIs are actually located in one of several DLLs provided by Microsoft. This is also true of many internal routines and system services. This makes it possible for Microsoft to distribute updates to the operating system and its APIs without requiring that you re-install the operating system.

DLL Hell!

The use of DLLs in Windows 2000 is a useful feature; however, it is not without its drawbacks. Sometimes a new application can come with a version of a DLL that is actually older than one already installed on your system. If the installation of the new application replaces the newer DLL with the older one, other applications could become unstable or fail to run. Most of us refer to this situation as

continues ▶

▶ *continued*

"DLL Hell," because finding the cause of this problem may not be easy. Windows 2000's new System File Protection Service does protect approximately 300 key operating system DDLs from being replaced accidentally. This, however, is only a partial solution to this problem. There are also some third-party products that claim to help in this area, but I have yet to find an adequate solution. ◆

Program Files

Program files in Windows 2000 are just sequential files that have been marked as executable programs. By convention, these programs end with an .EXE or .COM suffix. As mentioned in the preceding chapter, this dataset extension is used to associate the file with an appropriate processing program. (Note that this is similar to the use of the file extension in an OS/390 filename.)

Some examples of executable program files are the following:

```
CMD.EXE (The Windows 20000 Command Prompt)
XCOPY.EXE (The extended copy command)
ARREPORT.EXE (Our accounts Receivable reporting .program)
```

Source-Code Control Systems

As in the case of OS/390, many Windows 2000 installations use third-party source-code control systems. Perhaps the most popular one of these is Microsoft's Visual Source Safe, which comes with Microsoft's Visual Studio development toolkit. PVCS from Intersolv is also a popular choice.

As in the case of Panvalet and Librarian, these source-code control systems allow multiple versions of a program to be stored at the same time and also support the rollback of program changes. In addition, they keep a history of changes and who made them. ◆

The Program Development Process

Program development in Windows 2000 depends on the development tools that the programmer is using. It is generally a more interactive process than the process of developing OS/390 applications. Assuming a program in C/C++ is being developed, the steps of program development are as follows:

1. Source program preparation
2. Compiling the program
3. Building the function library
4. Linking the program

Figure 8.2 illustrates these steps.

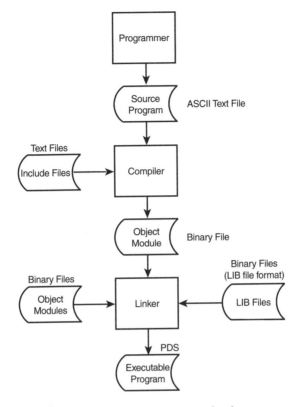

Figure 8.2 *The Windows 2000 program development process.*

Source Program Preparation

The following discussion assumes that the programmer is building a Visual C/C++ program using Microsoft's Visual Studio development package. Visual Studio integrates program editors, compilers, and linkers in a single package.

Visual Studio and Other Tools

There are of course development tools from vendors other than Microsoft. Some developers prefer Delphi from Inprise, or C and C++ compilers provided by Symantec and other compiler vendors.

Visual Studio is the favorite, however, because it is from Microsoft and because it integrates almost all of Microsoft's development tools in a single package. It includes Visual Basic, Visual C/C++, and Visual FoxPro, for instance. It also includes Visual Interdev (for Internet/intranet development), and even the Visual Source Safe source-code control system.

continues ▶

▶ *continued*

If you are more comfortable with mainframe editors, you can even use SPF/PC from Computer Technology Corporation to prepare your source code for compilation. ◆

In the scenario here, a programmer develops his source program using the Visual Studio *Integrated Development Environment* (IDE). This IDE is common to all language products except Visual Basic. (Visual Basic has its own IDE. Microsoft has indicated that they will integrate Visual Basic in a future release.) This IDE enables the programmer to edit, compile, link, and test applications in a common environment, much as the OS/390 programmer uses the TSO/SPF environment.

If the programmer is not using a source-code control system, he will use directories and subdirectories the way that an OS/390 programmer might use multiple PDSs. A development project might use the following directory structure, for example:

```
C:\ARProject
    \Source    (C source files)
    \H         (Common C Header files)
    \Lib       (Include libraries)
    \Bin       (Executables and DLLs)
```

The source directory would normally contain C source code and Makefiles. (See the sidebar "The Make Utility" in this section.) Source programs normally have an extension based on the programming language, like those in Table 8.1

Table 8.1 Programming Language Extensions

Extension	Programming Language
.C	C
.CPP	C++
.CBL	COBOL
.ASM	Assembler

The Make Utility

The Windows NT Make utility is a minimal Make utility with origins in the UNIX world. It uses the compiler, linker, and librarian (LIBR) utility to build an executable program based on a script defined in a Makefile with a .Mak *extension. It is smart enough to rebuild only those components whose constituent parts have changed. This cuts down on the amount of work that must be done when a change is made. OS/390 has nothing like this! OS/390 programmers normally recompile everything when in doubt just to be safe.*

An IBM product, called SES, is used by systems programmers to install, update, and modify the operating system itself. This is a kind of Make utility that keeps track of the state of the operating system and only does what is needed to update it. Although it is normally used only by systems programmers, you could define an application in SES format and use SES to manage changes to it. To my knowledge, this is not used very often. ◆

In the preceding example, the \H directory is for common C header files that are to be included in the program by the compiler #include statement. The \Lib directory is for prebuilt application libraries that will be input to the linker, and the \Bin directory is for the created .EXE and .DLL files that will be used at runtime.

Compiling the Program

After the program has been entered, the programmer can select a compiler-specific menu option in the IDE to "make" the program. This will compile the program into an object module and store the result in a directory specified by the programmer. It may also link the program with other library functions using the linker. (Note that interpretive languages, such as Visual Basic, may omit the compile and link step and allow the programmer to execute the source program directly in the IDE.)

As in the case of OS/390 program development, the compile step converts the source program into an object module. Because Windows 2000 does not have built-in program libraries, this object module is normally stored in a subdirectory.

Building Libraries for the Linker

In an application with many separate DLLs, the library utility (LIBR.EXE) is used to package related functions into a single .LIB file. LIB files can then be specified as input to the linker. Vendor products, such as compilers, already come with related functions packaged in LIB files. The programmer can use the Library utility to package up his own functions. This is similar to the way that OS/390 object PDS libraries are used.

Linking the Program

Where OS/390 has a Linkage Editor, Windows 2000 has a linker which performs a similar function. As discussed earlier, programs can call statically linked function. In most cases, however, DLLs are used. When a DLL is linked with a program, only a stub routine is actually combined with the program. When the stub is called, it instructs the operating system to load and call the program. Most of the APIs provided by the operating system are also implemented as DLLs. This makes it easy to update them as fixes are released by Microsoft.

The linker is normally provided by the compiler vendor, such as Microsoft. As in the case of the OS/390 Linkage Editor, the linker is used to build an executable program out of main programs, subroutines, and library functions.

The Linker can accept as input individual object files or it can accept a mix of individual files and libraries as discussed earlier. The output of the linking process can be an executable program or a DLL. Where executable programs normally end in .EXE or .COM, a DLL normally ends in .DLL.

Problems Replacing DLLs

Packaging functions in replaceable DLLs aids in system maintenance. There is one aspect of DLLs that could be improved upon: When a DLL is referenced, it is loaded into memory by the program that uses its services. After it is used, it normally remains in memory on the assumption that it will be used again. Because operating system DLLs and DLLs used by system services always remain in memory, they cannot be replaced without rebooting the system. This contributes significantly to system downtime. Windows 2000 drastically reduces the number of reboots required to do system maintenance compared to Windows NT. Nevertheless, a reboot is still required to replace an in-use DLL under Windows 2000.

Under OS/390, shared library modules are loaded into a common area called the Linkpack area. You can dynamically unload programs loaded in the Linkpack area and replace them to change the libraries in a running system. There is no way to do this in Windows 2000. In my opinion, this capability should be added to the Windows 2000 operating system architecture to increase system uptime. ◆

This chapter explained how programs are managed by OS/390 and Windows 2000, how programs communicate with each other, and how programs are prepared for execution. The next chapter shows how these programs are actually loaded and run, as well as what happens to the output of these programs.

9

Job and Task Management

This chapter focuses on the layers of software in each operating system used to manage units of work that are more complex than the execution of a single program.

OS/390 Job Management

OS/390 is extremely efficient at processing batch jobs. That should come as no surprise because mainframes were originally developed for this kind of processing. It was only when TSO and SPF were added that an appreciable part of their workload began to be devoted to supporting interactive users. And, even in the case of interactive users, the result of interactive processing is normally the submission of one or more batch jobs to be executed later by the operating system.

A mainframe job is specified to OS/390 as a sequence of JCL statements in a language that (by an extreme stretch of the imagination) can be considered to be a programming language that deals with datasets and programs.

What Is an OS/390 Job?

For purposes of this discussion, an OS/390 job is a series of related program execution steps defined and controlled by statements in a JCL. It is also a resource accounting and performance entity because the operating system keeps track of resource usage on a job basis and dynamically alters its performance based on job characteristics.

The typical job consists of input control statements, normally in the form of card images, in a *Partitioned Dataset* (PDS) member. This includes statements that define the overall job, each program to be executed, as well as statements that define the characteristics, location, and disposition of the datasets to be used by the job. These DD statements may point to datasets on disk or tape. DD statements—for instance, Sort utility control statements—that point to control statements may also point to other PDS members.

Note that this definition of a job is geared toward batch processing. In fact, when a user logs on to a TSO session, the operating system treats the session like a single-step job. Because each TSO user appears to the operating system as a separate job, each user session automatically gets its own address space and work files. These work files consists of private PDSs used to hold source code (in the case of a programmer), jobs, and/or control statements used by the job. TSO users also have some internal work files allocated for them at the start of their session.

In addition to batch jobs and TSO session, there is one other type of job worth mentioning. Chapters 2, "Operating System Architecture," and 5, "Multiprogramming," discussed the use of teleprocessing monitors such as CICS (discussed more fully in Chapter 15, "Transaction, Database, and Message Processing"). When the operating system is started, one or more CICS regions may also be started. JCL statements are used to execute the CICS startup process just as if it were a batch job or another TSO session.

The design of OS/390 job management is based on the philosophy that no single job is more important than the overall integrity of the operating system or the integrity of other jobs running at the same time.

Job Control Language

OS/390 JCL consists of statements that define the resources needed by a job. JCL includes the JOB statement, which is used to specify overall information about the job. It includes the DD statement that is used to specify information about the datasets used by a job. It also includes the EXEC statement, which is used to specify information about the programs to be run at each step of the job. A typical job is shown in the following sample code. (The line numbers in the example are not part of the file. They are just there for reference in the text.)

```
1.    //ZACKA    JOB  (1648666,34567-A),'WEEKLY AR REPORT',
2.    //                CLASS=1,NOTIFY=ZACK,MSGCLASS=X
3.    //OUTPUT01 OUTPUT COPIES=10
4.    //STEP1    EXEC PGM=IGHRCO00,REGION=4096K
5.    //STEPLIB  DD   DSN=SM01.LOADLIB,DISP=SHR
6.    //SORTLIB  DD   DSN=SM01.SORTLIB,DISP=SHR
7.    //SYSUDUMP DD   SYSOUT=*
8.    //SYSOUT   DD   SYSOUT=*,OUTPUT=*.OUTPUT01
9.    //SORTWK01 DD   UNIT=SYSDA,SPACE=(CYL,(10,10),RLSE)
10.   //SORTWK02 DD   UNIT=SYSDA,SPACE=(CYL,(10,10),RLSE)
```

```
11.   //SORTWK03 DD  UNIT=SYSDA,SPACE=(CYL,(10,10),RLSE)
12.   //SORTIN   DD  DSN=ZACK.RAWARDAT,DISP=SHR
13.   //SORTOUT  DD  DSN=ZACK.SRTARDAT,DISP=(NEW,CATLG,DELETE),
14.   //             UNIT=DISK,
15.   //             SPACE=(CYL,(16,6),RLSE),VOL=SER=ARVOL1
16.   //SYSPRINT DD  SYSOUT=*,OUTPUT=*.OUTPUT01
17.   //SYSIN    DD  *
18.   SORT FIELDS=(1,9,CH,A,17,25,CH,A)
19.   /*
20.   //STEP2   EXEC PGM=ARREPORT,PARM='01-01-1999',COND=(0,EQ,STEP1)
21.   //STEPLIB  DD  DSN=PROD.PROD.AR.LOADLIB,DISP=SHR
22.   //SYSUDUMP DD  SYSOUT=*
23.   //SYSPRINT DD  SYSOUT=*,OUTPUT=*.OUTPUT01
24.   //INFILE   DD  DSNAME=ZACK.SRTARDAT,DISP=OLD
25.   //WORK2    DD  DSN=&&TEMP,UNIT=VIO,SPACE=(1700,(300,50))
26.   //OUTFILE  DD  DSNAME=ARREPT.LIST,DISP=(,CATLG,DELETE),
27.   //             UNIT=DISK,VOL=SER=ARVOL1,SPACE=(CYL,(70,50),RLSE),
28.   //             DCB=(RECFM=FB,LRECL=120,BLKSIZE=12000)
29.   //
```

The following sections discuss some of these JCL statements and their key parameters. This explanation does not attempt to give you an exhaustive definition of JCL syntax; for after all, this is a book on Windows 2000 and not OS/390. Besides, it is assumed that you come from the mainframe world and already know OS/390 JCL. This discussion just reviews the basics, building a foundation from which to discuss Windows 2000 alternatives later in this chapter.

The JOB Statement
The JOB statement (line 1 and continued on line 2) has several important parameters, such as the following:

- Job name
- Accounting information
- Programmer's name
- Job class
- Completion notification
- Message class

The Job Name Field
The Job Name field (ZACKA) uniquely defines the job to the operating system. All output of the job is spooled under that name, and all operator messages use it to identify the job that generated them.

Accounting Information

The Accounting Information field ((1648666,34567-A) in line 1) follows
the JOB keyword. It is used to specify accounting information for the job.
(It can also be used to specify additional information, but that is not the
concern here.)

OS/390 keeps detailed resource-usage information on CPU time, disk
I/O, and other resources. This information is then normally processed by
job accounting software to charge back the cost of processing to user
departments.

Programmer's Name

The Programmer's Name field is used to identify the output of the job on a
printed output separator page. For a programmer-submitted job, it is the
name of the programmer. For a production job, it is usually used to identify
the job. This is the case in the example above where 'WEEKLY AR REPORT' is
specified in this field.

Job Class

The Job Class field (CLASS=1 in the example) is used to tell the JES2 what
scheduling class to place the job into. (See the JES2 discussion, below.) Note
that this parameter is on a continuation line (line 2). Lines are continued by
ending the preceding line with a comma and starting the next line with a
double slash (//) followed by additional parameters starting in column 16.

Completion Notification

The Notify parameter (NOTIFY=ZACK in line 2) instructs the operating system
to send a TSO broadcast message to the specified TSO user's session when
the job completes. This is primarily useful for jobs submitted by a programmer while in a TSO session.

Message Class

The Message Class parameter (MSGCLASS=X in line 2) is used to route output
to one of the JES2-managed output queues. These queues are normally
serviced by one or more JES2 output writers.

Class X in this example is a queue that does not have an output writer
assigned to it. In this case, it is assumed that someone will review the
output while it is still in the queue and either delete it or move it to a
queue serviced by an active output writer.

The EXEC Statement and JOB Step Execution

The EXEC statement (lines 4 and 20) has several important parameters that control the execution of a specific program. The key EXEC statement parameters are as follows:

- PGM or PROC
- PARM
- COND
- REGION
- TIME

PGM or PROC

The PGM or PROC field is used to specify the name of the program or cataloged JCL procedure to be executed in this step. A single step can result in the execution of a single program (PGM=) or it can result in the execution of a multistep cataloged procedure. In the case of a cataloged procedure, the PROC= is usually omitted because it is the default. The EXEC statement for a COBOL compile, link, and execute procedure might look like://STEP1 EXEC COB2CLG (Compile, Link, and Go), for example. In the example, IGHRCO00 (line 4) is the name of the OS/390 sort utility program and ARREPORT (line 20) is the name of an application program that will be used to print a report.

PARM

The PARM field is used to pass parameters to the program. For instance, it is used on line 20 to pass a run date to the report program.

COND

The COND parameter controls whether a step should be executed based on the success or failure of a prior step (or steps) in the job. The COND parameter makes the EXEC statement into an awkward "If" statement. (JCL, is after all a crude programming language for manipulating datasets and programs rather than data records!)

Is JCL Really a Programming Language?

I cannot resist adding a personal anecdote here. In the early 1970s, I was working as a consultant to IBM in Poughkeepsie, New York. The group that I was working for was charged with prototyping an experimental procedural job control language. Because, at the time, IBM's favorite language was PL/1(!) that was the language that we based our prototype on. This processor would accept a subset of PL/1 and generate JCL internally. The JCL would then be passed to the operating system JCL Interpreter to be executed step by step.

This made conditional execution of job steps a simple matter of coding an "If" statement. It also made it possible to loop through a group of datasets creating a job step to process each dataset based on a name template. This capability, however, did have its dangers. One of us (and I am not saying who) accidentally caused a loop that created a job with an infinite number of steps. This filled up the job queue and brought down the operating system!

The reason I bring this up here is that many of us have complained over the years about the awkwardness of using the COND parameter to control conditional step execution. Most modern control languages, such as REXX, are more procedural in nature. Later in this chapter, you will see how Windows 2000 rates in this category. ◆

REGION

The REGION parameter (line 4) is used to specify the size of the region that the job should be run in. In the example, the REGION parameter for the sort step specifies 4MB (4096KB). Because no Region parameter is specified for step 2, an installation default will be used. Note that the Region parameter, like several other EXEC statement parameters (such as TIME), can also be specified on a global basis with the JOB statement.

TIME

The TIME parameter (not shown in the example) can be used to specify the maximum CPU time that a job can use. After that the job will be cancelled. Information about the reason for cancellation will be written to the SYSUDUMP data dataset.

The Data Definition (DD) Statement

The DD statements in a job define all the datasets that will be used by the job. Table 9.1 summarizes the DD statements used in the preceding example.

Table 9.1   Datasets

Step	DD Statement	Explanation
Step 1	STEPLIB and SORTLIB	Libraries (PDSs) containing the sort program and user-provided exit programs
	SYSUDUMP	Dataset to hold the storage dump in case the program is abnormally terminated
	SYSOUT	Destination for status, warning, and error messages
	SORTWK01, SORTWK02, and SORTWK03	Temporary disk work datasets to be use by the program
	SORTIN	The input dataset to be sorted
	SORTOUT	The output file of sorted records
	SYSPRINT	Destination for printed output
	SYSIN	Sort control statement used to specify information about the fields to be sorted
Step 2	STEPLIB	Library containing the report program
	SYSUDUMP	Same as above
	SYSPRINT	Same as above
	INFILE	Sorted records from the previous step
	OUTFILE	Output report, in this case directed to a real file rather than a SYSOUT class

There are a large number of DD statement parameters, but only a few of the key ones are discussed here.
They are as follows:

- SYSOUT
- DSN
- DISP
- UNIT and VOL
- SPACE
- DSORG
- RECFM, LRECL, and BLKSIZE

SYSOUT

Specifies a JES2 output class. This will direct the output to an output queue. In the preceding example, sysout=* indicates that the output should go to the default output class specified by the MSGCLASS parameter of the JOB card. (The OUTPUT parameter is discussed later in this section.)

DSN

This specifies the actual name of the dataset. Dataset names are not specified in a program. Instead, a program specifies *a data definition name* (DDNAME). This DDNAME corresponds to the name immediately following the "//" in the DD statement. In this way the DD statement is used to associate the DDNAME used in the program with the actual dataset to be used by the job. This enables a program to process many different datasets based only on JCL changes.

DISP

The DISP parameter is used to specify the disposition of a dataset. Some datasets are temporary. They are created for use in a single job step and are scratched when the step is completed (see lines 9 through 11). Others are more permanent and are passed from step to step to finally be released at the end of the job. Still other datasets (lines 13 and 26) are more permanent—that is, they remain after the job is ended. A permanent dataset may be kept (KEEP), or it may be kept and cataloged (CATLG). If only KEEP is specified, subsequent JCL references must indicate the location of the dataset using the UNIT and VOL parameters discussed in the next section. On the other hand, the operating system keeps track of a cataloged dataset so that these parameters do not have to be used. This makes it possible to relocate a dataset without having to change the JCL. (The following chapter discusses OS/390 catalogs and Windows 2000 equivalents.)

UNIT and VOL

As indicated earlier, the UNIT and VOL parameters specify the location of a dataset. The UNIT parameter, if used alone, can also refer to a pool of disk volumes (such as SYSDA in this example).

Note the use of UNIT=VIO in line 25. VIO does not allocate space on disk at all! Instead it is allocated in OS/390 expanded memory. Remember the earlier discussion of memory-mapped files in the preceding chapter? This is how you can create a temporary OS/390 memory-mapped file using JCL. Although this can improve performance, many installations have limits on the maximum size of VIO files. Check your local standards on this subject.

SPACE
The Space parameter indicates the space allocation and the size of subsequent increments. You should remember from the preceding chapter that a limit is placed on the maximum size of a dataset based on this parameter.

DSORG
The DSORG parameter specifies the dataset organization, record length, and blocking factor. (You should also remember these from the preceding chapter.)

RECFM, LRECL, and BLKSIZE
The RECFM, LRECL, and BLKSIZE parameters are used to specify the logical and physical characteristics of records in a dataset. (Chapter 7, "Data Management," discussed these parameters.)

The OUTPUT Statement
Originally DD statements that specified SYSOUT distribution also contained additional parameters to specify special processing options. There were a large number of these parameters, and they often had to be coded on several SYSOUT statements in the job. To simplify, specifying the same parameters on multiple SYSOUT statements IBM added the OUTPUT statement to the JCL.

The OUTPUT statement can be coded before the first job step, or after an EXEC statement in the job (see line 3). When it is coded before the first step, it is considered to be a job-level statement. It can also be coded after an EXEC statement, as in the example. In that case, it is considered to be a step-level statement.

The OUTPUT statement has a symbolic name immediately following the "//". This name can be referred to by subsequent SYSOUT DD statements in the job (as shown in lines 8, 16, and 23). In the example shown, five copies of this job's output will be printed.

JCL Odds and Ends
SYSIN DD * is used to specify that the input data is in-line in the JCL. (Often the SYSIN DD statement specifies a member of a PDS containing the data instead.)

References of the form SYSOUT=* indicate that the output is to go to the same output class as the job's JCL listing.

A line with "//" all by itself is an end-of-job delimiter. It is not strictly necessary because the end of the input dataset will also indicate the end of the job. Nevertheless it is often used out of habit.

A line starting with "//*" can be used to add comments to a job. Commenting a job is always a good idea. It will help others (and yourself) understand the job when changes are required at a later date.

In addition to the traditional JCL statements discussed already, a number of additional control statements (such as the Output statement) have been added in recent years to extend JCL control of JES2 operations. These statements are also now considered to be part of the JCL, although they do have a slightly different format. These are not covered here.

Some additional JCL statements are not shown in the example, but by now you should have the basic flavor of JCL. If you want to learn more, you can refer to the IBM manual *OS/390 MVS JCL Reference (GC28-1757)*.

Now that you understand the language used to define and control the execution of jobs, it's time to take a look at the lifetime of a job and see the stages that a job goes through.

The Job Entry Subsystem

Jobs are managed in OS/390 by the Job Entry System, normally JES2. As mentioned in Chapter 1, JES2 is an outgrowth of HASP, which was used to augment early mainframe operating systems and which was integrated with IBM's later operating systems. Although OS/390 supports both JES2 and JES3, this chapter focuses on JES 2 because that is the most widely used version. JES3 is similar, and although it does have some unique capabilities, these are not covered in this book.

The major components of JES2 correspond to the phases of job processing as illustrated in Figure 9.1. They are as follows:

- Input phase
- Conversion phase
- Processing phase
- Output-processing phase
- Hard-copy phase
- Purge phase

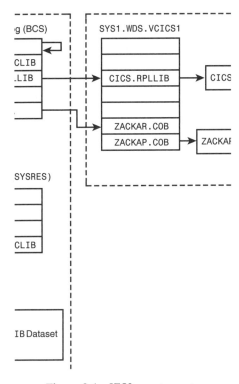

Figure 9.1 *JES2 components.*

Input Phase

JES2 input processors accept input jobs. Jobs are submitted to JES2 in the form of JCL in card-image text-line format. Normally this is submitted from a partitioned dataset member using the TSO SUBMIT command, although JES2 can also accept jobs submitted from network devices. Jobs can also be submitted directly from other jobs using a JES2 internal reader. This is an operating system component that accepts JCL lines one at a time from a program. This allows the execution of one job to request the execution of another.

First, JES2 assigns an internal number to the job for tracking purposes. Then, it writes the card images to the JES2 spool dataset. This dataset is keyed by job number and job class.

Conversion Phase

Multiple JES2 conversion processors continually scan the spool queue looking for jobs to process. When a conversion processor finds a job that has been spooled by a JES2 input processor, it reads the JCL lines from the job. If the JCL refers to a cataloged procedure, it merges the input JCL lines with the lines taken from the cataloged procedure.

After this merge, the conversion processor checks the merged job for errors. If there are errors at this stage, the job is immediately queued for the output-processing phase. If there are no errors, the job is converted to an internal format and re-queued for the processing phase.

Processing Phase

Responsibility for the processing phase is shared by JES2 and the base operating system. Strictly speaking, job execution is not really a part of JES2. It is actually handled by the base operating system in cooperation with JES2. Because this appears to be seamless, however, it is covered here.

OS/390 initiators take jobs to be run from one or more input queues. These queues are defined with class IDs and each initiator can take jobs with one or more class IDs. Therefore, it is possible for one initiator to be dedicated to a certain type of job. High-priority accounting jobs, for instance, could be processed by one initiator and background-program compiles could be scheduled at a lower priority through another initiator.

When JES2 finds an initiator capable of running a waiting job, it passes the job to the initiator. The initiator then allocates a region and runs the first step in the job. As each step ends, the initiator runs the next step. At the end of the job, the system datasets (SYSOUT, Messages, and so on) are queued for the output-processing phase (see Figure 9.2).

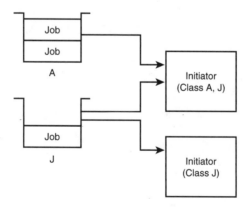

Figure 9.2 *OS/390 initiators.*

The operator can start and stop initiators and change their classes to control the flow of jobs through the system.

Output-Processing Phase

This phase determines the disposition of all SYSOUT and MSGCLASS datasets in the job. It groups datasets with similar output in the output queue.

Hard-Copy Phase

The processors of this phase select output for processing by class, routing code, priority, and other criteria. Local jobs are re-queued for processing by an operating system component called an output writer. This component of the operating system reads the data from the queue and prints it. In the case of remote jobs, the datasets are transmitted to the remote JES2 node.

Purge Phase

Purge processing is the final phase of job processing. After all other processing for the job is complete, all traces of the job are completely removed from the system queues.

The following section explains how Windows 2000 handles job management.

Windows 2000 Job Management

Windows 2000 is weak in the area of job management. Windows 2000 does not have a built-in JCL that is as powerful as OS/390 JCL. Windows 2000 does have some job-control capabilities, however, and additional ones can be provided through add-on products.

As indicated in the preceding chapter, the Job object of Windows 2000 is new with this operating system release. As such, its properties are only accessible by program APIs and not at the operator interface. As a result, no GUI or command-line interfaces to this object can be used to enforce limits on disk use, CPU time, and execution priority. (These omissions will probably be rectified in a future release of Windows 2000.) Nevertheless, Windows 2000 does have significant job-control capabilities.

Windows 2000 provides the capability to run a set of programs in a sequence much like the steps of an OS/390 job. Two built-in components of Windows 2000 can be used to build jobs consisting of the execution of multiple program steps: the batch file programming language inherited from DOS, and the newer Windows Scripting Host.

Batch File Programming

Batch file programming is not covered in this book. Instead the focus here is on the Windows Scripting Host. (If you want to know more about how to use batch files and even how to extend them to perform complex job-management tasks, you should definitely read *Windows NT Shell Scripting*, by Tim Hill, Macmillan Technical Publishing, 1998, ISBN 1-57870-047-7.)

The Windows Scripting Host

This chapter presents an overview of the Windows Scripting Host, which has replaced batch files for serious job-management tasks in Windows 2000.

The Windows Scripting Host is a new technology in Windows 2000. It provides a host environment that allows Windows 2000 to support multiple scripting languages. Windows 2000, as delivered, includes interpreters for VBScript and JScript, for example. (JScript is Microsoft's dialect of JavaScript.) Other vendors provide additional script interpreters. Active-State provides the PerlScript Windows Scripting Host engine, for instance.

This book concentrates on VBScript. VBScript is a dialect of Visual Basic, which is the most widely used Windows application development language. VBScript is an interpreted subset of this language developed especially for use in scripting. Because of limited space here to cover VBScript in detail, this review explains only the few language constructs that appear in the examples as they are used here. For a more detailed treatment of VBScript, see Learning VBScript, by Lomax and Petrusha, (O'Reilly & Associates, ISBN: 1565922476).

Script files can be run in one of several ways. You can double-click on a file icon on the desktop GUI. You can open a command-prompt window and type the name of a command file at prompt. You can also select the *Start* button on the desktop command bar and then choose *Run* from the resulting pop-up menu. These actions bring up a program open dialog box in which to type the command. When you choose any of these methods, the command interpreter that Windows 2000 invokes will depend on the extension of the file. A file ending in .vbs is passed to the VBScript interpreter, for example, while a file ending in .js is passed to the JScript interpreter.

The Windows Scripting Host is an ActiveX Automation Client (see the sidebar on Active-X Automation). This makes it possible for it to host ActiveX components and use their methods and properties. The Windows Scripting Host comes with several useful components, some of which are discussed later. It also supports the use of Microsoft Office components that can handle ActiveX Automation, such as Word and Excel. In addition, a number of third-party components add additional features. You can even write your own components in Visual Basic, C, or Delphi.

ActiveX Automation

In ActiveX Automation, there are ActiveX servers and ActiveX clients. An Active-X client can use the internal resources of an ActiveX server by setting and retrieving its properties and by calling methods that it supports internally (see Figure 9.3).

Properties are internal variables that hold information about an object. Methods are processing functions embedded within the object. Property and method references are in the form ObjectName.Reference, as you will see in subsequent examples.

ActiveX servers can be built-in objects such as the WScript and WShell objects provided with the Windows Scripting Host. They can also be whole applications such as Microsoft Excel, Word, or Access that have been written to act as ActiveX servers. They can also be objects developed by third parties.

New ActiveX objects are created with a call to WShell.CreateObject. After they are created, you can then refer to their methods and properties. ◆

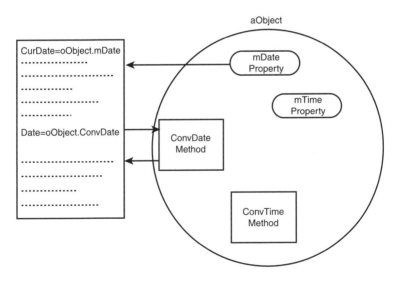

Figure 9.3 *ActiveX object methods and properties.*

The Windows Scripting Host Built-in Objects

There are five built-in Windows Scripting Host objects, as follows:

- `Wscript`
- `Wscript.Shell`
- `Wscript.Network`
- `Wscript.Shortcut`
- `Wscript.UrlShortcut`

This brief section covers only three of these objects: `Wscript`, `Wscript.Shell`, and `Wscript.Network`. The discussion also covers only a few of their more interesting properties and methods. This limited treatment should be enough to give you the flavor of what you can accomplish with the Windows Scripting Host.

The `Wscript` *Object*

The `Wscript` object is the base object of the Windows Scripting Host. One instance of the `Wscript` object exists when a script starts. The `Wscript` object provides properties that give information about the currently executing script. This includes the name of the script file, the path to the script file, and any arguments provided to the script at the time that it was executed. The following script is an example of the use of the Wscript object to retrieve and display information about the currently running script. (The line numbers in the example are not part of the script file; they are just there for reference in the text.)

```
1.  '-----------------------------------
2.  ' Wscript example
3.  '-----------------------------------
4.
5.  Page= "Wscript.Application=" & Wscript.Application &vbCrLf
6.  Page=Page & "Wscript.FullName=" & Wscript.FullName & vbCrLf
7.  Page=Page & "Wscript.Name=" & Wscript.Name & vbCrLf
8.  Page=Page & "Wscript.Path=" & Wscript.Path & vbCrLf
9.  Page=Page & "Wscript.ScriptFullName=" & Wscript.ScriptFullName
10.
11. Wscript.Echo Page
```

In a VBScript program, lines beginning with a single quotation mark are comment lines. Anything after a single quotation mark on a line is also treated as a comment. Use comments to document what your script is doing so that others (and you) will be able to understand them in the future.

Lines of the form `name=value` are assignment statements. They are used to assign a value (string or numeric) to a variable. Note that line 5 first sets the value of the Page variable to a string made up of multiple parts joined

together with the VBScript concatenation operator (&). Lines 6–9 are
subsequently used to add additional data to the variable also using the
concatenation operator. Also note that in lines 5–8 the variable VbCrLf is a
built-in VBScript constant that adds a carriage return and line feed to the
output string being built. Without it, all the lines would just run together
in the output.

In a VBScript program constructs of the form Wscript.Name are references
to an ActiveX object. For instance, the preceding reference is used in line 7
of the example to retrieve the Name property (value) of the Wscript object.

In line 11, the Wscript Echo method is called to display the final results
of building the output string. Figure 9.4 shows the result of running this
script.

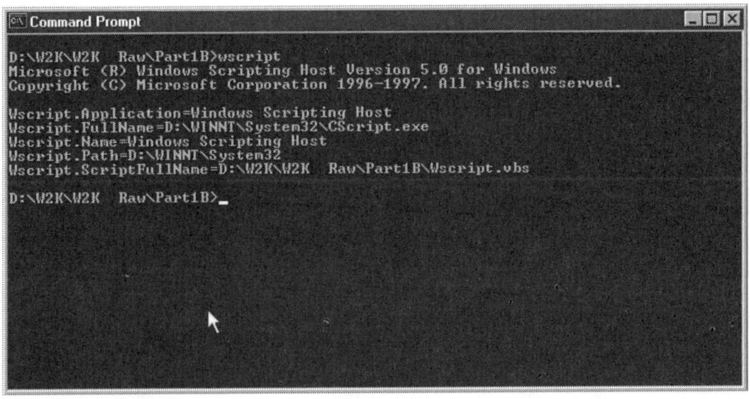

Figure 9.4 *WScript example results.*

One of the more interesting methods of this object is the CreateObject
method that can be used to create other objects to be used by your scripts.

The Wscript.Shell *Object*
The Wscript.Shell object makes it possible to retrieve information about
the machine on which the script is running (such as the number of
processors, as well as the path to special folders such as the desktop). It
also makes it possible to access and update settings in the Windows 2000
Registry.

One of the more useful methods provided by this object is its Run
method. This method can be used to execute any external program. In
the following script it is used to start execution of the Windows 2000
Notepad utility.

```
1. '-------------------------------------------------------------
2. ' Wscript.Shell Example
3. '-------------------------------------------------------------
4
5. option explicit
6.
7. Dim oWShell
8.
9. set oWShell=Wscript.CreateObject("Wscript.Shell")
10. oWShell.Run "notepad.exe"
```

Regarding this script, it is prudent to explain a few new language constructs before discussing the script. As you saw in the preceding example, you do not have to define variables before you use them. For instance, the Page variable was just created by referencing it for the first time in the script. Defining variables in this way can cause script errors, however. VBScript is not case sensitive. That means that Page, page, and PAGE all refer to the same variable. If you misspell a variable, however, you will accidentally create a new variable. Because the value of the real variable may not be what you expect it to be after such a mistake, this can be very difficult to debug. To prevent this, VBScript enables you to code the Option Explicit statement at the beginning of your script. (An example of this is shown in line 5.) VBScript will then produce an error message if you have an undefined variable in your script.

You define variables with the Dim statement, as is shown in line 7. Variables in VBScript are typeless—that is, they can hold any type of data. X=5 and x="hello" are both valid assignment statements. Their actual type is determined when you assign data to them.

Also in this example, a new form of assignment statement that begins with the keyword Set is used. Set is used to assign a name to a created object. Then their methods and properties can be referenced by the form name.method or name.property (see lines 9 and 10). Incidentally, you may have noticed that the object variables are prefixed with a lowercase letter o. That is used just as a reminder that the variable is a reference to an object and not a simple string or numeric variable.

Figure 9.5 shows the result of running this script.

Figure 9.5 Wscript.Shell *example results.*

The Wscript.Network *Object*

The Wscript.Network object makes it possible to access and modify network objects such as file shares. You can map a network drive with the following script, for example:

```
1.  -------------------------------------------------------
2.  ' Wscript. Network Example
3.  '-------------------------------------------------------
4.
5.  option explicit
6.
7.  Dim oWShell
8.  Dim oWNetwork
9.
10. set oWShell=Wscript.CreateObject("Wscript.Shell")
11. Set oWNetwork=Wscript.CreateObject("Wscript.Network")
12.
13. ' Don't abort if drive is already unmapped
14. On Error Resume Next
15. oWNetwork.RemoveNetworkDrive "Z:"
16. On Error GoTo 0
17.
18. oWNetwork.MapNetworkDrive "Z:", "\\BILLSPC\PUBLIC"
19.
20. oWShell.Run "cmd /k NET USE"      ' Show that it worked
```

This script is used to assign a drive letter (Z:) to a network directory shared as \\BILLSPC\PUBLIC. (See Chapter 14, "Networking," for more on this subject.)

Line 10 creates an instance of the Wscript.Shell object. This object will be used later to issue Windows 2000 commands using its Run method.

Line 11 first creates an instance of the Wscript.Network object. This is the object used here to map the drive letter. Line 15 attempts to unmap the drive, just in case it is already in use. The On Error Resume Next on line 14 indicates that the script is to continue execution even if there are errors. (The default behavior for a script is to stop on the first error. When you code this line in a script, you must check the return codes from commands and other operations yourself.) The On Error Goto 0 on line 16 resets this condition so that subsequent errors will cause the script to abort. The reason that was done here is because the RemoveNetworkDrive method will fail if the drive is not currently mapped. Because the objective is to unmap the drive, if it is already mapped is of no concern if the command fails because it is already unmapped.

Line 18 maps the drive using the MapNetworkDrive method of the Network object. Note that the Run method of the Wscript.Shell object could also have been used to issue a Windows 2000 NET USE command to achieve the same result. Line 20 does in fact use this method to prove that the drive was mapped correctly.

Using Normal Windows 2000 Commands with WSH

Normally a program would be executed directly using the Run method. To make use of input and/or output redirection, however, it is necessary to run the command under control of the Windows 2000 command processor (CMD.EXE). The use of CMD /K *in line 20 would only be necessary to capture the output of the command into a file for subsequent processing. In this case, the line would probably have read as follows:*

```
oWShell.Run "cmd /k NET USE > OutputFile"
```

This is often done to run a command and then read the output of the command back into the script for further processing. ◆

Figure 9.6 shows the result of running this script.

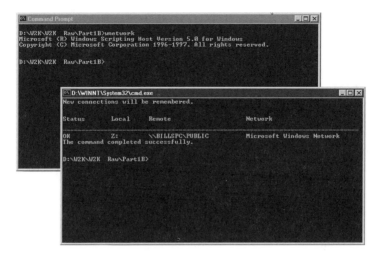

Figure 9.6 `Wscript.Network` *example results.*

Other Windows 2000–Provided Objects

In addition to the built-in Windows Scripting Host objects, many other applications have been written to be ActiveX servers and they can be used by Windows Scripting Host scripts to perform useful work. In addition to the Microsoft Office components discussed earlier, Windows 2000 provides the `Scripting.FileSystemObject` and the *Active Directory Services Interface* (ADSI) object.

The `Scripting.FileSystemObject`

Windows 2000 provides the `Scripting.FileSystemObject`, which enables you to create, read, and write to files. Using this object, you can create a new file or locate an existing one, open the file, read and/or write data to it, close it, and disconnect from it. The following script illustrates some of these operations.

```
1. '-----------------------------------------
2. ' Scripting.FileSystemObject Example
3. '-----------------------------------------
4.
5. option explicit
6.
7. ' Shell object stuff
8. Dim oWShell
9.
10. Dim oFileSystem
11.
12. ' Old file
13. Dim OldFileName
```

continues ▶

▶ *continued*

```
14. OldFileName="d:\ArFiles\Oldfile"
15. Dim oOldFile
16.
17. ' New file
18. Dim NewFileName
19. NewFileName="d:\ArFiles\Newfile"
20. Dim oNewFile
21.
22. set oWShell=Wscript.CreateObject("Wscript.Shell")
23. set oFileSystem=Wscript.CreateObject ("Scripting.FileSystemObject")
24.
25. ' Old file
26. On Error Resume next      'Ifgnore not-found condition
27. set oOldFile=oFileSystem.OpenTextFile (OldFileName)
28. On Error Goto 0
29.
30. ' New file
31. set oNewFile=oFileSystem.CreateTextFile (NewFileName, True)
32.
33. ' Copy the file
34. While Not oOldFile.AtEndOfStream
35. oNewFile.WriteLine oOldFile.ReadLine
36. Wend
37.
38. oOldFile.Close           ' Close the input file
39. oNewFile.Close           ' Close the output file
40.
41. oWShell.Run "CMD /k DIR D:\ARFILES"     ' Show that it worked
```

In this example, lines 10 through 20 define the file system objects and filename character strings needed by the rest of the script. oFileSystem is an object variable that will be set to reference the file system. OldFileName and NewFileName are the text strings that name the old and new files.

First, line 22 creates the Wscript.Shell object so that its Echo method can be used just as in previous examples. Next, line 23 creates the Scripting.FileSystemObject. This object has methods and properties that enable you to access new and existing files, as well as information about drives and folders. (This chapter concentrates on only the file-access capabilities of this object.)

The Limitations of the Scripting.FileSystemObject

The Scripting.FileSystemObject *currently works with sequential text files only. Hopefully a future enhancement will add binary and random/keyed file support. This enhancement will be necessary if this object is to be truly useful in an enterprise setting.* ◆

Line 27 opens a pre-existing file. The statement on line 31 is used to create a new text file. Without the `On Error Resume Next` in line 26, this file creation call will fail if the file already exists. Because this is not important in this example, the error is just ignored here.

The following logic (lines 34 through 36) defines a loop that reads records from the old file and writes them to the new file. Line 35 gets a little bit fancy. That line nests one VBScript statement inside another. The `oOldFile Readline` method returns the next line in the file. The `oNewFile Writeline` method then takes the returned line as its argument and writes it out to the new file.

Some of you may be thinking at this point that it would have been easier to have just used the `Wscript.Shell Run` method to execute a Windows 2000 `COPY` command. If so, give yourself a gold star! It would have been easier, but it wouldn't have given me the opportunity to demonstrate the use of the File System object. Note that we do use the Run method on line 41 as a quick way to execute a Windows 2000 `DIR` command to prove that the new file did get created. Often with the Windows Scripting Host, you will find that there are multiple ways to accomplish the same task.

As a final note, the Close method of both file objects is used to ensure that the files are closed and that the data in the new file's internal buffers is flushed to disk. This is not strictly necessary. When the script ends, the files will be closed automatically. It is good scripting practice, however. Figure 9.7 shows the result of running this script.

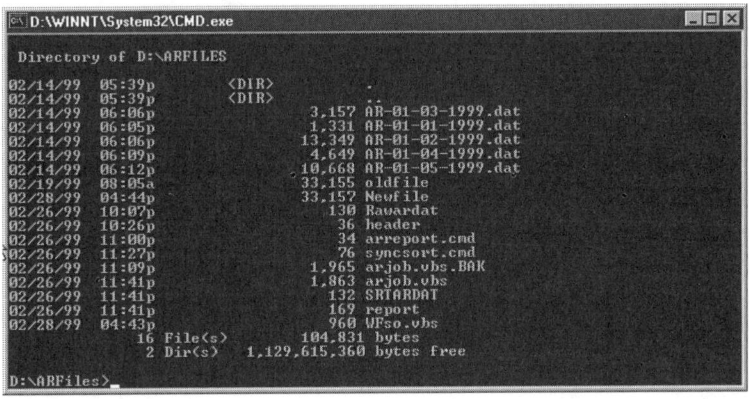

Figure 9.7 `Scripting.FileSystemObject` *example results.*

The Active Directory Services Interface Object
The Windows 2000 Active Directory Services (discussed in the next chapter)
includes Windows Scripting Host access in the form of the *Active Directory
Services Interface* (ADSI). ADSI enables you to script Active Directory
operations as an alternative to using the GUI. This is invaluable for
performing mass changes to the directory, such as adding a large block
of users with similar characteristics.

Microsoft Office Objects

The sample Windows Scripting Host scripts here are made up of statements
in the VBScript programming language. VBScript is a dialect of Visual
Basic, much like the *Visual Basic for Applications* (VBA) that is used to
write Word and Excel macros. Most components of Microsoft Office are
already ActiveX servers, clients, or both.

The Windows 2000 Resource Kit

The Windows 2000 Resource Kit is an absolute requirement for anyone
serious about running Windows 2000 on a workstation or a server. It is full
of handy utility programs and other software that Microsoft, for one reason
or another, did not want to make a supported part of the base Windows
2000 operating system. These programs were originally written to extend
the power of batch files. Although they are not ActiveX servers, they can
still be used via the Wscript.Shell Run method. The Resource Kit includes a
Sleep.Exe program, for example, that can be used to insert a time delay into
your script, as shown in the following example:

```
1.  '--------------------------------------------------
2.  ' Pausing a script
3.  '--------------------------------------------------
4.
5.  Option explicit
6.
7.  Dim oWShell
8.  Dim StartTime
9.
10. set oWShell=Wscript.CreateObject("Wscript.Shell")
11.
12. StartTime=Time
13. oWShell.Run "cmd /c Sleep 5", 0, True
14.
15. WScript.Echo StartTime & " - " & time
```

Line 12 first stores the current system time in the StartTime variable using
the built-in VBScript Time function. Then line 13 runs the Sleep.Exe
program from the Windows 2000 Resource Kit. In this example, the Run
method parameters 0 and True indicate that the command is to be run in a

standard window and that the Run method is to wait for completion of
the command to return the completion code to the script. (Otherwise,
the command will be started and the script will immediately continue
execution.) The Sleep.Exe program itself takes the number of seconds to
delay as its only argument.

Line 15 displays the original time, and the time after the delay, to prove
that the script was indeed delayed by the specified amount. Figure 9.8
shows the result of this script.

Figure 9.8 *Pausing a script example results.*

The Windows 2000 Resource Kit also includes many other useful utilities
that can be used in scripts. In addition to Sleep.exe, for example, the
following utilities are included:

- *WHOAMI.EXE* returns the username of the currently logged-on user
- *IFMEMBER.EXE* determines whether a user is a member of a specific group
- *DHCPCMD.EXE* can be used to administer DHCP from a script
- *FINDGRP.EXE* will list the group memberships of a specified user
- *NETSVC.EXE* is used to query, start, and stop the services running on a remote system.

Creating Your Own Objects

In addition to the ActiveX objects available from the previously listed
sources, you can also create your own in Visual Basic or (if you are more
adept at programming) in languages such as Visual C/C++ or Delphi. The
DIR function of Visual Basic does not exist in VBScript, for example, nor
it is available as part of the current `FileSystemObject`. Using Visual Basic,

however, you can "wrap" the Visual Basic DIR function in an ActiveX object that you can call from your scripts. Note, however, that this capability is also available in some of the third-party objects that you can download from the Web.

What Needs to be Added

The Windows Scripting Host and the objects that Windows 2000 provides are a good start. There are, however, a number of additional objects that could be added to make life easier. It would be nice to be able to access internal Job object properties for enforcing quota limits on a job basis, as in OS/390 JCL, for instance. (Remember quotas are currently enforced only on a user and process basis.) It would also be useful to be able to set disk space, printer output, and/or CPU time limits on a job basis. Implementing job-level accounting would also be useful, although third-party products could fill the gap here.

Windows 2000 includes a large number of useful administrative tools, such as the Disk Manager, Local Storage Manager, and other Microsoft Management Console (MMC) snap-ins. It would be nice if these tools could expose their properties and methods to the Windows Scripting Host. Perhaps these capabilities will be provided in a future release. ◆

Putting It All Together

The OS/390 section of this chapter used a sort and report example to illustrate the use of a job defined with OS/390 JCL. The following script converts the JCL example in the OS/390 section into a form that it might take if it were written for the Windows Scripting Host under Windows 2000. Note that this is a conversion in spirit only, because not all features of JCL are achievable in the Windows Scripting Host. Note that certain JCL features, such as printing multiple copies, had to be explicitly coded in the earlier example. Also, any form of job-level accounting and control is missing in the Windows Scripting Host.

OS/390 and Windows 2000 Sorting

OS/390 comes with a full-featured, industrial-strength sort utility capable of sorting thousands of records on multiple fields. Despite this, many OS/390 shops purchase one of the available third-party sort utilities, such as SyncSort. (At one time, SyncSort was the most popular third-party product in use in mainframe data centers. This is quite remarkable in light of the fact that IBM originally provided a free sort program with the operating system.)

Windows 2000 does have a built-in sort command; however, it is definitely not an industrial-strength program. Fortunately, SyncSort also sells a Windows 2000 version, which we recommend highly if you have major sorting requirements. We have chosen to use SyncSort in the example in this section. Because this is a book about how to integrate mainframes with Windows 2000, we think that it makes sense to use the Windows 2000 version of SyncSort. This is especially true if you already use the mainframe version. ◆

```
1.  '---------------------------------------------------------------
2.  ' AR Sort and Report Example
3.  '-------------- --------------------------------------------------
4.  Option explicit
5.
6.  '---------------------------------------------------------------
7.  ' Step 1 - Sort Input data
8.  '---------------------------------------------------------------
9.
10. ' SyncSort parameters
11.
12. Dim Fields      ' Sort fields
13. Fields="/fields Name 1 Character 9, Amount 17 25 Character "
14.
15. Dim Keys        ' Sort keys
16. Keys="/keys Name ascending, Amount descending "
17.
18. Dim Sortin      ' Sort input file
19. Sortin="/infile RAWARDAT "
20.
21. Dim Sortout     ' Sort output file
22. Sortout="/outfile SRTARDAT "
23.
24. Dim Sysout
25. Sysout="REPORT "    ' Report file
26.
27. Dim CommandLine     ' Command line for Wscript.Run methods
28.
29. Dim oWshell         ' Shell object variable
30. Dim Step1Rc         ' Step 1 return code
31. Dim Step2Rc         ' Step 2 return code
32. Dim I               ' Loop counter
33.
34. Dim Ncopies         ' Number of copies to print
35. Ncopies=2
36.
37. Set oWShell=Wscript.CreateObject("Wscript.Shell")
38.
39. On Error Resume Next    ' Don't abort if any step fails
40.
41. ' Build sort command line
42. CommandLine="SyncSort " & Fields & Keys & Sortin & Sortout
43.
44. Wscript.Echo CommandLine
```

continues ▶

▶ *continued*

```
45. Step1Rc=oWShell.Run(CommandLine, 1, True)
46.
47. '.............................................................
48. ' Step 2 - Print Report
49. '.............................................................
50.
51. If Step1Rc=0 then    ' OK to do Step 2
52. CommandLine="ARREPORT 01-12-1999 "
53. Wscript.Echo CommandLine
54. Step2Rc=oWShell.Run(CommandLine, 1, True)
55. Else                 ' Skip Step 2
56. Wscript.Echo "Step 1 failed with Step1Rc=" & Step1Rc
57. Wscript.Quit
58. End if
59.
60. ' Now print multiple copies
61.
62. CommandLine="PRINT  " & Sysout
63. For i=1 to Ncopies
64. Step2Rc=oWShell.Run(CommandLine, 1, True)
65. Next
66.
67. Wscript.Echo "End of Job"
```

You have already seen most of the language constructs used in this script in previous examples in this chapter. Rather than explain each line in detail, just a few overall comments about this script will be made here.

Note the use of the If statement in the script. This is, in my opinion, an improvement over the COND parameter of OS/390 JCL. Also note that the Windows Scripting Host does not expose any methods or parameters of the Windows 2000 Job object. You cannot set disk space or CPU time quotas for the individual job, for example, as you can in OS/390 JCL.

Also note the use of SyncSort in the example. This example uses only the basic command-line features of SyncSort to make the script as much like the sort example in the OS/390 section as possible. This does not really do SyncSort justice. SyncSort for Windows 2000 comes with a beautiful GUI sort procedure builder that can be used to create stored sort procedures that can be invoked from the command line or from an application program. It also can be called dynamically from Microfocus COBOL programs running under Windows 2000 in the same way that SyncSort on the mainframe can be called from a mainframe COBOL program.

Additional Information

Additional information on the Windows Scripting Host can be found at the Microsoft Web site at http://www.microsoft.com/scripting. (Note: At the time that I write this, Microsoft is reorganizing their Web site. If you have trouble locating the information on Microsoft's site, you can use the Search button on their Web page masthead to search for references to "Windows Scripting Host.")

Third parties are also developing a growing number of scripting objects. One good source of script examples and ActiveX objects that you can use to extend your scripts can be found at the Windows Scripting Web site http://cwashington.netreach.net.

Over time, Web site addresses have been known to change. If you cannot locate one of these references, try searching the whole Internet using one of the public Internet search engines, such as http://www.altavista.com. This should lead to other useful references as well.

This chapter compared the features of jobs and job control in OS/390 and Windows 2000. This included contrasting the features of OS/390 JCL and the Windows Scripting Host.

The next chapter discusses OS/390 catalog management and the use of the Windows 2000 Active Directory. The Active Directory is one of the most revolutionary features included in Windows 2000.

10

Catalogs and Directories

This chapter covers the catalog and directory services provided by OS/390 and Windows 2000. These services are provided to enable end users and programs to locate operating system resources, by name, without knowing the exact location of the resource. Be warned up front, however: This chapter is quite lopsided! The catalog services provided by OS/390 exist only to locate datasets in a single installation. On the other hand, the Active Directory and Active Directory services supported by Windows 2000 can be used to locate many other types of objects such as servers, directories, files, printers, fax servers, applications, databases, and even people. These objects can be located on multiple computers located anywhere in a distributed computer network.

OS/390 Catalogs

As indicated above and in the preceding chapter, OS/390 catalogs exist to allow datasets to be located by name, without specifying the serial number of the volume on which the dataset is located. In addition, an OS/390 catalog contains ownership and security information that can be used by the operating system to control dataset access.

OS/390 catalogs have had three different implementations over the years. In its early years, OS/360 supported catalogs called CVOLs; these catalogs were eventually superseded by VSAM catalogs. The most recent implementation is the *Integrated Catalog Facility* (ICF). I would feel obligated to explain each of these implementations were it not for the fact that the former two implementations self-destruct at the end of 1999 thanks to the infamous Y2K problem. (They maintain file creation and expiration dates with two-digit years internally.) Therefore, I will cover only the ICF catalog.

Logical Catalog Organization

OS/390 has the following two types of catalogs:

- Master catalogs
- User catalogs

Every OS/390 system has one active master catalog. It also normally has many active user catalogs. The master catalog is defined at IPL time. It contains dataset locations and property information on all the system datasets required to IPL the system. In addition, it contains pointers to all the defined user catalogs. User catalogs contain information similar to the information in the master catalog, but for user datasets. The master catalog holds information about the datasets located in each user catalog and a pointer to the user catalog (see Figure 10.1).

Remember from Chapter 3, "Central Processing Units," that OS/390 datasets are named with a dotted multipart naming convention. A dataset name can be up to 44 characters in length. Each part of the dataset name can be eight characters long. For instance, the name of the system procedure library would be SYS1.PROCLIB. System datasets are normally fully defined in the master catalog.

User datasets are cataloged in a user catalog that is pointed to by the master catalog. This user catalog defines the location and attributes of the user datasets. The first-level dataset name qualifier of all datasets defined in each user catalog is also defined in the master catalog. The master catalog entry also contains a pointer to the appropriate user catalog. For example, the name of a user dataset could be ZACK.AR.COB. The ZACK level would be listed in the master catalog (see Figure 10.1.)

Catalog Search Order

When the operating system receives a request to locate a cataloged dataset, the search process begins at the master catalog. If the dataset is defined in the master catalog, the information is retrieved from it. If not, the first-level qualifier is used to locate the user catalog that describes the dataset.

Physical Catalog Structure

An ICF catalog consists of two dataset types: *a basic catalog structure* (BCS) dataset, and a *VSAM volume dataset* (VVDS). There is only one BCS for an entire ICF catalog. There are multiple VVDS datasets, one for each disk volume that contains catalog-managed space. The BCS is normally located on one of the system volumes, such as SYSRES. Each VVDS is located on the disk volume containing the controlled datasets.

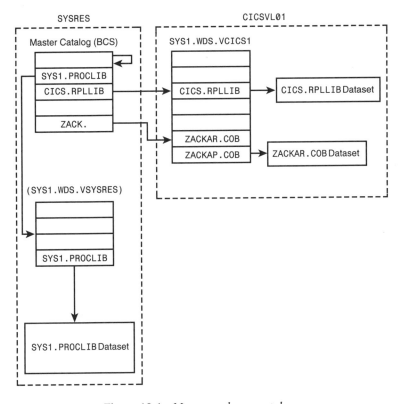

Figure 10.1 *Master and user catalogs.*

The name of the BCS consists of 44 bytes of zeroes. (The BCS also defines itself so that this name ensures that the BCS itself will appear first in the catalog.) The VVDS name is in the format SYS1.VVDS.Vvolser. For example, the VVDS on WRKVL01 would be named SYS1.VVDS.VWRKVL1.

Some non-VSAM non-system-managed storage datasets are defined partly outside of this catalog structure using another disk-resident control block, the *volume table of contents* (VTOC). This is a holdover from earlier catalog types. As time passes, more and more installation datasets will be put under control of system-managed storage.

Catalog Creation
Catalogs are created using the *Access Method services* (AMS) IDCAMS utility using the IDCAMS DEFINE command. The following example shows the creation of a new master catalog:

```
//MASCAT JOB MSGLEVEL=1,MSGCLASS=A
//CREATE EXEC PGM=IDCAMS
//VOL DD UNIT=3380,VOL=SER=SYSRES2,DISP=OLD
//SYSPRINT DD SYSOUT=*
//SYSIN DD *
 DEFINE MASTERCATALOG (NAME(SYSRES2.BACKUP.SYSTEM.MASTER.CATALOG) -
 FILE(CVOL) -
 ICFCATALOG -
 VOLUME(SYSRES2) -
 CYLINDERS(3, 2))
 /*
```

In this example, a new master catalog is created on a systems-residence volume that will be used as an emergency backup IPL volume. Note that it specifies a catalog name, the volume on which it is located, and a primary and secondary space allocation for the catalog. Creating a user catalog would be done in a similar fashion. If you were creating a user catalog here, you would also need to update the master catalog with a pointer to the new user catalog.

Catalog Integrity

When it comes to locating datasets, catalogs are extremely important. An installation may have hundreds of cataloged procedures and jobs that all reference datasets using the catalog. If the catalog were to become damaged, these cataloged procedures and jobs would become unusable. To protect the integrity of ICF catalogs, the systems programmer needs to take periodic backups of the BCS dataset and full disk volume backups of the disks containing the datasets and VVDSs. If the catalog is damaged for any reason, a backup copy of the catalog will need to be reloaded. IBM provides an *ICF Forward Recovery utility* (ICFRU), which uses a restored catalog copy and SMF log records to update a backup with changes that occurred after the backup was taken. In general, however, most installations still perform forward catalog recovery manually, a painstaking and error-prone process.

For more information on OS/390 catalog management, you should refer to the IBM publication *DFMS/MVS V1R4 Managing Catalogs* (SC26-4914).

The Windows 2000 Active Directory

Comparing the Windows 2000 Active Directory to OS/390 catalogs is a little unfair to OS/390! Both provide information on the location of datasets. Active Directory, however, has a much broader scope. It can be used to locate any defined object such as users, groups, services, network file shares, and print queues. It can be used to locate these resources wherever they occur in your network, be this locally or across the world. The Active Directory is primarily a namespace. It provides a way for users and programs to name and locate directory objects by name, just as you can locate OS/390 datasets or Windows 2000 files in their native namespace.

To use the Active Directory to locate resources, you must be running an Active Directory Server service in a domain. After you install Active Directory, all servers and workstations can make use of its services.

The Windows 2000 Active Directory provides a namespace that can be used to resolve the names of Windows 2000 objects just as the Windows 2000 file system provides a namespace in which to resolve the names of files.

The Windows 2000 Active Directory is object-oriented, hierarchical, and extensible. All objects in the directory can be described by the path to the object within the Active Directory namespace. You have already been exposed to namespaces, because the Windows 2000 file-naming convention used a namespace that includes the names of directories and files to locate a specific file. The namespace for directories, for example, is the familiar path name of a Windows 2000 file system directory such as `C:\ARFiles\DataDir` (see Chapter 7, "Data Management").

All objects in the Active Directory can be described by the path to the object within the Active Directory namespace. Active Directory objects also have properties (such as names) and can be located via one or more of those properties using the Active Directory. Note that using the Active Directory requires one or more Windows 2000 servers configured as a domain controller. Typical uses of Active Directory information are authenticating users, locating resources, and acting as a store for application-specific information to be used by directory-enabled applications

Information about directory objects is contained in an internal object-oriented database implemented by Microsoft. According to Microsoft, this database can scale to thousands of servers and millions of objects with good performance. Naturally this depends on your hardware and network topology as well as other performance factors. As always, your mileage may vary.

The Active Directory has the following characteristics. It is

- *Distributed*—Information about any resource in the network can be obtained at any other point in the network, even across vast distances.

- *Partitioned*—Partial copies of the directory (called replicas) are maintained in each domain.

- *Replicated*—Changes to this distributed directory are automatically replicated between systems in your network.

- *Secure*—Every directory object and every property of an object is subject to access controls that restrict or permit specific types of access by individual users and/or groups of users.

- *Extensible*—Administrators can add new object types to the directory and they can also add new properties to objects in the directory.

The Active Directory Database

The Active Directory can store up to 17 terabytes of data describing millions of objects. (This should be sufficient to accommodate very large organizations in a single directory.) Data describing the database itself, and all the objects contained within it, is stored in this database. This data is stored in several database structures. Each component of the directory has its own naming context or namespace. In the section titled "Sites and Replication" later in this chapter, you will see that the naming context is also the primary unit of replication.

These naming contexts are as follows:

- The schema
- The global catalog
- The configuration
- The domain

The Schema

The Active Directory database schema describes all the valid object classes (types) that can be stored in the database. It describes the position of these objects in the directory class hierarchy. In addition, it describes all the attributes of these objects. The attributes of an object are the characteristics or properties that an object of a given class can have. Some attributes are mandatory (must-have) and other attributes are optional (may-have). To add an object to the database, all of its must-have attributes must be specified. May-have attributes, however, are optional. Examples of must-have attributes for a user account object would be the user's name and password. A user's telephone number is an example of a may-have attribute.

The schema is dynamically extensible. Administrators can add new object types to the schema, although this is a fairly advanced option and should only be undertaken by an experienced administrator.

The fact that the Active Directory schema is extensible enables the creation of new applications that can take advantage of Active Directory as a distributed directory service. An email application can create new classes or attributes, for example, such as distribution lists, to integrate the application more fully with Windows 2000.

The schema is also protected by Windows 2000 security. Windows 2000 *access control lists* (ACLs) can be defined to protect any Windows 2000 resource, including Active Directory objects (see Chapter 13, "Security").

The Global Catalog

The Active Directory for a large organization needs to be distributed (or partitioned) across many geographic locations. To support this organization, Active Directory uses a global catalog. Copies of the global catalog (called replicas) exist at most Active Directory sites. (Sites are discussed in more detail throughout the rest of this chapter.) At a site, the global catalog replica is a partial copy of the total Active Directory. It contains all the defined objects together with a full list of object attributes in the current domain and a subset of the attributes of each object located in another domain. (A domain is a security and delegation boundary; domains are also discussed in more detail later in this chapter.)

The main function of the global catalog is to support a query based on the name of an object or a subset of its attributes. The global catalog makes it possible to determine the location of a full replica of the directory where more information about an object can be found.

The global catalog is built dynamically by the Windows 2000 replication system described later in this chapter. Any domain controller can be set up to be a global catalog server. There is usually one global catalog server per site. Clients locate their nearest global catalog server by using the Windows 2000 *Domain Name Service* (DNS).

The Configuration

The Active Directory configuration holds information for replication and other metadata about Active Directory. For instance, it stores the trust relationship data that connects Active Directory domains. (This particular Active Directory component is discussed in more detail in the section titled "Sites and Replication" later in this chapter.)

The Domain

The Windows 2000 domain is the basic Windows 2000 security boundary, just as it was in Windows NT. The Active Directory is made up of one or more related domains. Domain administrators can set domain-wide security policies and delegate a subset of the administrative rights in a domain to other users. Domain controllers located in the domain house a full replica of Active Directory objects in its own domain and a partial replica of Active Directory objects in other domains. These replicas are used to locate all resources.

An administrator can define the security policies that apply in a given domain (see Chapter 13). A Windows 2000 domain contains all defined users and groups as well as resources such as printers, applications, and disk volumes—in fact, almost anything that you want to locate and/or use.

The Domain Name Service (DNS)

The purpose of a DNS in a TCP/IP network is to locate distributed services. It functions by translating the symbolic name of an object into the specific TCP/IP address used to locate the object itself. Although it predates the Active Directory service, the DNS has been integrated with Active Directory to act as the locator service for Active Directory objects.

The Windows 2000 DNS is the same one that you are probably familiar with if you have ever browsed the Internet. In fact, the Windows 2000 DNS system can be spliced into the big Internet DNS and used to name and offer location services to your publicly available resources such as Web servers, as well as for internal resources.

Active Directory clients locate Active Directory servers in a domain by querying the domain name in DNS. This means that the Active Directory domain name has to correspond to a DNS domain.

Register Your Domain Name!

Because Windows 2000 integrates so completely with DNS, and because DNS can be used to provide a lookup service that can be used both inside and outside your corporation, it makes sense to register your domain name with the Internet name registration authority. This is true even if you currently have no intention of providing access from the Internet. You may want to change your mind later. Furthermore, there are some unscrupulous operators out there that go around registering other company's domain names and selling them back to them. You will want to avoid this. ◆

Objects defined in DNS have Internet style names such as: `PuplicWebServer.Whzco.Com` for a Web server, or `Wzack@WhzCo.com` for a user. A typical DNS hierarchy, which extends the Internet-naming scheme to the corporate intranet, might be set up as shown in Figure 10.2.

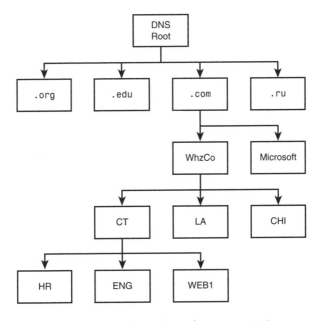

Figure 10.2 *The WhzCo domain in DNS.*

In Figure 10.2, the WhzCo.Com domain name can be used to locate the William H. Zack and Associates Web server (WEB1) located in Connecticut (CT).

This example, of course, ignores the question of whether it is actually advisable to provide direct access from the Internet to an internal server inside your network. In reality, you would probably protect your internal network from malicious access by installing a firewall between the Web server and your internal network. You might even use a different root domain name to disguise the relationship between your internal network and the Internet. (The use of disjoint root domain names is fully supported by Active Directory forests, as discussed later in this section.) In some cases, you may want to use a contiguous namespace for internal and external access. In other cases, however, a disjoint namespace makes more sense.

The DNS configuration and naming of your Active Directory domains is a major planning issue (an exhaustive explanation of which is beyond the scope of this discussion). The "bottom line" here is that your Active Directory domains must be supported by the DNS service. Regardless of whether you use the same DNS domain name on the public Internet as you use internally, you can configure DNS to accommodate Active Directory. Clients must be able to query DNS for the Active Directory domain and find entries that point them to Active Directory servers. There are lots of ways to handle this. For more information on this topic, refer to *Planning for Windows 2000* by Cone, Biggs, and Perez, New Riders Publishing, ISBN: 0-7357-0048-6.

Users

Users are represented in the Active Directory by user accounts created by an administrator in a specific domain. User objects in the Active Directory have attributes such as usernames and passwords. A workstation user normally logs on with a DNS style name such as wzack@WhzCo.Com.

When a workstation boots up, the nearest domain controller is located. When the user attempts to log on, the workstation is referred to a domain controller in a domain that can authenticate the user. If the client is a Kerberos client, the domain controller of the trusting domain provides a referral so that the workstation can contact the appropriate domain controller to be authenticated (see Chapter 13).

Groups

A typical Windows 2000 installation could have hundreds, or even thousands of user accounts defined. It could take an administrator a very long time to perform operations that affect a large number of these users. In general, these users will fall into a smaller number of categories, such as members of the marketing department, consultants, and accountants. So that administrators can avoid dealing excessively with individual users, Windows 2000 enables the administrator to add these users to logical groups and to use those groups to assign permissions and access rights to resources.

The Windows 2000 Active Directory supports three types of groups. These groups can be nested as follows:

- *Universal groups*—Appear in ACLs anywhere in a forest (see the discussion of forests later in this chapter). They can contain other universal groups, global groups, and user accounts from anywhere in the forest. The universal group appears in the global catalog. The advantage of this type of arrangement is that a small company can use only universal groups for simplicity. In a Windows 2000–only environment, for instance, it would be more natural to nest only universal groups.

- *Global groups*—Appear in ACLs anywhere in a forest. They can contain user accounts and other global groups from their own domain. Global groups appear in the global catalog, but not its members. Changes to global groups are effective throughout the forest.

- *Domain local groups*—Appear in ACLs in their own domain only. They can contain user accounts, global groups, and universal groups from any domain in the forest, as well as other domain local groups from their own domain. Typically, you will define your users in a domain and then add them to a global group for export to other domains. In a foreign domain, you can then add this global group to a universal group in that domain. The advantage of this is that the definition of global groups and their security attributes will not change very much over time. Most of the changes will be made to members of the global groups in their home domain. The current recommendation from Microsoft is to use universal groups rather than global groups, unless you have a mixed Windows NT/Windows 2000 environment.

Directory Partitions

A domain is also a partition of the Active Directory. It contains a full global catalog replica of the objects in it. (As discussed earlier, global catalogs in remote domains contain only partial replicas of the objects in other domains.)

Domain Controllers and Member Servers

Windows 2000 has two types of servers: member servers (sometimes called standalone servers), and domain controllers. Member servers act just as resource servers. They cannot authenticate domain users because they lack a copy of the Active Directory. A domain controller starts out life as a member server. It is promoted to domain controller status by the execution of the DCPROMO utility. It can also be demoted back to member server status using DCPROMO. This is a big improvement over Windows NT. In Windows NT, a domain controller had to be installed as such. A member server could not be promoted to domain controller status, nor could a domain controller be demoted back to member server status. As soon as you promote your first member server to domain controller, you create a domain.

There can be multiple domain controllers in a domain for redundancy and logon load balancing. (If you are familiar at all with Windows NT domain controllers, you will note that there is no longer a distinction between primary domain controllers and backup domain controllers. All domain controllers are now equal, even if more than one domain controller is located in a domain.)

Domains can span more than one location. This makes it possible to define a domain on a functional rather than on a geographical basis. A corporation with branches in two cities could define a marketing domain, for example, that holds users accounts and resources belonging to the marketing department. This would allow a marketing domain administrator to control the domain even though it spans multiple locations. (Later you will see how you can establish relationships among different domains that are grouped into domain trees and forests.)

Trust Relationships

Prior to Windows 2000, the domain was the top dog in the organizational hierarchy. To support multiple domains and allow the management of users and resources across these domains, some pretty complex interdomain organizations had to be constructed using relationships called *trusts*. A trust relationship between two domains allows one domain to accept that another domain (called the trusted domain) has authenticated a user wanting access to resources in the second domain (called the trusting domain).

A trust relationship could be set up between domain A and domain B for example, where domain B trusts domain A. In this scenario, a domain A user could log on in domain A to access resources in domain B. Domain B would then use a feature called pass-through authentication to verify the identity of the user in domain A. Based on this and the trust relationship between the two domains, the user would be granted access to domain B resources.

In Windows NT, these trust relationships were, by default, one way. Just because domain A trusted domain B, that did not mean that domain B trusted domain A. To support bidirectional trust relationships between two domains, two one-way trust relationships had to be set up between the two domains.

In Windows NT, these trust relationships were also nontransitive. If domain B had been set up to trust domain A and domain A had been set up to trust domain C, for example, that did not mean that domain A also trusted domain C (see Figure 10.3).

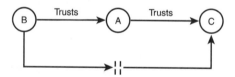

Figure 10.3 *Trust relationships.*

It is easy to see that the need to create two-way trusts among multiple domains could escalate to a large number of difficult-to-maintain connections. Fortunately, Windows 2000 trust relationships are automatically bidirectional and transitive. This means that a user can log on or be assigned permissions on any computer in the forest.

Organizational Units

As mentioned earlier, the Windows NT domain was originally the only organizational unit in a network. In that capacity, it served both as a physical and a logical organization unit. To delegate authority over a selected group of users and resources, a new domain had to be created. Then the desired administrators could be defined in that domain. This often led to a proliferation of domains with overlapping and confusing trust relationships between them. (If you have ever worked with Windows NT, you may have had to deal with the different domain-management models such as the single-domain model, the master-domain model, the multimaster-domain model, and the complete-trust model.)

In addition to the domain organizations present in Windows NT, Windows 2000 also adds a new structure, the *organizational unit* (OU). This structure enables you to partition domains into smaller security units and to delegate access to them on a finer basis than that provided by Windows NT domains (see Figure 10.4).

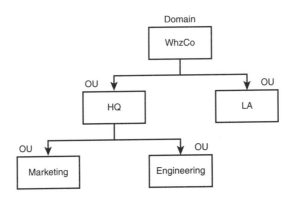

Figure 10.4 *Organizational units.*

A Windows 2000 OU resides completely within a single Windows 2000 domain. An OU is primarily a container object located in a domain that an administrator can define to delegate a subset of the administrator's authority to other users.

Figure 10.4 illustrates a single domain with functional areas divided into OUs rather than multiple domains. This organization enables an administrator to partition the network without having to have multiple domains and domain controllers. Delegation of administration in Active Directory is accomplished through the use of security descriptors on directory objects.

OUs, like all objects in the Active Directory, have names in a namespace. These names may look odd to you because they are based on the international X.500 standard for object names. OU-distinguished names follow the convention described in the following sections.

Distinguished Names

Every object in the Active Directory has one, and only one, formal name, called a *distinguished name* (DN). An object's DN fully identifies the domain in which it resides. It also defines the Active Directory path to the object from the root of the Active Directory. This name can be used to retrieve data about the object from a global catalog server (limited set of attributes) or a domain controller from the object's domain (full set of attributes).

As you will see in the following description, an object's DN can be fairly long. Furthermore, it can also change as objects (users, printers) get moved around to accommodate network changes. To enable users and programs to locate objects even in the face of these changes, the Active Directory allows queries by object attributes as well as by full or partial object names.

The "Real Name" of an Object

If you move an object, you will change its DN. Because an object's distinguished names can change, Windows 2000 also assigns a unique 128-bit identifying number (called a GUID) to all objects in the Active Directory when they are created. The algorithm used for this guarantees that this number will be unique for all objects ever created. ♦

The following is a typical DN:

```
CN=Bill Zack,CN=Users,DC=WhzCo,DC=Com
```

This DN identifies Bill Zack as an object in the Users container in the domain WhzCo.com. It defines the name of the object and all the object containers in its path from the root of the Active Directory.

Relative Distinguished Names

Even if you do not know an object's full DN, the Active Directory enables you to locate an object based on a subset of the DN called the *relative distinguished name* (RDN). The RDN is an attribute of the object itself. The RDN of the object in the preceding example is CN=Bill Zack.

User Principal Names

Security principals (such as users and groups) also have a more "friendly" name, called *user principal names* (UPN). The UPN for a user might look like wzack@WhzCo.Com, for example.

Delegation of Authority

As discussed earlier, domain administrators can delegate a subset of their authority to other users. An administrator could delegate the right to reset user passwords and unlock locked user accounts to a help-desk technician, for example. This would free the administrator from having to perform these chores every time that a user forgets his password and locks up his account by attempting to log on too many times with the wrong password. (Chapter 13 discusses logon security.) Another example would be an administrator in the information systems department who delegates administrative rights over the human resources OU to an administrator located in the human resources department.

Domain Trees

A domain tree consists of a hierarchy of related domains. Each domain is a partition of the Active Directory.

All domain controllers in a domain share the domain-naming context. The only thing unique about a "tree" is that it is a contiguous namespace for the naming of the domains. A single domain directory contains a single forest and a single tree.

Transitive bidirectional trust relationships are automatically set up among member domains in a tree (see Figure 10.5).

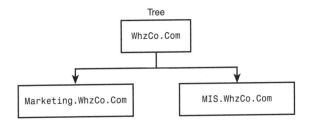

Figure 10.5 *Domain trees.*

The domain hierarchy forms a contiguous namespace where the shape of the tree is determined by the DNS namespace used. For example, the domain WebServer.Master.WhzCo.Com defines that the domain WebServer is a child of the domain Master in the WhzCo.Com domain.

As soon as you create the first domain in your network, you will also be creating your first directory tree. When you install a new server, you are given the following options:

1. Create the first tree in a new forest.
2. Create a new tree in an existing forest.
3. Create a new replica of an existing domain.
4. Install a child domain in the same tree.

When you select option 4, you will be prompted for the name of a parent domain. Then the new domain will become part of the parent domain's namespace.

The current beta version of Windows 2000 comes with a MoveTree utility, which can be used to reorganize the domains in a tree. Windows 2000 does not have a tool to enable you to join two or more trees together. Hopefully Microsoft, or a third party, will fill this gap soon.

Forests

A *forest* is a collection of one or more trees. The domains in a domain tree have names that are part of a contiguous namespace. This enables you to trace the ancestry of a domain by the segments of its domain name. Trees in a forest, on the other hand, do not share a contiguous namespace. The two domain trees shown in Figure 10.6, for instance, have a totally different domain root name. They do share a common schema, configuration, and global catalog. They are also completely joined by transitive trusts so that all domains in a forest trust each other (see Figure 10.6).

When you install a single domain, you automatically create a forest. There is currently no way to merge forests (although there may be a way provided in the released version of Windows 2000).

The ability to create a forest can come in handy in several situations. You may want to use different DNS namespaces for the Internet and for your internal network. You may also be faced with the chore of joining two previously unconnected networks. For instance, your company may merge with another company that also has a Windows 2000 network in place. In that case, you may not want to go through the trouble of changing all the domain names, organizational units, users, and groups of one network to match the other one. (The example in Figure 10.6 shows just such a merger of two dissimilar domains and the resulting forest created by joining them together.)

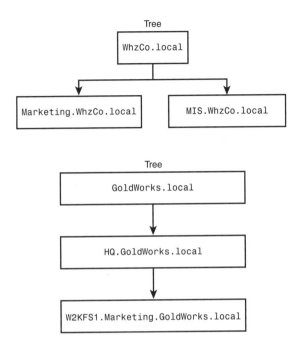

Figure 10.6 *Trees in the forest.*

Sites and Replication

As discussed earlier, the Active Directory needs to be distributed across multiple physical sites. A *site* is a location that contains a copy of the Active Directory. It is defined more precisely as a set of "well-connected" TCP/IP subnets. (See Chapter 14, "Networking," for a definition of TCP subnets.) Although the exact meaning of "well connected" can vary based on your network topology, in general it means locations connected by high-speed communications circuits that are not routed over slower wide-area links. This could be a 10Mbps Ethernet, for instance, or a 16Mbps Token Ring network. There is really no hard and fast rule here. In some implementations, locations connected with 1.544MBps T1 or 44.736MBps T3 lines could be considered local if they are dedicated to replication. On the other hand, they could be considered remote if they share network traffic with other applications (see Figure 10.7).

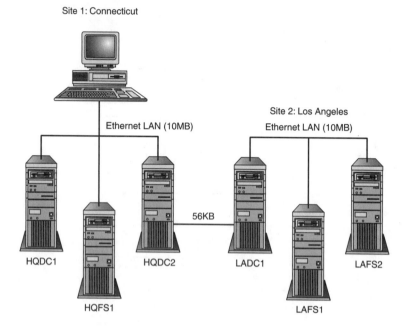

Figure 10.7 *Sites.*

How a Workstation Locates Its Site

A workstation discovers its site by querying DNS. The contacted server then uses the subnet address to direct the workstation to the appropriate catalog server to use. If the located server is not in the domain at that site (for instance, if the workstation has been moved), it notifies the workstation of a better server to contact. When a user logs on to a Windows 2000 domain, he is authenticated by the nearest domain controller located in the domain.

The main reason for defining sites is to set up and control the replication topology and frequency of updates to distributed replicas of the global catalog. Replication within a site (intrasite replication) is done via the *Remote Procedure Call* (RPC) facility, as discussed in Chapter 2, "Operating System Architecture." Replication across site boundaries (intersite replication) also normally uses RPC.

Intersite Replication Architecture

Many replicas of the global catalog can exist at geographically diverse sites. Changes to the directory can be made at any site. As changes are made at a given site, it is not possible to guarantee that all replicas of the directory will agree with each other at any given point in time. It takes time for a change to propagate to different sites. In addition, there may be only intermittent or slow connectivity between some sites. To accommodate this possibility, the Active Directory uses an intrasite and intersite replication architecture that is multimaster, with loose consistency, and convergence.

- *Multimaster*—In a multimaster network, there is no master directory site in the network. All directory replicas are equals. Updates made at one site are propagated (eventually) to the replicas at other sites. "Eventually" can vary depending on the way that sites are connected and the frequency of updates.

- *Loose consistency*—This refers to how different replicas of the global catalog may not agree completely with each other at the same moment in time. Over time, however, these replicas will reach the same steady state. The administrator can define a replication topology and schedule for the propagation of changes. This topology can contain loops for redundancy so that there can be more than one path that an update can take. To reduce update traffic, all replication is per property rather than per object. Each property update is given a unique serial number and conflicting changes are detected and resolved.

- *Convergence*—Loops in the replication topology are permitted and a damping scheme is used to ensure that all replicas converge to the same steady state and that unnecessary update propagation does not occur.

Access to the Active Directory

Now that you understand basic domain architecture and naming conventions, take a look at how to use the Active Directory to locate resources. Resources can be located via the Windows 2000 GUI or by commands and programs executed under Windows 2000.

GUI Access to Active Directory

The Windows 2000 GUI provides tools to locate resources using the Active Directory. Note, however, that at the time of this writing, Microsoft was still fine-tuning this part of the GUI. It may be a little different in the released version of Windows 2000.

To locate files in the GUI, just right-click the Start button and select the Search menu option. This will display a Search Results dialog box in which you can specify the name of a file or directory to find. Optionally, you can even specify a text string to match in the file (see Figure 10.8).

10.8 *Finding a user in Active Directory.*

Program Access to Active Directory

For performing simple tasks on a small group of objects, the Windows 2000 GUI provides an easy-to-use interface. It is not, however, as useful for making mass changes. If you have to add 200 new users as part of the setting up of a new domain, for instance, you will quickly tire of using the GUI. Fortunately, Windows 2000 provides scripted access to the Active Directory via the same *Windows Scripting Host* (WSH) as discussed in Chapter 9, "Job and Task Management." This access is provided by the *Active Directory Services Interface* (ADSI) ActiveX object that comes with Windows 2000. You can write a WSH script that invokes this object as shown in the following example. (Note that the line numbers are not part of the script. They are just so that I can refer to specific lines in the text.)

Additional Administration Tools

As I was writing this chapter, Microsoft announced that they would bundle domain reorganization tools from Mission Critical Software into Windows 2000. There will also be other tools for exporting and importing users to/from text files in the final version of the resource kit as well. Many other third-party companies will undoubtedly offer add-on tools as well. ◆

```
 1 ' ADSI Sample to create a new user account
 2
 3 Option Explicit
 4
 5 Dim sUsersC      'Path to the Users container
 6 Dim objUsersC     'The Users container object
 7
 8 Dim objNewUser     'The new user object to be created
 9
10 'Set the parent container path and get it
11 sUsersC="LDAP://cn=Users, dc=HQDomain, dc=local"
12 set objUsersC=GetObject(sUsersC)
13
14 'Specify the (required) cn for the new user account
15 set objNewUser=objUsersC.Create("user", "cn=BZack")
16
17 'Specify the only other (required) attribute
18 objNewUser.put "samAccountName", "BZack"
19
20 'Create it now!
21 objNewUser.SetInfo
22
23 wscript.echo "User account created"
24
```

This example uses ADSI and WSH to create a new domain user account. Line 11 and 12 specify that ADSI is to position the directory at the Users container in the HQDomain.local domain. Line 15 creates a new user account object (in memory) with the Common Name BZack. Line 18 adds the only other required parameter (samAccountName) to the object, and line 21 actually inserts the object into the directory.

Because this is the first release of Windows 2000, it does not have a very complete set of tools for administering the Active Directory. Although the resource kit does provide a few extras, it will be up to third-party developers to fill this need. The Windows 2000 resource kit does come with several useful utilities for managing the Active Directory. LDP.exe is a GUI tool that can be used to perform LDAP-based operations (such as searching, adding, and deleting objects). The resource kit also comes with several other useful WSH scripts. It includes Listmembers.vbs, which can be used to list members of any ADS container. It also contains CreateUser.vbs, which is a more powerful (and therefore more complex) version of the sample program shown here.

This chapter has covered how resources are located symbolically via OS/390 catalogs and the Windows 2000 Active Directory. Next you will see how one specific type of resource, printers, are handled under OS/390 and Windows 2000.

11

Printer Management

This chapter compares the printing services of OS/390 with those of Windows 2000. Early versions of the operating systems that evolved into OS/390 were dedicated to batch processing with the end result being printed reports. Windows 2000 evolved in the interactive PC world where printing reports played a smaller role. Nevertheless, you will see in this chapter how the printing features of Windows 2000 come close to the capabilities supported by OS/390.

OS/390 Printer Management

OS/390 is still primarily an operating system that runs batch jobs. In fact, even interactive processes such as TSO/SPF and CICS are started from the same JCL used to run batch jobs. In most mainframe shops, page printers, such as the IBM 3900, still produce mountains of output on a daily basis. This section examines the architecture of JES2, the OS/390 subsystem that manages printing. Then this chapter explains how printers are defined in OS/390 and wraps up with a discussion of how computer operators and end users control printers and the printing process.

JES2 Printing Architecture

As noted in Chapter 9, "Job and Task Management," JES2 handles all OS/390 printed output. Chapter 9 defined the processing phases of JES2 as follows:

- Input phase
- Conversion phase
- Processing phase
- Output-processing phase
- Hard-copy phase
- Purge phase

This chapter focuses on the two phases involved in print output processing: the output-processing phase and the hard-copy phase. You will remember that the output-processing phase determines the disposition of all SYSOUT and MSGCLASS datasets in the job, and that it groups datasets with similar output in the output queues. The hard-copy phase is responsible for selecting output for processing by class, routing code, priority, and other criteria. It then sends the output to the real printer.

JES2 uses a set of disk datasets to keep track of job information. These datasets are collectively called the *JES spool queue*. Two sets of datasets are used to implement the JES2 spool queue: a set of dataspace files, and a set of checkpoint/recovery files. Figure 11.1 shows the structure of the JES2 spool queue.

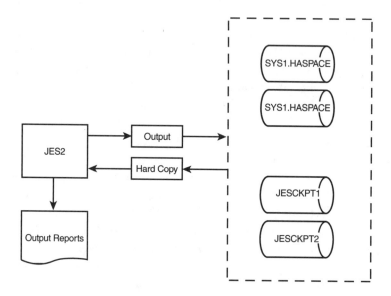

Figure 11.1 *JES2 printing architecture.*

The primary data area is made up of one or more datasets on separate volumes with the dataset name SYS1.HASPACE. There is also a set of checkpoint/recovery files named JESCKP1, JESCKPT2, and so on, which should be located on separate volumes. (The name HASPACE pays homage to HASP. As discussed in Chapter 2, "Operating System Architecture," JES2 descended from HASP.)

When a print dataset is created by an OS/390 job, it is placed in the JES spool queue output area. All the datasets produced by the job are grouped by similar characteristics such as form type or output class. JES2 supports up to 36 output classes for operating system messages and data.

Job output is queued in order of output priority. This priority can be specified via JCL, or JES2 can compute it based on the total number of print lines, punched cards, and pages of output (for page-oriented printing). The user can also specify printer character-set information in the form of a print-train name for line-oriented output or a *forms control buffer* (FCB) name for page-oriented output.

When the user codes his JCL, he can specify an output disposition for the print dataset. (If no disposition is specified, system defaults will be taken.) The valid dataset dispositions are as follows:

- *Hold*—This indicates that JES2 will not print the output. It will be left in the queue until you change the disposition to Write, Keep, Purge, or until you issue a command to Release it.

- *Keep*—This indicates that the dataset should be printed but not purged from the queue. After printing, the disposition will be changed to Leave.

- *Leave*—This specifies that the dataset is just to remain in the queue.

- *Purge*—This notifies JES2 to purge the output from the queue as soon as it can do so.

- *Write*—This indicates that the dataset should be processed and then purged.

Installing and Configuring Printers

Because your IBM customer engineer installs the mainframe printers, this discussion doesn't deal with that process. The systems programmer, however, must generate the operating system tables that define the printer device to the operating system and customize the sample JES2 parameter library members that define JES2 startup parameters. A subset of these startup parameters defines the devices JES is to use, the job output classes that they are to handle, and other output-related parameters.

JES2 output processing actually works by intercepting I/O operations destined for printer devices. JES2 then reroutes the output to the JES2 spool dataset. Because of this, the systems programmer can define multiple printers whether they actually exist or not! This makes it possible to have programs print to different devices where the actual output will be printed on the same physical device. In addition, JES2 supports the definition of multiple physical printers that take print jobs from the same print classes. These two features make it possible for multiple job classes to print to the same printer for priority output scheduling, and for one queue to feed multiple printers to support printer pooling. (The Windows 2000 discussion in this explains how to achieve the equivalent results in Windows 2000.)

Internal Readers

JES2 also supports the definition of one or more internal readers. An internal reader is a virtual print device that routes right back into the JES2 input queue. This makes it possible for subsystems such as CICS and TSO to submit a job to be scheduled for execution by the operating system. Normal application programs can also submit jobs as well. In fact, some third-party job-scheduling systems make use of this capability to schedule multiple jobs where the execution of one job depends on the completion of another. ◆

Operator Commands

Computer operators and TSO/SPF users have some degree of control over the output in the JES2 output queues. Computer operators have complete control. Users, on the other hand, can only control the output from jobs that they submit. This section first covers some of the operator commands that an operator has at his disposal, and then covers the commands that an end user can exercise.

Computer Operator Commands

The OS/390 operator controls printing with a combination of OS/390 and JES2 commands. After the system has completed initialization, the operator will normally notify the operating system that it can use the physical printer using the OS/390 VARY command. Then the operator can use JES2 commands to control further output operation.

JES2 operator commands are quite concise, often consisting of only a few letters. These commands all begin with the dollar sign character ($). The first command that an operator can issue is the $S (Start) command to start the printer.

Note that many commands such as VARY and $S can be automated to reduce the work that an operator has to do to get the operating system started.

Perhaps the most often used command is the $D (Display) command, which can be used to display the status of all the JES2 queues, the jobs in the queues, and the settings of various JES2 operating parameters.

For starting and stopping printers, operators can issue the $T command. This command halts printing between output jobs. Note that this command can be used only if the printer is currently inactive. Operators can use the $Z command to temporarily pause the printer in the middle of a job. They can use the $E command to reschedule the printing of another copy of a job.

Note that this command does not halt the copy of the job currently printing. (An operator would use this command to get additional copies of the output.) Operators can also issue the $I command to interrupt a job's output immediately and return it to the output queue for later printing. (For instance, an operator might use this command if the printer experiences a paper jam or runs out of toner. In this case, the output up to that point might be totally unusable.) To abort the print job completely, operators can issue the $C command, which will interrupt and purge the current job being printed. Operators can also use the $P command to deactivate the printer after it completes printing the current output group. (This is called *draining* the printer.) Operators can also forward space a printer a number of lines or pages with $F and backspace it with $B. The $H command can be used to place a job in the hold queue and a $O command can be used to release it.

End-User Commands

The previously listed operator commands give the computer operator quite a few options to use while controlling output. In early versions of the operating system, it was not unusual for the computer operator to receive many phone calls related to job output class and disposition changes in a day. When IBM introduced TSO/SPF, they added a facility for users to control their own jobs and output spool datasets. The *Spool Display and Search Facility* (SDSF) provides display panels that can be used to perform this function. By selecting an option (usually *S*) from the main SPF menu, you can call up the SDSF menu (see Figure 11.2).

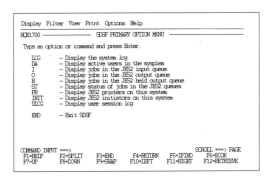

Figure 11.2 *SDSF menu.*

This menu provides quite a few job and output management options. (The next chapter discusses some of the non-printing-related options.) The output related options are as follows:

- *O*—This displays the jobs in the JES2 output queue waiting to be printed.
- *H*—This displays the jobs in the hold queue.

Although not exactly output related, the ST and DA commands, which display the status of running jobs, are also frequently used to keep track of a job. A user might submit a job with output directed to the hold queue, for instance. Later, the user might inquire as to the status of the job and browse through its datasets to make sure that the output is correct before releasing it to be printed. Figure 11.3 shows the result of entering *H* on the SDSF menu.

```
Display  Filter  View  Print  Options  Help

SDSF HELD OUTPUT DISPLAY ALL CLASSES   LINES 789        LINE 1-1 (1)
NP   JOBNAME   JOBID    OWNER   PRTY C CDISP DEST                 TOT-REC  TOT-
     ZACKA     TSU00538 ZACK     144 U HOLD  LOCAL                    189
     ZACKB     TSU00550 ZACK     144 U HOLD  LOCAL                    884
     ZACKC     TSU00621 ZACK     144 U HOLD  LOCAL                   1767
     ZACKD     TSU00630 ZACK     144 U HOLD  LOCAL                    206




COMMAND INPUT ===>                                  SCROLL ===> PAGE
 F1=HELP    F2=SPLIT   F3=END    F4=RETURN  F5=IFIND   F6=BOOK
 F7=UP      F8=DOWN    F9=SWAP   F10=LEFT   F11=RIGHT  F12=RETRIEVE
```

Figure 11.3 *The hold queue.*

Figure 11.3 shows four jobs that I have submitted from TSO/SPF. All of them have completed execution. This screen has quite a few areas where you can enter commands that control the display and disposition of your output. The top line of this panel is a menu, which enables you to control the overall display. (It is a recent addition to SPF and was not present on earlier versions.) Each subsequent line in the panel shows the status of a job in the queue.

The NP column can be used to enter one-letter commands that will change the status of the job. You can release a job to print in the specified class shown by using the A command, for instance. You can cancel the printing of a job with the C or P commands. You can also restart a job with the E command (for instance, to get another copy of the output), or move a job into the hold queue with the H command. (Naturally, you would have to be on the output queue display panel and not the hold queue display panel to do this. Afterward, it would show up in the hold queue.) Perhaps the most important NP column command is the s command, which enables you to display the output datasets in a job and browse through them.

In addition to the one-letter NP area commands, several of the fields on a line can be overtyped to change the disposition of a job. You can overtype the PRTY and c (output job class) fields, for example. Most of the other fields, such as Jobname, Jobid, and Owner are fixed and cannot be altered.

SDSF and "Real" Computer Operators

SDSF provides a pretty handy way to control jobs, in fact many computer operators prefer using SDSF to using JES2 commands to control individual jobs. SDSF, however, does not enable the operator to control everything that JES2 commands do. For computer operators, and other authorized personnel, the SDSF menu panel can be tailored to show options that end users cannot use. The PR *option, which can be used to display the status of JES2 printers, for example, and the* INIT *option, which can be used to display the active initiators, both require special authorization.* ◆

As you have seen, OS/390 provides a wide range of options to control printing. The next section shows how Windows 2000 compares with OS/390 in this area.

Windows 2000 Printer Management

Windows 2000 printer management has some of the same capabilities of OS/390 JES2 printer management. Windows 2000, however, has a single GUI interface that makes the job much easier. A whole book could be devoted to the subject of printing in Windows 2000, in fact, one has (sort of). Windows 2000 built-in Help has more than 60 pages of help on understanding and using printers in Windows 2000. No attempt is made to duplicate that material here. This discussion just touches on the most important topics that will help you make the transition from OS/390 to Windows 2000. To find this information, left-click on *Start* and then select the *Help* icon from the pop-up menu.

Windows 200 Printing Architecture

Before discussing the architecture of printing in Windows 2000, it is important to review a few components and some terminology.

Components and Terminology

When it comes to printing, Microsoft has defined a bewildering number of printer-related terms that are often confused with each other. The following sections summarize this terminology. Subsequent sections go into some detail about these terms and the entire printing process.

Print Job

A *print job*, in Windows 2000, is a file containing data to be printed, such as text, fonts, and graphics. A print job may be in one of several data formats (which Windows 2000 calls *types*). It could be in *Enhanced Metafile Format* (EMF) destined for a *page composition language* (PCL) printer, such as the Hewlett-Packard LaserJet family of printers. It could be pages of PostScript data destined for a PostScript printer such as an Apple LaserWriter. The data could even be pure text lines generated by a DOS application that only supports the output of raw text lines. This term is also used to refer to the icon of the print job displayed in a printer window.

Page Printing Languages

The Hewlett-Packard's page composition language (PCL) is similar to the Advanced Function Printing/Intelligent Printer Data Stream (APF/IPDS) facility supported by OS/390, OS/2, and other IBM platforms. Both printer control languages allow the definition of complex pages consisting of multiple data types such as text, images, graphics, and fonts. ◆

Printer

When the Windows 2000 documentation refers to a printer, it is not talking about a hardware device. Instead, it refers to a *logical printer*, which is actually a software component. It is roughly equivalent to a JES2 print queue.

Print Server

This is the computer that manages a remote printer accessed via the network.

Logical Printer

This refers to the logical interface between the operating system and the printer. It is software that runs on the print server.

It determines how a print job is processed and how it is routed to a network or locally attached printer port or a file.

Print Queue

A *print queue* is a group of print jobs waiting to be printed. This is also used to refer to the display of jobs in a printer window.

Printer Device

When the documentation refers to a *printer device*, it is actually talking about the real physical printer. A printer device has I/O lines that connect to the CPU bus over a parallel or serial port. Page-oriented printer devices often contain local storage to allow them to assemble a full page in local memory before printing it. They also often have a ROM-based interpreter language that can interpret and print files encoded with a printer page definition language such as PCL or PostScript.

Print Processor

This refers to Windows 2000 software that understands how to print a document on a specific type of physical printer. (See the discussion of the printing process in the remainder of this chapter.)

Print Spooler

This is the component of Windows 2000 that accepts a document to be printed. It either sends it to a remote print spooler or spools it to disk for later printing on the current machine. It also schedules and distributes the output.

Printing Pool

Two or more printers attached to a single print server and treated as a single logical printer by the operating system are called a *printing pool*. Spooled output jobs are printed on the first available printer in the printing pool.

Print Driver

This is the software that allows applications to print without worrying about the actual printer hardware or internal printer language (such as PCL or PostScript).

Line Printer Daemon (LPD)

This is a software service running on the print server that receives jobs from Line Printer Remote (LPR) clients for printing on the print server. Normally this utility is used to print output from non-Windows clients over a TCP/IP network connection.

Line Printer Remote (LPR)
This is the client-side utility used to send print output to an LPD processor normally running on a non-Windows print server.

Printer Window
This is a desktop window that shows information about jobs in the printer queue that are waiting to be printed. It shows key information about the job such the name of the job, the person who submitted the job, its size, and its print status. The printer folder in the Control Panel has an icon for every installed local and remote printer. Double-clicking on this icon opens the printer's window.

Print Sharing
This is the act of allowing remote users to see and spool print jobs to a server-managed printer. It may also include advertising the availability of the printer in the Active Directory.

Default Printer
This is the printer that will be automatically selected in the Print dialog box when you request printing from a Windows application. This should be set to the printer that you use most often. (For instance, I have mine set to a network printer located just outside my office.)

The Printing Process
Figure 11.4 shows the Windows 2000 printing process. This figure assumes a Windows 2000 network client system printing on a remote network printer attached to a Windows 2000 print server. (See the sidebar titled "Network Attached Printers and Non-Windows 2000 Clients" for other options.)

The components used in printing perform a function similar to the output and hard-copy components of JES2. The application program creates a page of output by drawing graphics and text into a logical memory work-space called a *device context*. The application program then calls the *graphics device interface* (GDI) for information on how to prepare the output for the particular printer type that it will eventually print on. The GDI requests this information from a copy of the *printer device driver* for the printer that will be used to print the document on the remote print server. It gets this information from a copy of the printer device driver located on the local system. Note that this is the same printer device driver that will be used on the remote printer server to actually print the job later. (The GDI is a software component that exists partially in the Win32 subsystem and partially in the operating system Kernel. It is responsible for communicating with a printer device driver to determine the capabilities of a specific model of printer. It is also called from the application when the print job is ready to be sent to the printer, as discussed shortly.) Printer device drivers are normally very platform specific. For instance, a driver for an Intel x86 system will not work on a Compaq Alpha system.

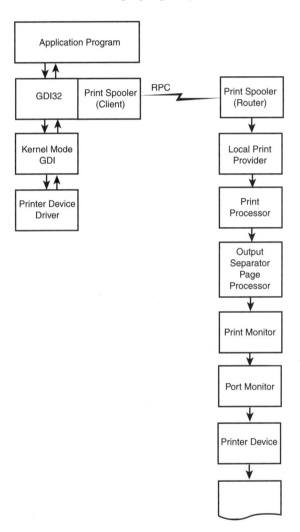

Figure 11.4 *Windows 2000 print processing architecture.*

The process that a print job goes through next is as follows:

1. When the job is ready to print, the GDI calls the local print spooler to route the job to the appropriate spooler service on the remote print server.

2. The *print spooler* is a set of distributed Windows 2000 processes that run on the client and the remote print server. The local print spooler uses *Remote Procedure Calls* (RPCs) to send the print job to the router component of the print spooler on the remote print server.

3. The *router* component of the print spooler running on the remote print server receives the job and passes the job to the local print provider, which writes the job to local disk storage.

4. The *local print provider* polls the available print processors. When a *print processor* recognizes a job type that it can handle, it receives the job and may also perform further operations on the data before sending it to the separator page processor.

5. The *separator page processor* may add an *output separator* page (similar to the JES2 output separator page) to it, if requested.

6. The job is next passed to the *print monitor*. The print monitor reads and sends the data to a port monitor process attached to the actual printer port controlling the printer device.

7. Finally, firmware in the printer device creates and prints bitmaps for each page of output.

Network Attached Printers and Non-Windows 2000 Clients

We have tried to keep the processing description as simple as possible by considering only what happens with Windows 2000 clients and print servers. There are, however, more complicated situations. Some printers can be attached directly to a network without being attached to a print server. A Hewlett-Packard LaserJet printer can be attached to a network via a JetDirect card, for example. Windows 95/98 clients can also be attached to a Windows NT print server or network. If a Windows 95/98 client is attached in this way, you do not have to install printer drivers on the clients. Windows NT will automatically download the driver to the client from the server.

Some vendors also supply products that can be used to route mainframe print data to Windows 2000 printers. One such product is MPI Tech's Blue Server. This product combines software that runs on a Windows 2000 Server with a plug-in card for a LaserJet printer. The plug-in card translates mainframe AFP/IPDS output to PCL. There are also products that run on an SNA Server being used to convert communications protocols from TCP/IP to SNA. (Chapter 15, "Client/Server, Transaction, and Message Processing," discusses the SNA Server and its use as a protocol converter and mainframe gateway.)

Windows 2000 also supports printing from a non-Windows client such as a computer running UNIX. In the interest of brevity, we have omitted discussion of these options. Refer to Windows 2000 online help (search for "LPR" and "LPD") for more information. ◆

Creating and Connecting to Printers

Because printers are really logical objects, care must be taken when describing the steps you required to create a printer. On a machine that has a printer physically attached to it (such as a print server), you *create* a printer. On a client that will print to a network printer attached to a print server, you *connect* to a printer. Both of these operations add an icon for the printer in your Printers folder. The difference is that you will not be asked to install a device driver when connecting to a network printer. This is because the Windows 2000 print server can download the required driver to the client when it is needed. (This, of course, assumes that the client is running Windows 2000, Windows 95, or Windows 98. On other operating systems, a matching driver would have to be installed manually.)

Although you can hook up a printer to a client system and create a printer for it in the printer's folder, the process is identical to creating the printer on the print server. The only difference is that you probably won't share the printer over the network or advertise its availability in the Active Directory. The following discussion assumes that your intention is to install the printer on the print server and make it widely available through the Active Directory.

Creating a Printer on the Print Server

Creating a printer on the print server is fairly easy under Windows 2000. In fact, if you have a printer connected to a USB port, your printer will automatically be recognized by Windows 2000 *Plug and Play* support as soon as you plug it in. Unfortunately, most of the printers that you will be dealing with connect to a parallel port and Windows 2000 Plug and Play support will not recognize the printer immediately when you plug it in. When you install this type of printer, you will have to reboot your computer, or start the *Add Printer Wizard* manually (as discussed later). Then Windows 2000 should automatically recognize your printer and install the driver for it. (If Windows 2000 cannot automatically recognize your printer type, it may prompt you for the information necessary to install the printer driver and port.)

You can initiate the printer creation process manually in one of several ways. One method is to use the Active Directory to locate a printer. To do this, you invoke the Search Results dialog box by right-clicking on the *Start* button and choosing the *Search* menu option. (The Search Results dialog box has replaced the Find option on the pop-up menu.) From this dialog box, you can specify the name or other attributes of the printer that you are looking for. After you locate the appropriate printer, you can specify that a shortcut for the printer is to be added to your desktop (see Figure 11.5).

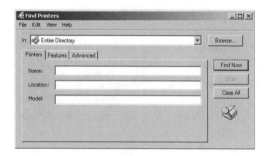

Figure 11.5   *Search results.*

After you start it, the Add Printer Wizard guides you through the rest of the installation process. It first asks whether you want to add a local printer or a network printer. If you are installing a physical printer on a print server, you should specify local printer. Otherwise, specify a network printer.

After creating the printer, the Add Printer Wizard asks whether you want to share it. If you agree, the wizard enables you to specify sharing options. It also gives you an option to publish the printer in the Active Directory. Not sharing it means that no one else will be able to use it. Not publishing it means that only people who know that it exists will be able to connect to it (assuming that they are allowed access to it). Publishing it will enable others to locate it by name or by its attributes in the Active Directory.

Creating Printer Pools

Normally Windows 2000 systems are set up with distributed printers located near the users that they serve. In some cases of high-volume output, however, a single printer may not be able to keep up with the workload. In this case, a central pool of printers may be required. As in the case of OS/390, you can set up multiple printers to print from the same printer queue. This would be useful if the print volume on any one printer is higher than the speed of the printer. To do this, you just create one Printer (queue) object and specify multiple output ports on the port page of the printer's properties notebook. (You will have to check the Enable Printer Pooling box to be able to select multiple ports.) Note that these printers must all be the same type and have the same driver. (For the users' sanity, the printers should all be located in the same area as well! Otherwise, users will not know where to find their output.) In addition, you will probably want to print output separator pages between jobs, just as you do with OS/390.

Servicing Multiple Printer Queues with One Printer
The converse situation may also exist. You may want to give priority to certain types of print jobs. The printing of payroll checks may be a little more important, for example, than the results of compiling a program. To implement this, you could create multiple printers that all print to the same physical printer. These printers could then be set up to print from multiple queues having different priorities. Output from the highest priority queues would then be printed first.

Creating a Printer on the Client
If you are adding a connection to a remote network printer, you must start the process manually with one of the methods previously discussed. When you do, you will be given the option to specify the printer name (if you know it) or browse for it using the Active Directory. You will also be presented with an option to connect to a remote printer over the Internet or via a corporate intranet. (This discussion assumes that you are going to browse for a printer and connect to it.) The Browse for Printer windows will present a list of the networks that you are attached to. Possible options here are *Microsoft Windows Network* or *NetWare or Compatible Network* (if you have support for NetWare installed on this machine). Double-clicking on either of these will expand a list of printers that you can connect to.

Connecting to Printers on Non-Windows Print Servers

There is another way to connect to a printer if you cannot browse for it. If you have OS/2 LAN Server or Warp Server print servers in your network, for example, you will have to install a printer driver for that printer as if it were a locally attached printer. Then using the Add Printer Wizard, you will have to specify the Universal Naming Convention (UNC) name of the printer in the Printer Name box. (The UNC name will be of the form \\servername\ printername. *Because you cannot browse for it, you will have to know this in advance.)*

You can also connect a client printer to a UNIX print server; however, that is beyond the scope of this book. (Again, the online help mentioned in the previous sidebar will assist you here.) ◆

Operator Commands

Four special predefined user groups relate to printing in Windows 2000: administrators, print operators, server operators, and power users. Anyone who is not in one of these groups is considered to be in the built-in group "everyone." (Chapter 13, "Security," discusses users, groups, security, permissions, and rights.) All users have the same tools at their disposal to control the printing process. What discriminates among them is the rights and permissions that they have on the local and remote systems, and over the individual jobs in the spool queue.

Printing

Printing features are subject to the same security system that protects all other Windows 2000 functions. Four possible permissions can be assigned to a user or group, as follows:

- No Access
- Manage Printers
- Manage Documents
- Full Control

To start with, even the right to print a job on a Windows 2000 printer is controlled by the Windows 2000 security system (discussed in Chapter 13). A user cannot even print on a remote printer unless he or she has permission to do so. The print permission allows the specified user or group to print on the specified printer. In addition, users can manage their own print jobs by using the options discussed in the following section. Figure 11.6 shows the printer Permissions dialog box. Note that if all the boxes under Print Permissions are unchecked, the user or group has no access.

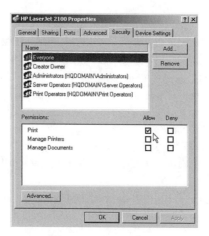

Figure 11.6 *Permissions.*

Managing Documents

All the printer management options discussed here are performed using the Printer Management window. This window opens when you double-click on a printer icon for a specific printer. This icon will be located in the Printers folder (or its shortcut if you followed the recommended tip and placed a shortcut to it on your desktop).

This window has a menu bar for global operations on jobs in the queue and the queue itself. In addition, right-clicking on a job produces a pop-up menu of options.

To manage documents, you must either be the creator of the print job or have the Manage Documents permission for the printer. The Manage Documents permission gives a specified user or member of a group permission to change the status of any job in the printer queue. These options include the following:

- *Pause* (hold) a job (or multiple jobs) that have not yet started to print
- *Resume* the printing of a job (or multiple jobs)
- *Release* a single job or the entire queue if it was previously held
- *Cancel* (flush) a single job or all the jobs in the queue
- *Restart* (reschedule) the printing of a job in the same order, to get another copy of the job output
- *Display* job properties of any job or all jobs (see Figure 11.7)

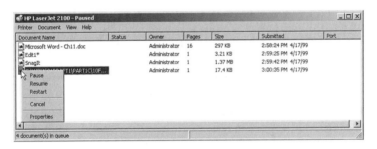

Figure 11.7 *Managing documents.*

Note that, unlike JES2, Windows 2000 does not give you any control over the job while it is in the process of being printed.

Managing Printers

By default, administrators, print operators, server operators, and power users have the Manage Printers permission. The Manage Printers permission give, the specified user or group functional control over the jobs in the printer queue and over the queue itself. This includes the right to change printer settings in the printer properties notebook for a job or the selected printer. One key setting in the properties notebook for an individual job is its priority, located on the general page of the document properties notebook (see Figure 11.8).

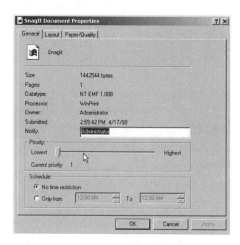

Figure 11.8 *Document print priority.*

By altering the slider values on these pages, the operator can alter the printing order of jobs in the queue much in the same way that the JES2 operator can change the printing order of OS/390 jobs. (It would be even nicer if we could just drag and drop jobs around in the printer window to achieve the same result. Perhaps that will be implemented in a future release.)

This chapter has shown how OS/390 and Windows 2000 operating systems support printing, and the management of printers, for end users and operators. The next chapter takes a look at some additional operating system tools and facilities that can be used to control the operation of OS/390 and Windows 2000.

12

Operator Control

In the world of mainframes, jobs have become quite specialized over the years. A Windows 2000 system may have a single system administrator responsible for installing, tuning, and day-to-day operations of a Windows 2000 system. In a typical OS/390 operation, however, these responsibilities would usually be partitioned between systems programmers and operators. This chapter focuses on the tasks performed only by operators. In some cases (especially with Windows 2000), the distinction may get a bit blurred.

OS/390 System Operation

The OS/390 operators are responsible for running the computer system. In a small OS/390 shop, a single person may perform all operator functions. Even in these shops, however, it is typical to find round-the-clock operations in place that require multiple shifts of operator coverage. In the medium-to-large mainframe shop, it is more typical to find even one shift manned by multiple operators, each with a specific responsibility.

Operator Types

In the typical OS/390 operation, a "console commander" may be stationed near the CPU and be responsible for operating the main system console and controlling the overall well being of the entire system. A printer pool operator may be stationed in the printer pool and be responsible for keeping printers fed with forms of the appropriate type, responding to forms' mount messages, and removing and distributing the printed output. A "tape jockey" may be located in the tape library, along with the tape drives, and be responsible for labeling and filing tape cartridges, staging tapes to be used in job processing, mounting tapes, and responding to mount messages related to that function.

In some OS/390 shops, you may also find more specialized operators responsible for running individual subsystems such as CICS and/or DB/2. This chapter does not attempt any such distinctions. Instead, it just briefly covers the tasks and responsibilities of all these operators and some of the tools that they use to do their job.

A modern OS/390 system often consists of a processor cluster called a Sysplex. A Sysplex may be partitioned into multiple *logical partitions* (LPARS), run as a single system, or be configured with processors running in both modes in the same complex. Because the operation of a Sysplex is touched on in the chapter on scalability (Chapter 19), this chapter does not cover the details of operating OS/390 in a processor complex. Although it adds to the complexity that an operator must deal with, they still perform the same basic functions covered in this section. Therefore, this discuss assumes OS/390 system operations controlled by an operator running a single-processor system.

The following section reviews the tasks that an OS/390 operator performs. Then this chapter contrasts these tasks to comparable operating tasks required of a Windows 2000 operator.

Console Management Functions

The operator interface of OS/390 is primarily command-line oriented. This makes it look pretty primitive to those used to GUI interfaces. In fact, this interface has changed little in more than 30 years. Most of the commands that an operator issues are short and appear quite cryptic. Although graphic consoles do add a full-screen display and a type-over mode of operation similar to the TSO/SPF panels discussed in the preceding chapter, command entry is still mostly line oriented. And as if that's not enough, operator commands can be in several different formats. Commands directly to the operating system are in one format, such as V 580,ONLINE. Commands to JES2 are in another format, such as $DA. Replies to operator messages that are directed at the base operating system are of the format reply 10,'U', while replies to JES2 take the simpler format such as 3u. A running commentary of all operator messages and operator replies is kept in the system log. (See the example later in this section.)

OS/390 has two kinds of consoles. There is usually a hardware console, which is used to IPL the system and to report serious hardware errors. There can also be several operator consoles used to support the distribution of operators (as discussed earlier). OS/390 supports routing the appropriate messages to these consoles using OS/390 *multiple console support* (MCS). This makes it possible for the appropriate operator to see and respond to the appropriate messages without cluttering up his console with messages for other operators. In OS/390, an operator can also use SPF consoles and SDSF (discussed in the preceding chapter) to perform some of his job functions.

Starting and Stopping OS/390

The OS/390 operator is responsible for starting the operating systems and all of its subsystems and for shutting them down when required.

Startup

Chapter 2, "Operating System Architecture," discussed the IPL and startup process, so that information is not repeated here. In addition to starting the base operating system, the operator is also responsible for starting various OS/390 subsystems such as JES2, VTAM, TSO, CICS, and DB/2. This also includes replying to any startup messages that the subsystems issue. (Hopefully the amount of work necessary here has been minimized by the systems programmer through the use of various automation procedures at his disposal.)

Shutdown

Shutting down an OS/390 system is a complex process that involves stopping all active subsystems (such as TSO, CICS, DB/2, VTAM), quiescing JES2 with $PJES2, and issuing the CPU halt command (Z EOD). Often this also involves using the send message (SE) command to broadcast a message to TSO and CICS users, notifying them that the system is shutting down.

Steady-State OS/390 Operations

After starting the system, the operator is responsible for keeping it going. This includes making sure that input is provided when necessary, that output is disposed of, and that exception messages are responded to. These responsibilities can be divided (somewhat arbitrarily) into the following categories:

- System monitoring
- Printing and offloading data
- Load balancing
- Job scheduling
- Servicing requests
- Overall housekeeping

System Monitoring

The operator is responsible for continuous monitoring of the health of the system. To perform this function, the operator may periodically issue display commands such as $DA (display active jobs and users), $DI (display initiators), D ASM (display page dataset status), D R (display outstanding replies), and DU (display status of units such as printers, disks, and tapes).

The operator is responsible for monitoring for communications problems with VTAM D NET display commands, which he uses to monitor the status of VTAM buffers, lines, nodes, and terminals. Some OS/390 shops also have a network-management package such as Netview, Tivoli, or CA-Unicenter installed. In these cases, the operator may also have the responsibility to monitor special management consoles as well.

Printing and Offloading Data

The preceding chapter discussed how operators are responsible for managing the printing process. In addition to the responsibilities discussed in that chapter, the operator is also responsible for archiving console logs, dumping and clearing *System Management Facility* (SMF) logs, printing *Resource Management Facility* (RMF) reports, and unloading standalone dumps. The operator may also be responsible for printing or archiving hardware error reports for the IBM customer engineer, using the *Environmental Reporting Edit and Print program* (EREP).

Load Balancing

The load-balancing tasks that an operator normally performs include the following:

- Dynamically starting and stopping initiators to control the number of simultaneous jobs, with the $SI command
- Setting initiator job classes
- Setting printer classes
- Setting the number of active printers with $T

In some shops, the operator may also be responsible for monitoring and even increasing the amount of page dataset and JES2 and spool space allocated to the operating system.

Job Scheduling

During normal operation, the operator is responsible for premounting tapes for jobs about to be run. In most large-scale OS/390 shops, production jobs are often scheduled for execution by a special group or even a third-party job-scheduling package. In many cases, however, the operator is responsible for submitting production jobs and/or for releasing jobs previously staged in an input hold queue. In a very small shop, the operator may even be responsible for making up the production schedule.

Servicing Requests

The OS/390 operator is charged with servicing requests from OS/390, its subsystems, and application programs. These messages include requests to mount tapes and disks and to reply to dataset security messages. See the following log file example.

```
 1  JOB02130 00000091  $HASP373 PAYREST  STARTED - INIT  18 - CLASS A - SYS AC21
 2  JOB02130 00000090  ACF9CCCD USERID BZACK    IS ASSIGNED TO THIS JOB - PAYREST
 3  JOB02130 00000090  IEF403I PAYREST - STARTED - TIME=09.00.01
 4  JOB02130 00000090  *72 FDRW24 FDRABR REQUEST FOR TAPES - 012448  REPLY YES NO OR
    BYPASS
 5  JOB02130 00000090  *TMS009  IEF233D M
    06D2,012397,,PAYREST,A,FDRABR.VSDDTST.B199064A,
 6  JOB02130 00080094  *IEF233D M 06B2,012496,,PAYREST,A,FDRABR.VSDDPAY.X199064A, 198
    00094
 7                       OR RESPOND TO IEF455D MESSAGE
 8  JOB02130 00000090  *73 IEF455D MOUNT 012397 ON 06D2 FOR PAYREST A OR REPLY 'NO'
 9  SY05TPE2 00000290  $DA
10  JOB01494 00000080  $HASP608 TESTCPMP EXECUTING A   PRIO 9 BB38
11  JOB02128 00000080  $HASP608 BACKUP1  EXECUTING A   PRIO 9 BB38
12  JOB01264 00000080  $HASP608 SDDAAOR1 EXECUTING G   PRIO 9 BB38
13  JOB01269 00000080  $HASP608 PAYREST  EXECUTING A   PRIO 9 BB38
14  JOB01455 00000080  $HASP608 TRIALBAL EXECUTING G   PRIO 9 BB38
15  JOB01483 00000080  $HASP608 BZACK    EXECUTING A   PRIO 9 BB38
16  JOB01492 00000080  $HASP608 CICSPROD EXECUTING G   PRIO 9 BB38
```

In this example, you see lines extracted from the OS/390 console log for a single job with JES2 job number 2130. (The actual log would be quite cluttered because it would have lines from all running jobs intermixed with each other.)

You can see that job 2130 was started by a Class A initiator (lines 1–3), and that a mount message for tape volume serial number 012397 was issued to access dataset FDRABR.VSDDTST.B199064A (lines 5–6). You can also see a $DA command issued by the operator (line 9) and the reply to this command listing all the active jobs (lines 10–16).

Another operator responsibility is handling hardware errors and performing device reconfiguration operations in the event of unrecoverable hardware errors. Finally, the operator is also responsible for handling user requests to cancel hung TSO sessions with the C U=userid command.

Overall Housekeeping

The operator may also be responsible for clipping volumes (changing volume serial numbers) and initializing and labeling tape cartridges. The operator may have to scratch lost temporary datasets on scratch disk volumes. (Temporary datasets used by jobs are supposed to be deleted at the end of the job. Often, due to abnormal conditions, this does not happen as it should.)

One of the most important responsibilities of a mainframe operator is to run the jobs that make backups of key datasets and volumes. The operator uses DFSMS backup utilities to perform this function. These backups will be used in case of a lost disk dataset or volume.

Problem Determination and Recovery

Problem determination is one of the most important responsibilities of an OS/390 operator. In addition to keeping the system running, the operator must be constantly on the lookout for any exceptional conditions that would interfere with smooth operation of the system. An operator must determine when system degradation or failure occurs. The operator must determine the cause of the problem, and then take the necessary action to correct the situation. Some possible error conditions that the operator must detect and respond to include determining whether the system is experiencing waits, hangs, or looping conditions. It may also include monitoring for job Abends on critical production jobs. As part of this process, the operator may use tools such as traces and dumps (although this is often the system programmer's job instead). Finally, in the case of a condition resulting in termination of system or subsystem operation, the operator must restart the affected system or subsystem.

As you can see, an OS/390 operator performs fairly complex jobs. Next you will see how these responsibilities compare with the tasks and responsibilities of Windows 2000 operators.

Mainframe Operating System Reliability

Most mainframe installations maintain a 24-hour, 7-day-a-week operating schedule. These shops normally have as an objective a 99.999% uptime. This amounts to only a few minutes a year of downtime. Windows 2000 still has a long way to go to meet this criteria. Recently, however, several major vendors announced that they will agree contractually to 99.99% availability using techniques such as clustering (discussed in Chapter 19.) The Datacenter version of Windows 2000, which will ship 90 days after Windows 2000 Server and Advanced Server, will target even greater reliability. ◆

Windows 2000 System Operation

Windows 2000 is descended from Microsoft Windows, which started life as a desktop operating system (although it does owe some of its networking heritage to Microsoft LAN Manager, an early LAN operating system). Partly because of its desktop heritage, there is often a lack of distinction between tasks such as installing and tuning the operating system, which are normally performed by a system administrator, and tasks such as system monitoring and performing backups, which are normally done by an operator.

Operator Types

In the Windows 2000 world, the term *systems administrator* (and the companion term *systems administration*) often encompasses all setup and operating job functions. Even in Windows 2000, however, the security system allows privileges to be assigned to several different types of operators. (As Windows 2000 continues to make inroads into the data center, I expect to see further operator specialization occur, just as it has with OS/390.) Briefly, these operator types and their Windows 2000 rights and privileged are as follows:

- *Administrators*—They have all the built-in rights and abilities defined in the system. In addition, they have the right to take ownership of any resource in the system (although, as you will see in the next chapter, this does leave an audit trail). For instance, an administrator can set up and administer domain controllers, create user and group accounts, and assign users to groups.

- *Account operators*—These are users who have had some administrative authority delegated to them by the administrator (see Chapter 13, "Security"). An account operator can create and administer new users and groups, but cannot change user and group accounts created by administrators. In addition, an account operator cannot modify administrator, server operator, account operators, or print operator local groups. An account operator also cannot assign user rights.

- *Server operators*—These are the guys who run the servers. They can start and stop servers and manage printers. In addition, they can start, stop, and pause all services.

- *Backup operators*—As members of the backup operators group, they can back up and restore all files regardless of any security restrictions placed on those files. (They also have other rights, discussed more fully in Chapter 13.) The right to back up and restore files makes this right a dangerous one to give out freely.

- *Print operators*—They have the right to manage printers and printer devices. They can also manage all documents in the printer queues regardless of the owner.

- *Users*—Even users can be considered operators (of a sort), because they can operate their own workstation, run applications, and use local and network printers. (This assumes, of course, that they are given permission to do so). They can start and shut down their workstations. They can also lock and unlock the workstation using their logon password. Users cannot share any resources on their computers such as folders or local printers. (Again, as with all these groups, users have additional rights covered in Chapter 13.)

Most of these built-in groups exist to assign specific rights to users who perform specific job functions, such as the backup operator group. Other groups exist to be assigned rights to system processes. (The next chapter covers the rights and privileges of these other groups. For now, this chapter just illustrates some of their rights as they pertain to system operation.)

The OS/390 section of this chapter discussed how an OS/390 operator may be working in a clustered-processor environment such as that provided by an IBM System/390 Sysplex. In the case of Windows 2000, clusters also exist. Clustering, however, is still a relatively rare situation. Windows 2000 clustering, code-named Wolfpack (discussed in Chapter 19), has only appeared on the scene in recent versions of Windows NT. It is still nowhere near as functionally well developed as the IBM Sysplex form of clustering.

Now it's time to take a more detailed look at the responsibilities of a Windows 2000 operator and how they match up with, and differ from, the responsibilities of an OS/390 operator.

Console Management Functions

The most obvious difference between OS/390 and Windows 2000 operations is that the primitive command-line or pseudo–full-screen interface of OS/390 is replaced with a *graphical user interface* (GUI). This GUI is rooted in the familiar Windows Desktop Explorer interface that was introduced with Windows 95 and earlier versions of Windows NT. (This book does not attempt to cover the detailed use of this interface. Dozens of other books on the market deal with that. Instead, this book concentrates on examples that illustrate how an operator might use it to perform his responsibilities.)

All administrative tools are located from the *Start* button on the taskbar. Left-click on the *Start* button, and then click on the *Programs* menu option. A pop-up menu will appear. This menu contains entries that you can click on to execute programs. Menu entries that have a right-pointing arrow on them will produce another cascaded menu when selected (see Figure 12.1).

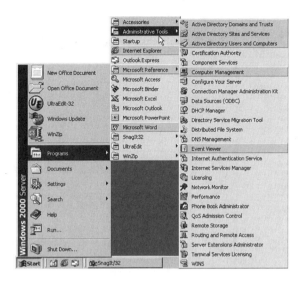

Figure 12.1 *The Start Programs menu.*

(Note that you may initially see only a subset of these menus including the entries for selections that you have used recently. To expand the menu to the full list, double-click on the double down-pointing arrows at the bottom of the menu.) The *Administrative Tools* menu entry leads to a long (and at first bewildering) list of administrative tools that you can invoke.

All the tools inherited from earlier Windows NT and the new tools developed for Windows 2000 are gradually being integrated into Microsoft's new management architecture, the *Microsoft Management Console* (MMC). The MMC is Microsoft's attempt to gather all the scattered administration tools that Windows NT provided and the new Windows 2000 administration tools into one place for easier access. In the MMC architecture, Microsoft provides a two-pane view of management tools (see Figure 12.2).

The left pane shows a tree view of various system-management applets called snap-ins. The reason that they are called snap-ins is because the MMC is nothing more than a shell into which you can install the various applets that you can use to control a particular service or function. In fact, you can build your own tool collections in the form of private MMC "consoles." You can then save them as files and even delegate the use of them to lower-level administrators in subordinate domains or organizational units. A discussion of this, however, is beyond the scope of this book.

You can refer to the document titled "Microsoft Management Console: Overview," which you can download from http://www.microsoft.com/ NTServer/management/Techdetails/prodArchitect/mmc.asp. (For an explanation of domains and organizational units, refer to Chapter 10, "Catalogs and Directories.")

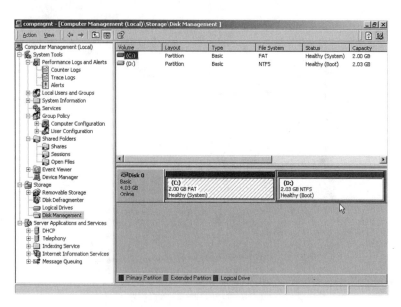

Figure 12.2 *The Microsoft Management Console.*

Microsoft has provided several preconfigured consoles such as the computer management console shown in Figure 12.2. In that figure, you can see a tree that contains three snap-ins: System Tools, Storage, and Server Applications and Services. As an example, the Storage branch of the tree has been extended to access the Disk Management snap-in. Disk Management shows the status of all disk volumes and partitions. It can be used to repartition and extend existing disk volumes. It can also be used to create various fault-tolerant configurations such as the mirrors and stripe sets discussed in Chapter 7, "Data Management."

Starting and Stopping Windows 2000

The Windows 2000 operator is responsible for starting and stopping Windows 2000. Starting a Windows 2000 system is a lot simpler than starting the typical OS/390 system. Normally this just involves turning on the power switch. In larger Windows 2000 installations, such as those found in a data center, there may be external units such as tap silos and/or raid towers. These units may have to be turned on in a pre-determined power-up sequence just as early predecessors of System/390 had to be started.

Startup

Chapter 2 discussed the Windows 2000 system startup process, so that information is not repeated here. Just as in OS/390, the startup of the various Windows 2000 subsystems is normally automated. Most of these subsystems run under control of the Windows 2000 Services Manager. The Services Manager is another MMC snap-in. Figure 12.3 shows the Services Manager.

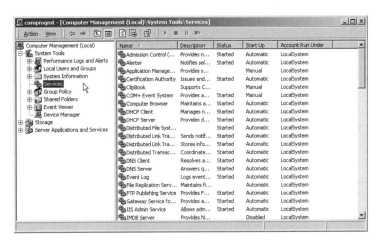

Figure 12.3   *The Services Manager.*

The display in Figure 12.3 is for the headquarter's domain controller. This figure shows only a partial list of all the services installed on it. (A complete list would take several pages to display.) Each of these services can be set to start manually by the operator, or automatically at boot time. Normally all the required services are set to start up automatically so that the operator has only to turn on the machine.

Shutdown

Shutting down a workstation is simple compared to shutting down a server on a network. Nevertheless, some of the same tasks required to shut down a mainframe may be required. Network user may be in the process of using resources on the server. Critical system functions, such as replication, may be in process on those servers. In addition, the server may be running Web Server software offering system content to browsers via your corporate intranet or the World Wide Web.

Prudence dictates a controlled quiesce and shutdown procedure, just as you would find in a mainframe shop. Perhaps the operator will be required to notify all connected users that the server is going out of service.

(Domain users can be notified with the Windows 2000 NET SEND command, which behaves similarly to the OS/390 SEND command. Internet and intranet users may be notified via a special redirect Web page that performs a similar function.) Users with file shares open on the server should be notified and allowed to wrap up their work. If you shut a server down with open files on the server, important data could be lost.

The actual act of shutting down a Windows 2000 system is fairly simple, just left-click on the *Start* button, and then select *Shutdown*. When you do, you will be given several shutdown options: Logoff Administrator, Shutdown, Restart, Standby, and Hibernate. (Standby and Hibernate are power-saving options used mainly on workstations.) The shutdown process takes care of quiescing all the services, flushing data buffers to disk, and stopping the system.

Steady-State Windows 2000 Operations

Just as in the case of OS/390, the operator is responsible for keeping the computer system running smoothly. Here too operator responsibilities can be divided into the same categories, as follows:

- System monitoring
- Printing and offloading data
- Load balancing
- Job scheduling
- Servicing requests
- Overall housekeeping

System Monitoring

Active system monitoring involves monitoring the general health of the operating system and the health of whichever Windows 2000 subsystem(s) and application(s) the operating system is running.

One tool that can be used for system monitoring is the Windows 2000 Performance Monitor. The Performance Monitor can be used to monitor and display a large number of operating system and subsystem performance counters. In addition, it can be set up to generate an alert message to an operator or an administrator when one of these counters goes above or below a given threshold (see Figure 12.4).

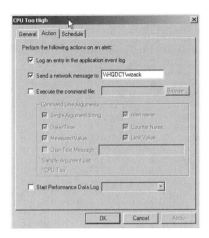

Figure 12.4 *Performance Monitor alerts.*

As the figure shows, I have requested that an alert be sent when the percent of CPU time exceeds 90%. (This is just for an example. In reality this is probably not a good idea, because CPU time in a loaded Windows 2000 system will often exceed 90% for short periods of time.)

Also in the figure, note that I have specified that the CPU threshold alert is to be posted to the Windows 2000 event log. The Event Viewer (which is used to examine event logs) is another extremely useful system monitoring tool. As you can see in Figure 12.5, the Event Viewer has snap-ins that can be used to display the event logs for application events (such as the Perfmon alert that I requested), Directory Services, DNS, File Replication Service, the security system, and another log for general system events.

In case you need more than the built-in reporting capabilities of Perfmon, you can purchase one of many add-on third-party tools such as AlertPage from Geneva Software, Inc. AlertPage can be set up to send email or dial a pager and send a message to an operator or an administrator when an important event occurs. (Products such as AlertPage often go beyond just monitoring the event log. Many of them can trigger an alert if a critical subsystem fails or when an application error message log file receives a key error message.)

Your company may also use a third-party management system such as the Windows 2000 version of Tivoli or CA-Unicenter. In this case, the operator may also have monitoring tools from that package at his disposal.

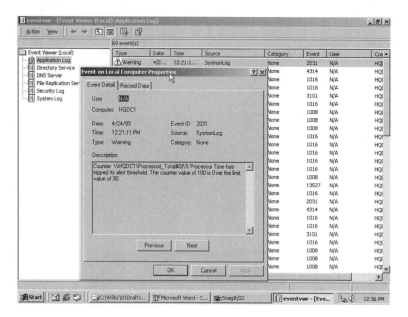

Figure 12.5   *The Event log.*

Printing

The preceding chapter discussed the rights and responsibilities of the printer operator, so these are not repeated here. Refer back to Chapter 11, "Printer Management," for details.

Load Balancing

The Windows 2000 operator does not have much to do in this category because the whole concept of jobs and the Job object is new to Windows 2000 (see Chapter 9, "Jobs and Task Management"). The whole infrastructure that would allow the operator to control the number of active jobs in the system does not exist in Windows 2000. The operator can use the Services Manager to stop noncritical services (such as disk indexing) during periods of system stress. (I expect more capabilities in this area in future releases as the Job object and batch-processing capabilities of Windows 2000 mature.)

Job Scheduling

As stated previously, the Job object is new to Windows 2000. Windows NT lacked any real form of JCL such as OS/390 JCL. With the advent of the Windows Scripting Host (see Chapter 9) and the Windows 2000 Task Manager, scheduling batch processing will most likely become a larger part of an operator's responsibilities. The Windows 2000 Task Manager can be used to perform middle-of-the-night disk defragmentation and to run other off-shift production jobs (see Figure 12.6).

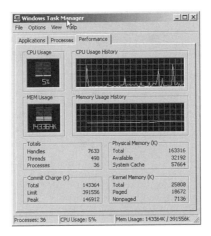

Figure 12.6 *The Task Manager.*

The Task Manager has not been converted to run as an MMC snap-in yet. You must start it from the Windows 2000 Control Panel inherited from prior versions of Windows; just left-click on the *Start* button, select *Settings*, and then select *Control Panel*. To open the Task Manager, select its icon in the Control Panel folder.

Servicing Requests

Some Windows 2000 subsystems, such as the Removable Storage Manager (discussed in Chapter 6, "Input/Output Device Management") can issue requests to the operator to mount tape cartridges and perform related actions. The operator can satisfy the request and then reply to the message to inform the system that the operation is complete.

Housekeeping

As in the case of OS/390, the operator may be responsible for initializing and labeling tape cartridges. Again, one of his most important functions is to run any required jobs that perform backups of key directories, files, and volumes. In some cases, this job may be automated by Windows 2000 backup software or third-party utilities.

Problem Determination and Recovery

The steps of problem determination and recovery performed by a Windows 2000 operator are similar in spirit to those performed by an OS/390 operator. A Windows 2000 operator, however, may have more hardware troubleshooting responsibility. (An IBM customer engineer usually handles most of the hard-core hardware troubleshooting in a System/390 installation.)

This chapter has covered only some of the tools available to OS/390 and Windows 2000 computer operators. Many others are discussed in other chapters in the book. The next chapter discusses the Windows 2000 security system, which has already been mentioned many times here and in previous chapters. This is the security system responsible for controlling access to all Windows 2000 components and services.

13
Security

Any industrial-grade operating system must protect itself and the resources that it manages from unauthorized access. This chapter examines the features of OS/390 and Windows 2000 to see just how secure these operating systems really are.

OS/390 Security

OS/390 has extremely tight security. In OS/390, the *System Authorization Facility* (SAF) acts as an intermediary every time a job is run or a user attempts to access OS/390 resources. The SAF, in turn, calls on an access control component to determine whether the requested access will be allowed. In OS/390, this is normally either the *Resource Access Control Facility* (RACF) provided by IBM, or the *Access Control Facility* (ACF) sold by Computer Associates, Inc. (see Figure 13.1).

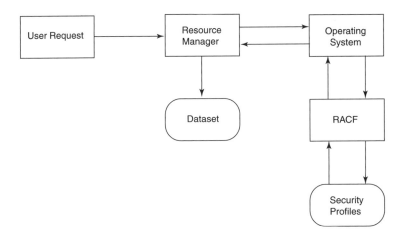

Figure 13.1 *RACF security.*

Because RACF is used in more installations, it is discussed here. Bear in mind, however, that both of these products perform essentially the same function. RACF is used to perform the following tasks:

- Identify and authenticate uses
- Grant users and jobs access to protected resources
- Permit only allowed access types
- Audit and report unauthorized access attempts

Using RACF, a security administrator creates profiles in a security database. These profiles describe users, groups of users, and resources, such as datasets, together with their access rights and permissions.

Identifying and Authenticating Users

Users are defined by a unique user ID comprised of one to eight characters. A password for the user is also specified in the user profile; however, the user is normally required to change it the first time that he logs on. (Additional RACF profiles can be used to define installation standards for minimum password length, password aging, and other overall security parameters.) In most installations, a user cannot reuse a password that he has recently used, nor can he change his password more frequently than after an installation-specified minimum time limit. Passwords are stored in the security database using one-way encryption. When a user enters a password, it is encrypted, and then it is compared with the password stored in the database. If they match, the user is allowed access.

Alternative Forms of Identification

It has become a popular expression in articles on security to say that authentication is based on "something you know (such as a user ID and password), something you have (such as a magnetically encoded pass card), or something you are (fingerprint recognition, retinal scan, and so on)." The expression is too cute not to use, and it does get the idea across.

OS/390 RACF supports the user ID/password combination. In addition, it supports the use of a pass ticket generated by another authorized subsystem. Pass tickets expire within 10 minutes, so they have to be used as soon as they are created. RACF also supports the use of a machine-readable operator identification card in place of, or in addition to, the user's password. ◆

Controlling Access to Resources

RACF, like Windows 2000 supports discretionary access control. The owner of a resource can control whether other users have the right to access a resource and how they may access it.

When a user logs on to a TSO terminal, or when a batch job begins to run, the SAF calls on RACF to determine whether the job or user has the required privilege level to log on or run. When a batch job or a user's TSO session subsequently asks to access a resource, such as a disk file, RACF will determine whether the caller has the right to access the resource. First, it performs a series of two security-level tests to determine whether the request should be rejected.

Security-Level Tests

First, RACF compares a security level specified in the user or group profile with one specified in the resource profile. If the security level of the resource is higher than the security level of the user or group, the request is denied.

Category Tests

Next, RACF compares a list of categories in the requester's profile with a list in the resource's profile. This list of categories normally contains installation-defined names, such as departments or business functions. If the category is not in the user's profile, the request is denied.

Following these two tests, RACF will allow access to the resource if any of the following conditions are met:

1. The resource is a dataset and its high-level qualifier is the user's RACF user ID. (TSO/SPF encourages the creation of datasets with your user ID as the high-level qualifier.)

2. The requestor's user ID is contained in the access list of the resource with sufficient authority to access the resource.

3. The requestor's current connect group is in the access list of the resource with sufficient authority to access the resource.

4. The requestor's *universal access authority code* (UACC) is sufficiently high. Access can be permitted or denied by assigning a specific access authority in a resource profile. It can also be allowed implicitly by specifying a UACC in the resource profile. This method permits any users or groups to access the resource.

Controlling Type of Access

When a caller passes these access tests, RACF is still not finished with him. There is the issue of determining the type of access that the caller can have to the resource. The owner of a resource has full access rights to a resource. The owner can grant specific access types to other users. The meaning of these access types varies by the type of resource (such as dataset, program, and terminal). The access types are as follows:

- *None*—Prevents the user or group from having any access at all to the resource

- *Read*—Allows the authorized user or group read-only access (in the case of a dataset)

- *Update*—Allows the authorized user or group to read and write data to the dataset

- *Alter*—Allows the authorized user or group to rename and/or delete the dataset

---

RACF and Other Resources

In addition to DASD, RACF also can be used to protect datasets on tape, and prevent unauthorized access to terminals, programs, and subsystems such as CICS, IMS, and DB/2. In fact, any installation-defined resource can have profiles defined for it and be protected in this way. Datasets in OS/390, like files in Windows 2000, have an owner who can be given complete access privileges for the dataset when it is created. Other users can be granted more limited access rights, if required. ◆

Security Administration

RACF includes a security administration component that uses TSO/SPF panels and TSO commands. Using these tools, a security administrator can create new user, group, and resource profiles; and modify existing ones. They can also create an administrative hierarchy and delegate a subset of their responsibilities to a subordinate administrator. For instance, the headquarters security administrator may set up a local security administrator at a branch office. The local security administrator then has full control over the creation of profiles at their level. (This hierarchical structure is used strictly for administrative delegation. It is not used for access determination.) They could also use this feature in a single installation to delegate a subset of the security administrator's responsibilities. For instance, a help-desk operator may be given the right to reset locked user accounts and change passwords that a user has forgotten.

RACF provides extensive security-auditing capabilities. Each resource profile contains a specification of the audit reporting that is to be done whenever anyone attempts to access the resource. This audit data is stored in the *Systems Management Facility* (SMF) log dataset. RACF includes a generalized report writer that the administrator can use to generate a wide variety of security reports.

Using RACF is a complex subject, and this discussion has just scrapped the surface. To learn more, you should refer to IBM publication CG28-1912, *Security Server (RACF) Introduction*. That publication also has an excellent bibliography and a list of other information resources on the Internet and elsewhere. (I recommend it highly.) Now, let's take a look at Windows 2000 security.

Windows 2000 Security

As discussed in Chapter 12, "Operator Control," the Windows 2000 domain is the primary security boundary in Windows 2000. It contains the Active Directory replica, which holds all properties for accounts in the domain and a subset of all the properties of accounts in other domains. It also holds the domain policies set by the domain administrator. The Active Directory is automatically synchronized across the domains. Conceptually, Windows 2000 has two types of domains: account domains and resource domains. Account domains are responsible for authenticating users when they log on. Resource domains normally contain resources, such as printers, directories, and files that the authenticated user wants to access. All Windows 2000 domains are connected with transitive trust relationships. This means that a user can be authenticated in any single domain in a domain tree or forest (see Chapter 12). A user can then access resources in any other domain (subject to the access permissions discussed later in this chapter).

We have already covered quite a lot about Windows 2000 security in previous chapters of this book. In fact, security pervades almost every aspect of Windows 2000. Everything that Windows 2000 deals with is managed by the creation of an operating system object, and all objects can and do have security protection associated with them. As discussed in this part of the chapter, Windows 2000 has extremely powerful distributed security capabilities.

All objects in Windows 2000 are created and managed by the Windows 2000 Object Manager. When a user of an application attempts to create and/or access an object, the Windows 2000 security subsystem is used to determine whether the user or application will be allowed to perform the desired operation.

Identifying and Authenticating Users

Users, groups, and computers must all be identified so that they can be authenticated to determine their scope of authority over resources that they will try to access. Users are identified externally by their user account name. Because user accounts can be renamed, Windows 2000 uses a unique encoded identifier for all security principals (users, groups, and computers). The *Security ID* (SID) is a 96-bit number guaranteed to be unique. Windows 2000 generates this number when it is installed and when a new account is created. After authentication, users, and the groups that they belong to, are identified by their Security ID and the Security IDs of any groups to which they belong.

User accounts have properties such as user IDs and passwords. These properties are used to authenticate the user. For the user, Windows 2000 security begins with the Windows 2000 logon process.

Logon Processing

The components that participate in the Windows 2000 logon process are the Win32 subsystem, the logon process, and the security subsystem, which includes the *Security Accounts Manager* (SAM) and the *Local Security Authority* (LSA) (see Figure 13.2).

You log on to Windows 2000 when you enter the trusted logon sequence (Ctrl+Alt+Del). When you start a Windows 2000 Server, or when you enter the trusted logon sequence at a computer, the WINLOGON program executes. WINLOGON next loads a *Graphical Identification and Authentication* program (GINA). This component of logon can be replaced by security vendors; in the standard Windows 2000 system, however, it is MSGINA, the version provided by Microsoft. Next, the GINA presents the Logon dialog box. After the user enters his user ID, password, and workgroup or domain name, the GINA passes this information on to the LSA via a local procedure call.

The LSA first encrypts the password and then calls an authentication package to perform authentication. Windows 2000 supports three authentication packages; Kerberos for domain logons; *Secure Sockets Layer* (SSL) for Internet logons; and *NT LAN Manager* (NTLM) for local computer logons, and logons from Windows NT and other down-level clients such as Windows 95/98 and Windows 3.x. For this discussion, it is assumed that the user is executing a domain logon from a Windows NT client. (Internet logons and SSL are discussed a little later in this chapter.) If the logon is a local logon to the current machine, or if the logon is a domain logon and the current machine is a domain controller, the logon is processed locally. If not, the logon must be shipped to a domain controller elsewhere in the network. For simplicity, it is assumed here that this is a domain logon. In this case, the local computer ships the logon request to the nearest domain controller using a pair of NETLOGON processes running on the two machines. (Remember, as discussed in the preceding chapter, that a workstation discovers a domain controller near it on the basis of its physical site.) In either case, the logon data is passed to the appropriate LSA on the target system.

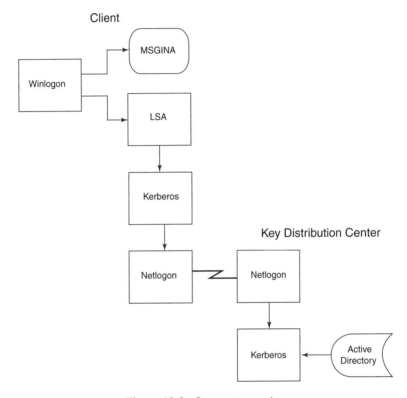

Figure 13.2 *Logon processing.*

Next, the LSA on the domain controller will authenticate the user using the appropriate authentication package. In this case, it will use Kerberos. Kerberos is an industry-standard security protocol originally developed at MIT. Windows 2000 domain controllers are also Kerberos *key distribution centers* (KDCs), as defined in the Kerberos standard. The Windows 2000 implementation of Kerberos uses the data in the Active Directory to perform the actual authentication.

After authenticating the user using the Kerberos authentication package, the LSA creates an access token for the user. An *access token* is a complete security description of the user. This access token contains a list of the Security IDs that represent the user, and any groups to which the user belongs. It returns this list as a token wrapped in a Kerberos ticket called a *ticket-granting ticket* (TGT) (see Figure 13.3).

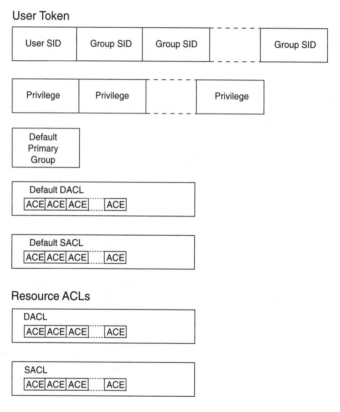

Figure 13.3 *Tokens and ACLs.*

The access token that is created contains the account name, account Security ID, group Security IDs, and a list of privileges (rights) that the user holds. It also contains a *discretionary access control list* (DACL). This DACL is used by default whenever the user creates a new object. (This token is one half of the security equation. Object permissions, which are the second half of the security equation, are discussed later in this chapter.) After the user is authenticated at the domain controller, the security token is wrapped in a TGT and passed back to the client. The client then caches the TGT locally, and can use the TGT to identify itself when making requests to use other services in the network. The ticket also contains an encryption key that can be used to encrypt application data so that the recipient can decrypt it.

When a client wants to access a network resource, it uses the user's TGT to get a *service ticket* (ST) from the KDC. The ST is then passed to the target service to prove that the user has been authenticated in the domain. Service tickets expire after a time interval specified by the domain security policy. (Typically, this is eight hours.) When they expire, the client and the KDC can renew them so that the connection can continue. To reduce traffic, the ST is cached at the workstation and can be reused if the resource is needed again.

The "Evils" of Cloning

The Security Identifier (SID) *is the fundamental identifier in Windows 2000. Windows 2000 will normally create a brand-new, unique Security ID for every domain, user, group, workstation, and server when it is created. All user accounts created on a computer that has a security database (such as workstations, member servers, and domain controllers) have this Security ID as their parent "authority" and increment a subauthority value starting at 100.*

There is one dangerous exception to this rule. To roll out large numbers of Windows 2000 systems rapidly, many companies have resorted to a process known as cloning. During cloning, a disk-image copy of a system is made and then copied to load many new systems. (Several utilities on the market do this. The most popular of these are Ghost from Ghosts Software and Image Drive from Powerquest). The problem with this technique is that every system created in this fashion has the same Security ID. Because new account Security IDs all increment from 100, this will almost surely create duplicate account Security IDs on multiple systems. This will create havoc with security that is based on the Security ID uniquely identifying a user account. This was a minor problem with Windows NT, but it is guaranteed to be a problem with Windows 2000.

If you have used this method to clone systems, you should use one of the available Security ID change programs, such as the free NewSID utility from Mark Russinovich and Bryce Cogswell. You can download this utility from their Web site at www.sysinternals.com. *(Free, of course, is a relative term. You will still have to visit all the affected systems to change their Security IDs. I would not want to have to do this to large numbers of workstations, for instance.) The cloning packages mentioned here have also recently added Security ID changer features to their products. Unfortunately, countless systems have already been created without duplicate SIDS. ◆*

This concludes the discussion of the Windows 2000 domain logon process. The following sections discuss NTLM (briefly) and the SLL authentication packages supported by Windows 2000. Following that, the focus is on how the result of this process is used to protect Windows 2000 resources.

NTLM Security

NT LAN Manager (NTLM) security was used in Windows NT as the primary authentication protocol. As previously discussed, Kerberos has largely replaced NTLM for authentication in Windows 2000. For down-level Windows NT and Windows 95/98 clients, Windows 2000 still supports NTLM. NTLM uses a fairly secure challenge-response protocol, which is not as secure as Kerberos. Because this is a book about Windows 2000, this protocol is not covered here in any detail.

Internet Logons and SSL

As previously discussed, Windows 2000 uses Kerberos to authenticate Windows 2000 clients connecting to a domain. Because these clients have Kerberos client software on them, this works fine. If a user is attempting to connect to a Windows 2000 Server using a Web browser across the Internet, however, this situation may not apply. The client cannot usually participate in Kerberos security, or even NTLM security. To support Internet access, Windows 2000 also supports the industry-standard SSL security protocol.

You will recall from earlier in this chapter that Windows 2000 supports three authentication packages: Kerberos, SSL, and NTLM. Also, as discussed earlier, the LSA passes the logon request to the appropriate authentication package. SSL is the security package that Windows 2000 normally uses to support the authentication of Internet clients.

SSL works on the basis of a tamper-proof, encrypted document called a certificate, issued by a trusted certificate authority. A certificate includes the user's name and a private encryption key (see the sidebar "Public and Private Key Encryption"). The certificate is proof that the server is who it says it is. (The SSL standard also defines the use of client certificates in addition to server certificates. A client certificate proves the identity of the client to the server. This feature is not used as much as server certificates are. This is due to the cost and/or inconvenience of acquiring and installing a certificate on a browser when a user may visit a site only occasionally.) Some certificate authority that both parties trust normally issues certificates. Traditionally, this has been a public certificate authority, such as Verisigin. Starting with Windows NT 4.0, however, Microsoft has included a Certificate Server. This software allows a company to issue its own certificates and to be its own certificate authority. This is sometimes done

in applications where the company has some degree of control over the t
ype and setup of the client's Web browsers (for instance, in an internal
corporate intranet, or even an external extranet that the company shares
with its business partners.) In general, however, client certificates are still
not used very much.

When a certificate is issued to a company, it is normally installed as a
data file on their Web server. When a browser that can support SSL wants
to engage in a secure conversation with the server, it connects to the Web
server with a URL that begins with `//https` rather than `//http`. This "tells"
the Web server that the browser would like a secure channel connection.
(Hence, the name of the SSL authentication library: `schannel.dll`). Figure 13.4
shows the SSL handshake.

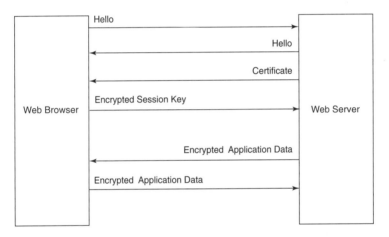

Figure 13.4   *SSL handshake protocol.*

The initial `//https` request is sent to the Web server in clear text
(unencrypted). When the server receives this request, it engages in an
SSL handshake exchange with the client browser. As in Kerberos authentication, the objective of the process is to encrypt data passing in both directions with a set of keys chosen so that the sender can encrypt the data and
only the receiver can decrypt it. In this case, however, no common key
repository is required. The first thing transmitted is the server's certificate,
so that the browser can be sure that the server is authentic and not an
impostor. (The Internet, after all, is not regulated by any central authority
and can be a scary place.) Following the SSL handshake, all application
data passing in both directions is encrypted.

Public and Private Key Encryption

I do not want to bore you here with the intimate details of public and private key encryption systems. A brief introduction, however, is appropriate. Windows 2000 uses two kinds of encryption: private key encryption is used by Kerberos, and public key encryption is used by SSL.

Kerberos was originally developed at MIT. It is considered to be a public key system, because it relies primarily on the use of a key distribution center that stores shared private keys. In private key encryption systems, both parties rely on their knowledge of the other party's private key. (This is often called a shared-secret system.) This knowledge is normally held in some secure repository such as the Kerberos KDC that was discussed earlier (actually, it is on a domain controller in the Active Directory).

The KDC holds private encryption keys that belong to all domain participants. (For those of you who may have come across Kerberos security on other platforms, the domain is synonymous with a Kerberos realm.) Thanks to the Active Directory, both the user and the KDC know the user's password. When a client requests authentication, Kerberos uses these keys to engage in a secure conversation with the client.

SSL was originally developed by Netscape. It is a private key encryption system. It uses two keys that are mathematically related, so that a public key can be used to encrypt data that only the corresponding private key can decrypt. A user's public key can be kept unsecured and even published in a public place for all the world to see. The user's private key, however, must be kept secret and known only to the user. Over a secure channel, each side of the SSL conversation will use the other party's public key to encrypt the data it sends. The receiving party will then use its private key to decrypt the data. To ensure that public keys are authentic, SSL uses the certificates mentioned earlier.

This has been just a brief overview of this subject. Variations of the protocol are in use in practical implementations. In fact, even the private key Kerberos system used by Windows 2000 actually includes the use of a public key as part of the initial handshake with the client. For more information on Windows 2000 security, you can read the Microsoft white paper "Secure Networking Using Windows 2000 Distributed Security Services" at www.microsoft.com/Windows/server/Technical/security/DistSecServices.asp. *The most comprehensive modern book on cryptography is* Applied Cryptography *by Bruce Schnier, ISBN 0-4711-1709-9, John Wiley & Sons. Although parts of this book are quite esoteric, the introductory chapters are excellent background reading on the subject.* ◆

Controlling Access to Resources

The preceding discussion of logon identification and authentication is only half of the security equation. The other half concerns itself with rights and permissions. Rights provide control of over actions that a user can have over the entire computer system. Permissions, on the other hand, are controls that apply to a specific object.

Rights

Rights normally allow an action on a system-wide basis (such as the right to shut down the computer). Permissions, on the other hand, normally pertain to a specific object, such as a file owned by a specific user. In some cases, there is some overlap, such as when a user or group is given the right *to back up and restore files and directories*. In these cases, the right effectively overrides the permissions. For instance, a backup operator with the preceding right can back up and restore files and directories, despite the fact that the backup operator does not have the permission to access the individual files and directories.

Rights are best administered at the group level for ease of administration. Because users inherit the rights of all the groups to which they belong, all the users who would be granted the right to back up the system should be placed in the built-in group called backup operators. This group has that right by default.

To further break down rights, Windows 2000 defines two categories of rights:

- Privileges
- Logon rights

Privileges

The privileges that Windows 2000 supports include the right to do the following:

- Act as part of the OS
- Add a workstation to a domain
- Back up files and directories
- Bypass traverse checking
- Change system time
- Create a token object
- Create a permanent shared object
- Create a paging file
- Debug programs

- Enable Trusted for Delegation on user and computer accounts
- Force shutdown from a remote system
- Generate security audits
- Increase quotas
- Increase scheduling priority
- Load and unload device drivers
- Lock pages in memory
- Manage auditing and security log
- Modify firmware environment values
- Profile a single process
- Profile system performance
- Replace a process-level token
- Restore files and directories
- Shut down the system
- Take ownership of files or other objects
- Unlock a laptop

No attempt is made to explain all these rights here. (Windows 2000 Help has a detailed explanation for all these privileges. You can access it from the Windows 2000 Start button.) As you can see, some of these are fairly obvious (such as the right to *shut down the system*); others are pretty esoteric (such as the right to *modify firmware environment values*). In general, you will not assign these rights at all. You will just use the built-in groups. These built-in groups normally will have the appropriate rights from the preceding list.

Logon Rights

Logon rights, as the name implies, relate to how a user can log on to the computer. These rights include the right to do the following:

- Access this computer from the network
- Log on locally (interactively)
- Log on as a batch job
- Log on as a service
- Deny access to this computer from the network
- Deny logon as a batch job
- Deny logon as a service
- Deny local logon

As in the case of the privileges, you will seldom have to specify any of these rights yourself. The built-in groups should handle this quite nicely for you. In a domain, for instance, the *Domain Users* group has the right to *access this computer from the network*. To allow the various Windows 2000 subsystems and services to access resources freely, the special user account *LocalSystem* has almost all these privileges and logon rights assigned to it. All processes that run as part of the OS are associated with this account and have these rights.

Built-in Groups

To provide you with commonly used bundles of rights, Windows 2000 provides two types of built-in groups:

- Domain local groups
- Global groups

Domain Local Groups

The domain local groups are used to define the rights of specific types of users when logging on at the computer (an interactive logon). They include

- Account operator
- Administrator
- Backup operator
- Guest
- Print operator
- Replicator
- Server operator
- User

Administrators have most of the possible rights on the local computer. Account operators have a subset of these rights. Server, print, and backup operators have a set of rights that allow them to do their jobs, and users and guests have the fewest rights of all. A complete treatment of the rights owned by these groups is included in the Windows 2000 online Help.

Global Groups

Global groups are groups defined to enable you to grant users authority at the domain level. They include

- Domain administrator
- Domain user
- Domain guest

Domain administrators have the same rights as local administrators, but over the entire domain. Domain users (and domain guests, if allowed) have the right to log on anywhere in the domain.

Special Identities

In addition to the previously discussed groups, Windows 2000 also defines several special identities. (Windows 2000 does not call them groups; but, because they can contain multiple users, they act like groups.) These identities are not in the list of built-in groups, and do not exist for you to add users to. Only Windows 2000 can add users to these groups. You can, however, use them in assigning permissions to resources. They include

- Everyone
- Network
- Interactive

Everyone means exactly that. It is the group of users that is now, or could ever be, logged on to the system. This includes domain users and guests, as well as users from other domains. When access to a resource is granted to everyone, it is not really protected at all. (One of the first steps in securing a system is often to remove *everyone* from the list of permissions specified for an object.)

Network is used to represent all current and future users who connect over the network (as opposed to users who log on locally at the computer holding the resource).

Interactive represents all current and future users who access a given resource by logging on locally at the computer where the resource is located (as opposed to users who access the resource over the network).

Permissions

So far this discussion has focuses on the rights that protect the system as a whole. *Permissions*, on the other hand, protect individual resources such as directories and files.

As you will see later in this section, all objects, such as directories and files, have an owner. The owner of an object can permit other users to access an object. The owner of the object can also limit the type of access that another user has. Windows 2000 also allows the granting of special privileges, called rights, to a user or group.

To protect individual objects, Windows 2000, like RACF, uses discretionary access control. All control over the operations that a user can perform on an object is at the discretion of its owner. All access is controlled by the presence (or absence) of security descriptors associated with an object. Two access control lists are used for this purpose: a *discretionary access control list* (DACL), which is used to control access to the resource; and a *security access control list* (SACL), which is used to control the auditing of attempts to use the object (see Figure 13.3). This section discusses DACLs. The section titled "Security Auditing," later in this chapter, discusses SACLs.

Discretionary Access Control
As in the case of OS/390, the owner of an object can permit or deny another user or group access to an object that he owns. The owner can also specify exactly what type of access is allowed. Security over an object is implemented by attaching ACLs to an object. Note that in Windows NT an ACL governed access to a complete object. In Windows 2000, however, an ACL is per property. That means that different permissions can be specified for different parts of the same object. Assuming, for instance, that the Active Directory schema includes the user's home phone number as a property, the user could be granted the permission to change that property of his account without letting the user change any other properties (see Chapter 10, "Catalogs and Directories"). This is a powerful feature.

Access Control Lists
When an attempt is made to access an object, Windows 2000 will determine whether the object's security descriptor contains an ACL. Each ACL can have zero or more *access control elements* (ACEs) associated with it (refer to Figure 13.3).

The processing that Windows 2000 goes through to determine whether a user has the right to access the resource in the requested manner is as follows:

1. The owner of the resource has all rights by default. If the owner is asking, access is allowed.

2. If the object has no ACL associated with it, all types of access are allowed by everyone. If, on the other hand, the ACL exists, but has no ACEs in it, all access is denied to everyone.

3. If ACEs do exist, Windows 2000 will scan the list for one with a Security ID that matches the user's Security ID, or one of the user's group Security IDs. If one is found, and it specifies *deny*, the request will be denied.

4. If, on the other hand, the matching ACE specifies *allow*, further testing is performed to determine whether the specific type of access requested is allowed. (Access types vary by type of object. For instance, a file object has the access types open, close, read from, and write to.) If the type of access requested is *allow*, the request is allowed; otherwise, it is denied.

Inheritance

When an object is created, the ACL in the user's token is used to provide a default ACL for the object. In the case of objects with a hierarchical structure (such as a file system object), ACLs can be assigned in such a way that they are inherited by lower-level objects in the hierarchy. For instance, the permissions can be set on an existing directory and then propagated downward to lower-level directories and files.

Impersonation

To allow servers to access resources on behalf of a user, the server adopts the Security ID of the user while accessing the resource. When a client makes a request to a server, that server can act as the client and make a request to another server on the client's behalf. This is called *impersonation*. Windows NT supported single-level impersonation only. In Windows 2000, this impersonation can extend to multiple levels.

Security Administration

There is a lot to Windows 2000 security, and in fact, a whole book could be devoted to this subject. This chapter has only scratched the surface of this subject. Administering security settings related to individual user and group accounts in Windows 2000 is normally done by using the Active Directory Users and Computers snap-in. Windows 2000 also has other security-related tools that bear on different aspects of security.

An ACL Editor enables you to display and change the settings specified in objects' ACLs. With the available Policy Editor, you can lock down various aspects of Windows 2000. For instance, you can remove entries from a user's Start menu or otherwise restrict the changes that a user can make to his system. Windows 2000 also has a whole set of tools, collectively called the "Security Configuration Toolset." This toolset is a set of MMC snap-ins that allow a company to apply mass security changes based on a set of definition files.

For information on the Group Policy Editor, refer to the Windows 2000 "Walkthrough" document at www.microsoft.com/Windows/Server/Deploy/Manangement/GroupPolicyWT.asp.

At the time of this writing, Microsoft is reorganizing its Web site, and so a specific Web address is not available for more information on the Security Configuration Toolset. You can, however, search Microsoft's site for references to it. In any event, the Windows 2000 online Help has some information on this.

User administration is most often performed with the *Active Directory Users and Computers* administrative tool snap-in. A predefined MMC console contains this snap-in, and you can bring it up by left-clicking on the Start button, selecting Administrative Tools, and then selecting *Active Directory Users and Computers* (see Figure 13.5).

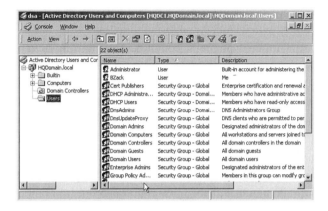

Figure 13.5   *Active Directory Users and Computers.*

Security Auditing

Auditing the use of critical resources is important in Windows 2000, just as it was in OS/390. To specify auditing requirements at the individual object level, all objects can have an SACL that is analogous to the DACL used to protect the resource. The SACL, however, can contain ACEs that specify that the operating system is to generate an audit event every time that an attempt is made to access a particular resource in a particular way. This event information is written into the Windows 2000 security log, which can be examined using the Event Viewer applet that you can access from Administrative Tools or from the Computer-management console using the Event Viewer snap-in.

Integrating with Mainframe Security

As discussed in Chapter 14 "Networking,"and Chapter 16 "Communicating with OS/390," Microsoft's SNA Server component is used to interface Windows 2000 computers with systems using IBM's *Systems Network Architecture* (SNA) protocols. SNA is the primary communications protocol used by OS/390. (IBM's AS/400 minicomputer also uses SNA.)

To support mixed Windows 2000 and OS/390 installations, SNA Server comes bundled with software that provides a basic single sign-on feature to allow a single user ID and password to be used to control access to Windows NT and RACF. Several third-party add-ons, such as Proginet's

SecurPass, can also be used to extend this capability to a fully integrated multiplatform security solution. SecurPass synchronizes Windows NT, RACF, and UNIX security; and provides single sign-on and synchronized administration on all connected platforms. At the high end, full network-management packages such as Tivoli and CA-Unicenter also include this type of support.

This chapter briefly introduced the Kerberos support in Windows 2000. If you want to learn more, you can read the Microsoft white paper "Secure Networking Using Windows 2000 Distributed Security Services." You can find this white paper at `www.microsoft.com/Windows/server/Technical/security/DistSecservices.asp`. For information on NLTM and Windows NT security, you can read a pair of articles written by Mark Russinovich for *Windows NT* magazine in May and June 1998. You can find these articles in the *Windows NT* magazine archives at `www.winntmag.com/Magazine/Article.cfm? ArticleID=3143` and `www.winntmag.com/Magazine/Article.cfm? ArticleID=3492`. (And, while you are at it, you may as well subscribe to their magazine. It is the best general source of information on Windows NT and Windows 2000 that you are likely to find outside of the Microsoft Web site.)

Having covered the OS/390 and Windows 2000 security that is used to authenticate users connecting via a network, the discussion can now focus on how these users actually get connected via OS/390 and Windows 2000 networking. This is the subject of the next chapter.

14
Networking

This chapter covers OS/390 and Windows 2000 networking. OS/390 networking is dominated primarily by IBM's *Systems Network Architecture* (SNA). The networking support in Windows 2000 is focused on the *Transmission Control Protocol/Internet Protocol* (TCP/IP), although Windows 2000 does support other networking protocols.

First, this chapter examines SNA from the perspective of IBM host computer–controlled networks. Then, the discussion focuses on the native networking support in Windows 2000. Chapter 16 covers the marriage of the two when the discussion turns to Microsoft SNA Server and how to couple SNA and TCP/IP networks together.

OS/390 Networking

Until the late 1960s, mainframe operations were typified by batch process-ing. In the mid-1960s, IBM did produce some terminal devices such as the IBM 2260 *cathode-ray terminal* (CRT). This was followed in the early 1970s by the IBM 3270 family of terminals, printers, and terminal-cluster control units. In addition, IBM also developed channel-attached communications controllers to support locally and remotely attached devices and at the same time to offload the communications-processing overhead from the mainframe.

In parallel with this development, operating system software was devel-oped with esoteric names such as *Graphical Access Method* (GAM), *Basic Telecommunications Access Method* (BTAM), and the *Telecommunications Access Method* (TCAM). Most recently, IBM has defined SNA, which includes the *Virtual Telecommunications Access Method* (VTAM). Also in the mid-1960s, transaction-processing software such as IBM's *Customer Information Control System* (CICS) was develop to allow the mainframe operating system to support transaction processing and communications (see Chapter 15, "Transaction, Database, and Message Processing" and Chapter 16, "Communicating with OS/390").

This section covers the current state-of-the-art technologies in mainframe networking, and includes a discussion of some of the hardware, networking architectures, and software that make it all possible.

Hardware

System 390 networking hardware utilizes the CPU and channel architecture discussed in Chapter 2, "Operating System Architecture." As you will recall in this architecture, I/O processing is offloaded to intelligent processors called channels. These channels, in turn, connect to device control units to which the actual I/O devices are attached.

The OS/390 communications architecture essentially follows this structure. When dealing with local devices, such as tape drives, disk drives, and printers, the devices are pretty reliable and their control unit hardware does not have to be very sophisticated. If an application program issues a command to read a record from a disk dataset, for example, the application can be pretty sure that the data will be received from the device and presented back to the application program with no errors (most of the time). This is because the whole structure of channels, control units, and devices is tightly coupled together with either huge bus-and-tag cables or fiber-optic ESCON channels.

The situation with respect to network connections and communications devices, however, is quite different. With remote (and sometimes even local) terminals, transmission errors are much more frequent. In addition, terminals often transmit their data serially, one character or a partial block of data at a time. Communications hardware must wait for this data, assemble it into meaningful chunks, and present it to the application that requires it. (We take this process for granted when dealing with local non-communications devices because it is fast and usually error-free.) This requires more sophisticated hardware and software. Figure 14.1 shows the networking hardware architecture. This hardware consists of the following:

- Terminals
- Terminal-cluster controllers
- Networks
- Communications controllers
- Host computers

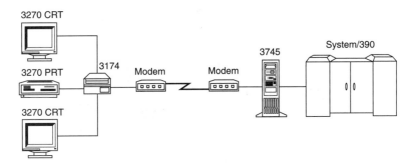

Figure 14.1 *Networking hardware.*

Terminals

Although IBM did produce crude terminals in the mid-1960s, it was the introduction of the IBM 3270 family of terminals in the early 1970s that introduced most of us to anything other than batch processing with punched cards. Even though most mainframe shops have replaced real 3270 terminals with PCs running 3270 emulator programs, mainframe software still operates as if it were dealing with 3270 terminals. In fact, this support has not changed much since the early 1970s. Current terminal support still uses the 3270 data-stream architecture described later in this chapter.

IBM 3270

The original 3270 family of terminals consisted of cluster controllers, CRTs, and printers. The 3270 CRT is a character-mode terminal capable of displaying text on a black background. Although the original 3270 CRTs were green on black, later models did support a limited number of colors for emphasis. Figure 14.2. shows a 3270 screen as presented by a popular terminal emulator package, Attachmate EXTRA!. (I tried to find a real 3270 to take a digital picture of it for you, but I couldn't find one anywhere! They are pretty rare.)

Figure 14.2 *3270 terminal.*

These terminals are block-mode terminals that send one block of data at
a time, unlike some terminals that send each character as it is entered.
The typical 3270 family terminal uses a 1920-byte buffer (24 lines of 80
characters). This buffer is sent to the terminal in a single block of data and
displayed onscreen. The data is in a structured format (see Figure 14.3).

Figure 14.3 *3270 data stream.*

Data is stored and manipulated in *Extended Binary Coded Decimal
Interchange Code* (EBCDIC) format to match the format used in the mainframe. The data buffer is broken up into some leading control information
and a series of definable fields prefixed by attribute characters that define
the fields. For instance, bits in an attribute byte can be set to specify that
a field is protected (display-only) so that it cannot be modified by the
operator. Other bits can be set to indicate that a field is to be displayed in
high intensity. (High intensity and protected are often used for field labels
that are placed in front of input fields.) The operator makes his changes and
then presses one of the attention keys on the keyboard, such as the Enter
key. Only at that time is the data transmitted from the terminal. Real 3270
terminals are attached to a parent cluster controller by coaxial cables. In
most shops, real 3270s are a thing of the past. Their place has been taken
by personal computers running terminal emulation software. This software
usually also emulates the cluster controller functionality as well.

Cluster Controller

IBM 3270 terminals are normally attached to a *cluster control unit* (CCU) such as an IBM 3174 Establishment Controller. This unit can control up to 253 terminal devices. The CCU provides network-management functionality and handles the physical unit connection services for the devices (as discussed shortly). These CCUs can be located at the host computer, where they are attached directly to a channel; or they can be remotely located and connected to a communications controller by modems, and dial or leased telephone lines. (The next section discusses communications controllers.)

Other Terminal Types

Although the 3270 terminal family accounts for the bulk of the terminal population, OS/390 does support other types of terminal devices. Once upon a time, IBM sold remote job-entry workstations. These workstations were little more than a card reader and a line printer in a box, together with a control unit and communications circuitry. The purpose of these workstations was just to remote the card reader and line printer used by JES for submitting jobs and receiving back output.

The most popular of these workstations were the IBM 3770 and 3780 workstation. Although it is not used much any more, their batch-oriented protocol has survived as the protocol that JES uses to transmit jobs submitted on one JES system for execution on another. VTAM still provides support for this protocol. ◆

Networks

CCUs, such as the IBM 3174, can be directly attached to a mainframe channel. The CCU can be attached to the same LAN as the terminals that the CCU supports. It can even be located remotely and attached via dial or leased telephone circuits. Channel attachment of a device is very reliable because the device is located quite near the computer itself. Attaching a device via a LAN is fairly reliable, but errors do occur, most frequently due to the distances involved and the electrical nature of the network.

A WAN connection is the least-reliable method of all because no one can guarantee the quality of the public network facilities used to make the connection. Software must exist that guarantees end-to-end, reliable, error-free communications between endpoints.

Communications Controllers

To offload communications processing from the mainframe, a *front-end processor* (FEP), such as the IBM 3745, is normally used. This is a relatively expensive specialized computer (about $300,000). It even runs its own operating system, the *Network Control Program* (NCP). The FEP can control multiple local and remote cluster controllers.

FEPs include special hardware and adapters for controlling communication lines. They are responsible for assembling received bits into bytes, and bytes into blocks. They are also responsible for interrupting the mainframe when there is data to transfer to and from it. FEPs are normally channel attached; however, they can also act as remote concentrators in a distributed network. FEPs are also responsible for data-link activation, remote-device polling, and error detection and correction. In addition, the FEP performs network-routing and flow-control functions.

Host Computers

As discussed earlier, FEPs and local cluster controllers can be locally attached to a host computer channel. These devices attach to the channel by one of two methods:

- Bus-and-tag cables
- ESCON fiber-optic cables

Bus-and-tag cables (also called parallel cables) hearken all the way back to the dawn of System/360. They are approximately 1-inch-thick cables with huge connectors that are usually at home only under the raised flooring of the data center. These cables are limited to connecting devices located only several hundred feet apart. Data transmitted over these cables is also limited to 3 to 4.5MBps. The newer ESCON fiber-optic cables, in contrast, can support data transfer to devices located up to several kilometers apart at a rate of up to 18MBps.

Now that you are familiar with the hardware, this discussion can focus on the networking architecture that provides the framework for implementing software to make this hardware useful. Following this architecture discussion, the focus turns to VTAM and NCP, the specific software implementation used in most OS/390 shops.

Systems Network Architecture

IBM's SNA is a proprietary layered architecture for implementing networking products, originally developed in the early 1970s. The original version of SNA was strictly hierarchical and host-computer controlled. As discussed later, hierarchical SNA is based on the concept of a subarea. (A subarea requires a mainframe to provide central control of a hierarchical SNA network.) To accommodate the AS/400, IBM later added a form of peer-to-peer networking support to SNA called *Advanced Peer-to-Peer Networking* (APPN). Recent versions of SNA products have tended to blur the distinction between these two flavors of SNA. In general, however, mainframe shops that do not include AS/400s primarily use the hierarchical flavor of SNA, so that is the one concentrated on here.

Most recently, IBM has attempted to integrate TCP/IP into this architecture, although few IBM mainframe shops support TCP/IP all the way through to the mainframe. The IBM 3174 cluster controller (Enterprise Controller) can operate as an APPN node and also carry TCP/IP traffic. IBM has even come up with a new "networking blueprint" to encompass all the popular network protocols and a set of products under the "ANYNET" label to support these protocols. Nevertheless, most IBM shops still use only the classical hierarchical flavor of SNA unless they also have AS/400s installed. This chapter concentrates on hierarchical SNA and pretty much ignores APPN.

SNA Layers and Protocols

SNA is a layered protocol. A layered protocol makes it possible to implement network software in a layered protocol stack where the operating system (or device) communicates with the upper layer, and each lower layer has a defined function. Conceptually, peer protocols connect each layer, even though the data actually travels down the sending stack layers and up the receiving stack layers.

In every communications book that you will read, you will most likely see a diagram of the *Open Systems Interconnect* (OSI) protocol layers. This is a neat division of communications functions into seven layers. Unfortunately, both SNA and TCP/IP do not map into these layers very well, because SNA and TCP/IP both came out well before this model was developed and accepted (see Figure 14.4).

A Bit of Trivia

Once upon a time, I managed a mainframe data center. As a result of converting older mainframe equipment to some newer equipment, I inherited a surplus bus-and-tag connector, which I used for several years as a paperweight. This connector weighed in at about 3 pounds and was about 6 inches long! The cable that it was originally connected to was more than an inch thick. ◆

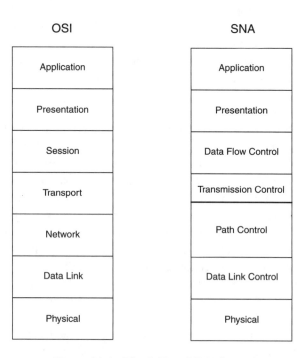

Figure 14.4 *The OSI and SNA layers.*

Working from the bottom of the protocol stack, the functional layers that IBM defines for SNA are as follows:

1. *Physical layer*—This layer includes physical hardware, such as interface cards that fit in the boxes and the physical wires (media) that connect them together. This includes considerations such as electrical-signal strength, size and shape of wires and connectors, and the number of wires in a cable. It also covers how bits are transmitted synchronously or asynchronously, and assembled into bytes.

2. *Data link control (DLC) layer*—This layer concerns itself with formatting data, flow control, and establishing and terminating network links. The DLC layer defines the *Synchronous Data Link Control* (SDLC) protocol, as well as the protocols used to communicate over Token Ring and Ethernet LANs.

3. *Path control layer*—This layer is responsible for routing data through the network, regulating network traffic, and segmenting and reassembling segmented transmission data.

4. *Transmission control layer*—This layer is responsible for ensuring reliable end-to-end communications. It also handles encryption, transmission pacing, sequence numbering, and security.

5. *Data flow control layer*—This layer is responsible for taking care of synchronizing the exchange of data between endpoints. It structures transmission data into units and is responsible for managing the direction and sequence of data flow.

6. *Presentation layer*—This layer is responsible for invoking application programs, and enforcing protocols between application programs and the lower layers. An application program communicates with these lower layers via an *Application Programming Interface* (API) normally provided by the presentation layer. Other presentation-layer services are responsible for transforming data from one form to another.

7. *Application layer*—This layer supports application services such as File Transfer, Distributed Database, and Document Interchange. Programs in the application layer interact with the presentation layer by issuing the API calls previously mentioned. For instance, an *Advanced Program-to-Program* (APPC) program can converse with another APPC program by invoking the APPC ALLOCATE API call.

Architectural Components and Where They Fit

SNA defines the following architectural components:

- Domains
- Subareas
- Nodes
- Links
- Network Addressable Units
- Sessions

Domains

In hierarchical SNA, a *domain* is the segment of the network managed by a single host computer. Multiple host computers require the definition of multiple SNA domains. If two FEPs and their associated peripheral nodes are connected to one host computer running VTAM, for instance, the host and the two FEPs form a single domain (see Figure 14.5).

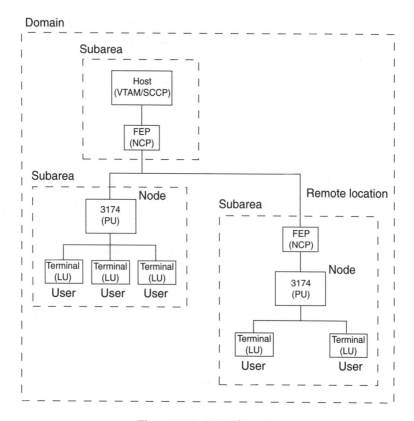

Figure 14.5   *SNA domains.*

Subareas

A *subarea* is defined as a portion of an SNA network that contains a subarea node, together with its attached peripheral nodes and associated resources. A host computer by itself is an example of a subarea node. A FEP, together with all its peripheral nodes, is also a subarea.

Nodes

In SNA, *nodes* are the physical devices that are at the endpoints of SNA links. SNA defines quite a few node types. This chapter ignores the APPN node types and concentrates on the hierarchical node types supported by classical mainframe-oriented SNA. The most interesting node types are as follows:

- *Type 5*—This node is a host (mainframe) node. It is represented by VTAM running under OS/390 on an IBM host computer.
- *Type 4*—These nodes are FEPs. They are implemented by a single copy of the *Network Control Program* (NCP) running in a FEP.
- *Type 2*—These nodes are peripheral nodes, and could be intelligent cluster controllers such as an IBM 3174 Enterprise Controller.

Links
The data link layer of SNA supports links. *Links* are the physical connections that make up your network. SNA supports a wide variety of local and remote data links. For WANs, such as those using telecom lines, it supports *Synchronous Data Link Control* (SDLC). For local connections, the two most common link types are IBM Token Ring, and channel attachment via ESCON or parallel channel attachments. (Ethernet is more popular in general than Token Ring; however, in most mainframe shops, Token Ring LANs are more prevalent.) SNA also supports other WAN link layer protocols, such as X.25.

Network-Addressable Units
The whole point of a communications architecture is for devices and programs to be able to address and talk to each other. To support this, SNA architects the following four kinds of *network-addressable units* (NAUs):

- System services control points
- Control points
- Physical units
- Logical units

Systems Services Control Points
In hierarchical SNA, the control point for a network runs in the host computer and is implemented by software that provides *system services control point* (SSCP) functionality. When a remote entity wants to connect up with another endpoint (for instance, TSO running on the mainframe), the SSCP receives the connection request and assists in making the final connection. (This processing is discussed in more detail when logical units are discussed later in this chapter.) A secondary purpose of the SSCP is to monitor and control network links and node resources.

Control Points

Intelligent communications devices need some of the services provided by an SSCP; however, due to their less-sophisticated nature, they do not need full SSCP functionality. In addition, peers in an APPN network do not have a host SSCP to assist in the connection process. In these cases, a scaled-down subset of the SSCP functionality exists in a *control point* (CP) located in the device. The 3174 Enterprise Controller is a device that can operate in either a hierarchical or a peer network. It can do this because it has a CP as part of its implementation.

Physical Units

Physical units (PUs) are hardware and/or software that are responsible for performing control functions for a device. They are responsible for activating and deactivating the device when instructed to do so by the SSCP. They are also responsible for error detection, correction, testing, and the collection of status information and operating statistics.

Although quite a few PU types have existed over the life of SNA, there are currently four major types of interest in hierarchical SNA:

- *PU Type 5 (host computers)*—These represent host nodes, and can support several different type of LUs.

- *PU Type 4 (FEPs)*—These are communications controller nodes that are responsible for flow control and routing.

- *PU Type 2.0 terminal*—This is a PU that can support simple terminal devices such as the original IBM 3270 family of terminals. It has largely been superceded by the Type 2.1 PU.

- *PU Type 2.1 terminals*—This can support more sophisticated terminals than a Type 2.0 PU can. It was originally developed for use in APPN networks, where devices do not need the services of an SSCP to connect LUs with other LUs. It is also used in most terminal emulation software that exists today. In addition, it is used by Microsoft's SNA server gateway products (discussed in Chapter 16, "Communicating with OS/390").

Logical Units

Logical units (LUs) represent the actual endpoints of an SNA network. These could be terminals or application programs.

There are two types of LUs: dependent LUs and independent LUs. Dependent LUs require the assistance of an SSCP to connect with another LU. It is this type of LU that is found in hierarchical SNA. In the case of this LU type, an application program ruining on the mainframe acts as the primary (master) LU and the terminal LU acts as the secondary (slave) LU.

Independent LUs (such as the ones found in APPN), do not need an SCCP to connect with another LU. This type of LU is found most often in APPN networks such as the ones typified by AS/400s.

The basic LU types are LU 0, 1, 2, 2.1, 3, 4, 6, 6.2, and 7.

- *LU Type 0* is a generic LU that exists so that vendors can build devices that do not follow any of the remaining predefined LU protocols. With LU 0, vendors can define a proprietary protocol that their own devices can use to communicate with each other.

- *LU Type 1* is used for routing host print-format data over a network, normally to a remote host or RJE workstation with a high-speed printer.

- *LU Types 2 and 2.1* define the capabilities of 3270 family terminals. LU 2 was used for the original 3270 terminals. LU 2.1 is used currently for interactive 3270 data-stream devices. It is also used for SNA gateways such as Microsoft's SNA Server, as discussed in Chapter 16.

- *LU Type 3* was originally used for printing to 3270 family printers.

- *LU Type 4* was used primarily for routing data between APPN hosts. It was an early predecessor of LU 6.2. It is not used much any more.

- *LU Types 6, 6.1, and 6.2* define LUs for program-to-program communications. The most common LU type used today is LU 6.2. LU 6.2 supports APIs such as the APPC and the *Common Programming Interface-Communications* (CPI-C).

- *LU Type 7* is used by the IBM 5250 workstation, which is the main terminal type supported by the AS/400 in an APPN network.

Sessions

A dependent terminal LU desiring to talk to a host LU (such as CICS or TSO) cannot do so until a session is established between it and the other LU. In hierarchical SNA, this requires the intervention of the SSCP running on the host. The LU first establishes a session with the SCCP in the host, and then the SCCP assists in making the connection through to the desired (partner) LU.

When you first turn on a terminal that is connected to your network, you may see a kind of welcome screen with a menu of applications that you can connect to. Some shops do not present a menu or otherwise identify themselves for security reasons. In these cases, you just have to know the options to enter. The strings entered are then mapped to the actual VTAM *application IDs* (APPLIDS) by a VTAM table built during VTAM configuration.

When you connect to VTAM, you are really talking to the SCCP in an LU-SCCP session. After you select an application, the SCCP assists in connecting you to it. At that point, the LU-SCCP session becomes an LU-LU session between the two LUs.

NCP

The NCP runs the FEP is responsible for managing the communications with all communications devices. It works in concert with VTAM running on the host. The responsibilities of the NCP are routing, polling remote devices, error detection, flow control, and protocol conversion. The NCP is actually built on the host and downloaded to the FEP when it is started.

VTAM

VTAM is the mainframe software subsystem that is used to support SNA. All program LUs, such as TSO and CICS, can be reached only via the SSCP component of VTAM. VTAM communicates directly with the NCP running in the FEP. It is responsible for monitoring the status of all these entities. VTAM also performs network-error recovery and reconfiguration. It is responsible for logging errors and statistical data, and keeping usage accounting data. VTAM is also responsible for providing operator commands to start and stop lines, terminals, PUs, and LUs.

Defining a VTAM Network

Creating the tables that define a VTAM network is a complex process, and this discussion cannot do it justice. In general, however, the process is to code a set of Assembly Language statements and PDS member resource definitions. These elements are processed into an executable NCP that can be downloaded and run on the FEP, together with a set of VTAM control statements and modules that are loaded from one or more PDS members when VTAM is started.

Although this is not a book on VTAM, I did want to give you the flavor of this process. The following example shows the beginning of the macros that define an IBM 3174 CCU that will be directly attached to a host processor running VTAM. (The line numbers in the example are not part of the example. They are just there to refer to the lines in the text.)

```
 1 **********************************************************************
 2 *                             *
 3 * DEFINE 3174 CLUSTER CONTROLLER A01 AND ATTACHED TERMINALS     *
 4 *                             *
 5 **********************************************************************
 6
 7 C3174A  VBUILD TYPE=LOCAL
 8 * DEFINE 3174 CONTROLLER PU
 9 PUA01  PU    CUADDR=140,    CHANNEL AND SUBCHANNEL ADDRESS   X
10               ISTATUS=ACTIVE,                 X
```

```
11                PUTYPE=2,    3260 CLUSTER          X
12                MAXBFRU=50,                   X
13                PACING=0,                     X
14                DLOGMODE=VT1BIND, SESSION CONNECTION PARMS    X
15                MODETAB=MT100,  LOGON MODE TABLE         X
16                SSCPM=VT1SSCS,                X
17                USSTAB=USSMENU
18
19 * DEFINE TERMINAL LUS
20 C3174A02 LU  LOCADDR=02
21 C3174A02 LU  LOCADDR=03
22 C3174A02 LU  LOCADDR=04
23 C3174A02 LU  LOCADDR=05
24 C3174A02 LU  LOCADDR=06
```

In this example, the VBUILD macro on line 7 specifies that the definition is for a locally attached device. Lines 8 though 17 define the PU characteristics of the cluster controller.

Most of the parameters of the PU macro are fairly esoteric, and this discussion does not go into them in any detail. Note, however, that CUADDR is the physical address of the device, and that PUTYPE=2 indicates that this is for a Type 2 PU. Lines 20 through 24 define LUs for five cluster controller–attached terminals.

Subsystems and APPLIDs

As previously discussed, when you initially power up a VTAM-managed terminal, you are allowed to enter a data string that VTAM can translate into the identifier of an OS/390 subsystem or user-developed VTAM application program. The most common OS/390 subsystems that use VTAM to communicate with terminals are as follows:

- *CICS*, which has been mentioned several times in this book (and which is covered in more detail in Chapter 15), provides transaction-processing access to interactive terminals. CICS relies on VTAM to manage these terminals.

- *TSO* is another product that uses VTAM to manage interactive terminals used by programmers, operators, and other users.

- *JES2* uses VTAM to route jobs between mainframes and RJE workstations, as well as between multiple mainframes.

You can also write or buy other application programs that use a VTAM-supported API to open a connection to VTAM that will allow you to accept connection requests from terminal LUs or other programs LUs. (The process is similar to the one you use when you open a dataset for the purpose of reading and writing data.)

Security Considerations
The preceding chapter discussed how RACF controls security in an OS/390 system. VTAM is a full participant in the RACF security scheme. When a user attempts to connect to a VTAM application, VTAM calls on RACF to determine whether the user should be allowed to connect.

VTAM Operations
As previously discussed, VTAM lines and nodes are configured by the systems programmer when he creates the VTAM definition tables and parameter lists in VTAM datasets. During normal operation of a VTAM-controlled network, very little operator intervention is required. In most cases, VTAM just runs itself. VTAM also has a fair amount of error recovery built in. In some cases, however, the operator must take action to assist in the error-recovery process. VTAM provides several operator commands for this purpose.

Monitoring
The OS/390 operator is responsible for making sure that the computer system runs efficiently and effectively. This extends to the communications network, as well. In a VTAM network, the operator is responsible for ensuring that communications are working correctly and that performance is acceptable. If the operator suspects that there is a problem with a VTAM resource, he can display the status of the node, link, or LU using VTAM Display commands. For instance, the command d net,id=C3174A02 can be used to display the status of one of the terminal LUs defined to VTAM earlier in this section of the chapter.

Starting and Stopping VTAM Objects
In case of errors, the computer operator can stop and restart VTAM nodes and links. To do this, the operator uses the OS/390 Vary (v) command to communicate with VTAM. The following example shows the commands to stop and restart a cluster controller that is experiencing errors:

```
v net,inact,id=PUA01
v net,act,id=PUA01
```

Similar commands can be used to deactivate and reactivate a network link or LU. The computer operator is also often called on to purge hung TSO sessions for users. In most cases, the operator can just cancel the user's TSO session (which just appears to the operating system as a job with the user's ID as the job name). If the problem was caused by a communications error, the operator may have to stop and start the terminal LU or link; in extremely rare cases, VTAM may have to be stopped with the z net command and restarted again.

Local Area Networks

LANs emerged in the 1990s as a connectivity solution for departmental computing. Part of their emergence was as a backlash against the centralized host computing typified by mainframes. Eventually, IS was called on to support and integrate LANs into the host network.

LAN Operating Systems

IBM and Microsoft, in cooperation with networking hardware vendors, provided several LAN solutions over the years. More recently, Microsoft developed and marketed LAN Manager, a LAN operating system that ran under OS/2. (This was back in the days when IBM and Microsoft were partners, as was discussed in Chapter 1, "Origins and Evolution of OS/390 and Windows 2000.") IBM made minor modifications to LAN Manager and sold it as IBM LAN Server. IBM LAN Server has since evolved into IBM's current offering, Warp Server. LAN Manager was eventually absorbed into Windows NT to form the core networking support in Windows NT and now Windows 2000. ✦

TCP/IP

In IBM mainframe shops today, SNA is still the most popular communications protocol in use. In the past couple of years, however, another communications protocol has emerged and is gradually forcing its way into this environment. More and more mainframe shops are finding it necessary to provide access to legacy mainframe data to users with Web browsers connected via the Internet. The protocol in use on the Internet is TCP/IP.

Most mainframe shops have resisted connecting TCP/IP traffic from the Internet through to their mainframe because of security considerations. In many cases, they have opted to set up a separate network of disconnected Web servers instead. With the appropriate use of firewalls and good security practices, however, this need not be a major issue. Chapter 17, "Integrating with Legacy Mainframe Applications and Data," discusses how SNA gateways, such as Microsoft's SNA Server, can be used to connect SNA and TCP/IP networks together to achieve the same purpose without carrying TCP/IP all the way to the mainframe. Thanks to the need to engage in e-commerce, we can expect more and more companies to use TCP/IP gateways or add native TCP/IP support to their mainframes as time passes.

IBM has recently begun to integrate TCP/IP support into its hardware and software offerings with products such as their ANYNET offering. The IBM 3174 can also act as a TCP/IP router and support TCP/IP traffic as well as SNA.

Because TCP/IP is covered in more depth in the Windows 2000 section of this chapter and because it is still not widely used in mainframe shops, it is not covered it in any more detail here.

Windows 2000 Networking

Windows 2000 Server is a network operating system (NOS). As such, it supports a wide variety of communications protocols. This section discusses these protocols.

Hardware

This analysis of Windows 2000 networking begins by examining the network-related hardware that Windows 2000 supports, and then focuses on the software architecture used to implement Windows 2000 networking.

Terminals

In the OS/390 world, everything is terminal-based with 3270 terminals or terminal emulators running on a PC. In the Windows world, almost everything is a Windows computer (of some flavor), whether it is running on a desktop or as a server. This makes Windows 2000 networking quite different from OS/390 networking.

Terminal Server

The closest thing to a dumb-terminal environment is when the Windows Terminal Server support in Windows 2000 is used to support Windows terminals. A Windows terminal is normally a special-purpose computer running a copy of Microsoft's Windows CE operating system. It can also be an X86 system running a less-capable operating system than Windows 2000. It may, in fact, be running one of Microsoft's older operating systems with Terminal Server Client software installed. Terminal Server makes it possible for remote users to execute applications that actually run on the server. ◆

Computers

As discussed under OS/390 networking, an SNA-based network is typically organized in a hierarchy with a single centralized host computer, FEPs, cluster controllers, and dispersed terminals. In a Windows 2000 network, the participants are all normally full-fledged computers. As such, Windows 2000 networking has more in common with the peer-to-peer style of networking used by AS/400s and APPN. In an APPN network, you will recall, there is no central or master computer. All computers are created equal. In Windows 2000 networks, this is also true. (Although, as discussed in earlier chapters, some Windows 2000 computers, such as domain controllers, are more equal than others!)

This architecture is reflected in the administrative tools provided with Windows 2000. In most GUI-based tools, for example, you first select the computer that you want the tool to operate on, and then perform the desired operation.

As previously indicated, Windows 2000 Server and Professional (Workstation) computers can participate as network peers. Other operating systems, however, are relegated to the lesser role of network clients. Windows 2000 can support clients such as legacy Windows NT, Windows 95 and 98, Windows 3.1, 3.11, and Windows for Workgroups. It can also support clients such as OS/2, NetWare, UNIX, and others, although effective interoperability may require software from the vendor of those operating systems or other third parties.

Networks

As in the case of OS/390, Windows 2000 supports a wide variety of network connections. OS/390 originated in the world of locally attached 3270 terminals and remotely attached 3270s connected over WANs. As discussed in the section on OS/390, locally attached terminals were often connected to their controller via coaxial cables. With the introduction of LANs into the enterprise, IBM added the capability to connect these terminals over LANs as well. Windows 2000, on the other hand, grew up in the world of LANs and then graduated to WANs.

LANs

Today, Windows 2000 networks are normally connected via LANs. Even in the case of geographically separated locations, they are still connected via LANs at each location. These LANs are then bridged or routed over WAN links between locations. In most non-mainframe environments, Ethernet is the LAN architecture of choice. In OS/390 shops, Token Ring is the most popular choice, although it is currently losing ground to Ethernet.

WANs

When it comes to WANs, Windows 2000, like OS/390, supports a wide variety of choices. These choices include T1 and T3 lines, X.25 packet-switched networks, ISDN, Frame Relay, ATM, and others. WAN access is usually via serial port and modem, data access unit, or other specialized adapters.

Routers and Bridges

LAN locations are often connected with bridges and/or routers. Some protocols, such as NetBEUI and DLC, are not routable. In these cases, bridges must be used or the protocol must be encapsulated in a routable protocol such as TCP/IP. Bridges operate below the network layer. As a result, they do not have to understand anything about the networking protocol being transported. This is both good and bad. It is good because they make the entire network look like a single logical network. It is bad because, unlike routers, which operate at the network level, they cannot filter and optimize traffic flow. Routed networks can be segmented and designed so that traffic flow between network segments is minimized.

Network Interface Hardware

To connect Windows 2000 clients and servers with the selected network type, an appropriate hardware adapter must be installed in the computer. This hardware adapter could be a Token Ring, or Ethernet NIC-installed, so that the computer can connect to a LAN. There are Windows 2000–compatible NICS for all the popular LAN and WAN protocols such as Token Ring, Ethernet, and *FDDI* (Fiber Distributed Data Interface).

Although it is not normally thought of as an NIC, a serial port connected to a modem also fulfills the role of an NIC when used in conjunction with the Windows 2000 *Remote Access Service* (RAS). With RAS, a remote computer can connect to a Windows 2000 system as if it were connecting via a local LAN connection.

Windows 2000 Networking Architecture

The Windows 2000 networking architecture consists of software and hardware layers, connected together with network bindings when you configure the network support in Windows 2000. As an example, this layered approach makes it possible for a NetBIOS application to be encapsulated in a TCP/IP protocol and sent over a router, despite the fact that NetBEUI is not a routable protocol. Windows 2000 uses a layered architecture that can be mapped roughly into the OSI model (see Figure 14.6).

In this architecture, upper layers can be bound to a number of lower layers. This makes it possible for the operating system to support multiple protocols over multiple protocol stacks through a single network card installed in the computer. (You can also have multiple network cards installed, either for performance or to have a computer connected simultaneously to more than one network or network segment at the same time.)

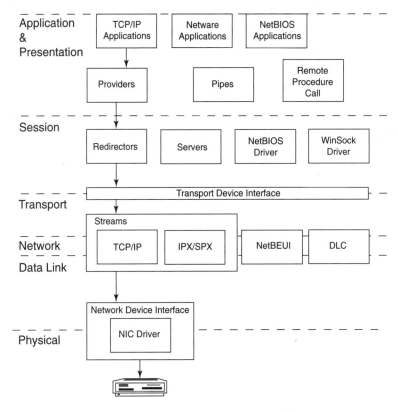

Figure 14.6 *Windows 2000 network architecture.*

Applications
Of course, the whole purpose of all of this networking infrastructure is to support network applications. Network applications make calls to services located on other computers, either directly by using one of several API sets, or indirectly by making I/O calls to files and directories located on another computer. In the latter case, the file system actually takes care of issuing the APIs to satisfy the request. The file system, in turn, interfaces with one of the service providers discussed in the following section.

Providers
Providers act as an interface between the Windows 2000 file system and the network redirectors that redirect requests to other computers. Their main function is to map file system names and device references to the location of a file or directory on a remote server.

Redirectors

Redirectors, as their name implies, redirect file system requests to other computers. These redirectors work in one of two ways. A file system request can reference a drive letter that does not exist on your computer. If this drive letter had been redirected to a network drive, the appropriate provider will determine the appropriate redirector to satisfy the request. Redirectors also handle file system requests made using a file's or directory's *universal naming convention* (UNC) name. When a redirector receives a request, it is converted to a message, and then sent to the appropriate server process on the remote machine. There, the operation is performed, and the result is returned to the requesting program.

Servers

Servers act as the remote partners of redirectors. They receive the I/O request and actually issue the request locally on behalf of the client. Then, they return the results to the client, where it passes up the protocol stack to the application program that originally issued the request.

The Transport Device Interface

The *Transport Device Interface* (TDI) provides a standard interface between drivers, such as redirectors and servers, and the various network transports provided by the operating system. It is an interface rather than a software layer.

Protocols

Network protocol modules support the appropriate network protocols in use on the network. This chapter has already discussed these protocols in some detail. To recap, Windows 2000 supports TCP/IP, Novell IPX/SPX, NetBIOS, DLC, as well as other popular protocols.

In addition to supporting direct access from redirectors to protocol modules such as TCP/IP and NetBUI, an additional level of abstraction exists to provide a common interface to multiple protocols. The *streams* interface in Windows 2000 is based on work originally done in the UNIX world to generalize network communications. This protocol was adapted by AT&T and incorporated into the UNIX Sockets protocol. Microsoft also provides the *Windows Sockets* (Winsock) API as a high-level interface to multiple transport protocols operating at the lower layers.

The Data Link Control Protocol

The DLC protocol is used for only two purposes. It is used by Windows 2000 to control network-attached printers. It is also used to communicate with SNA networks; however, to support this, it requires the use of additional software such as Microsoft's SNA Server (see Chapter 16). ◆

The Network Device Interface Specification

The *Network Device Interface Specification* (NDIS) is a standard developed by Microsoft, 3Com, and IBM for writing network device drivers. It allows multiple protocol stacks to support multiple protocols over a single network card. This software component is called an NDIS "wrapper" because it wraps the network card and coordinates its use.

Network Bindings

The software components discussed in this section can be bound together in flexible ways to allow various API requests to be carried over more than one protocol—although not all combinations are supported. To configure the protocol bindings on your computer, right-click on the Networks Near Me icon, and then select Properties. Next, select the Advanced menu option followed by the Advanced Settings menu entry (see Figure 14.7).

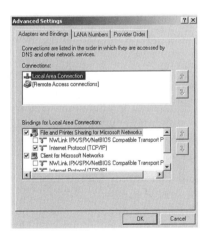

Figure 14.7 *Network bindings.*

After you do this, you will see the network bindings set for your computer. An experienced administrator can add or change the order of bindings by using this window. (Do not try this unless you really know what you are doing here. A mistake may disable your computer's networking support.)

TCP/IP

This section introduces you to the TCP/IP support in Windows 2000. It will not make you an expert on TCP/IP, however. Because whole books have been written on the subject, the focus here is on the material most relevant to the use of TCP/IP under Windows 2000.

TCP/IP Applications

Windows 2000 TCP/IP comes with quite a few TCP/IP applications (sometimes called TCP/IP utilities). Unfortunately most of them are little more than applets, and you will need to purchase a third-party product for serious work. Some of these applications are listed and explained in this section. Unfortunately, space considerations make it impossible to cover them all here.

The most interesting of these applications are as follows:

- *FTP* (File Transfer Program) is used to transfer files between TCP/IP systems.

- *Telnet* is used to connect a remote workstation to a server with a command prompt. The Windows 2000 TCP/IP suite also includes Telnet 3270 (TN3270). TN3270 uses the Telnet data-transfer protocol to transmit 3270 data streams between a TCP/IP client and either a mainframe running TCP/IP or an intermediate box that converts TCP/IP to SNA. Although Microsoft provides a primitive TN3270 applet with Windows 2000, third-party vendors provide more capable products.

- *SMTP* (Simple Mail Transfer Protocol) is used to send and receive email using TCP/IP. Most mainframe shops use mainframe-based email systems such as PROFS, or vendor-supported email systems such as Exchange, Lotus cc:Mail, Lotus Notes, or Novel GroupWise. SMTP is usually used only to retrieve email from *Internet service providers* (ISPs).

TCP/IP also defines other programs such as DNS, ARP, and RARP. These programs are used for special purposes more related to the functioning of TCP/IP networks.

IP Addressing

Computers in IP networks are called hosts. Hosts in a TCP/IP network are addressed definitively by their *Internet Protocol* (IP) address. An IP address consists of a 32-bit number normally represented as a four-part number in dotted-decimal form (such as 190.112.010.2). The exact representation depends on the range of addresses allowed. Depending on the class chosen, the number identifies a network ID and a host on the network. For instance, a Class C address uses the first three parts of the number to identify the network (there are lots of them!) and the last part to identify hosts on the network. These address ranges are as follows:

- Class A (0–127)
- Class B (128–191)
- Class C (192–223)
- Class D (224–239)
- Class E (240–255)

Normally, only Classes A–C are used in commercial applications. With the exception of some reserved addresses and some reserved address ranges, these addresses are available for use as host addresses in IP networks.

IP Address Assignment

In early versions of TCP/IP, all IP addresses had to be statically assigned. This often let to duplicate IP addresses in a network. This led to the creation of a dynamic address-assignment protocol known as BOOTP. Windows 2000 supports its own flavor of dynamic assignment of IP addresses to hosts. The *Dynamic Host Configuration Program* (DHCP) is used to assign an IP address and other TCP/IP configuration parameters to a new host when it joins a network. The IP address is allocated from a reserved pool of IP addresses and leased to the host for a predetermined time. The DHCP protocol also supports the renewal of these leases when they expire. This dynamic address assignment is normally used only for workstations. Servers usually need to have a static (and well-known) IP address so that workstations can locate them easily.

Sockets

Most TCP/IP utilities are addressed by using a combination of their IP address (which defines the unique host that they run on) together with a well-known socket address (port number). For instance, FTP uses port number 21 for control information, and port number 20 for data transfer. Web servers use port number 80 for normal (http) data transfer, by default, and port 443 for SSL (https) data transfer (see Chapter 13, "Security").

Name Resolution

To enable users to use more friendly mnemonic names rather than a string of numbers, the designers of TCP/IP defined a naming system and a name-resolution mechanism. Originally, TCP/IP defined a static name-to-IP address mapping file called the Hosts file. More recently, this has been replaced with the more dynamic *Domain Name System* (DNS). You have already seen something of DNS in Chapter 10, "Catalogs and Directories." DNS was originally developed for the Internet and used in conjunction with TCP/IP. Now, it has been integrated into Windows 2000 as its own name-resolution service.

DNS

In DNS, every host has a place in a domain hierarchy. If the host is publicly accessible over the Internet, it will be part of the worldwide DNS hierarchy. Even if your domain is internal to your company, you will still have your own DNS service to perform name resolution. Figure 14.8 shows the Internet domain hierarchy.

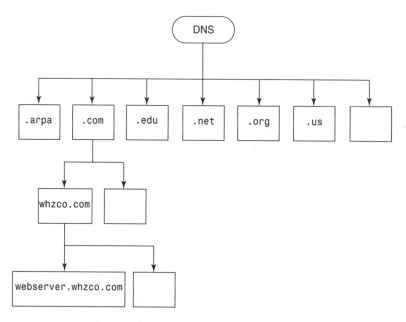

Figure 14.8 *The Domain Name System.*

In this hierarchy, hosts have a name such as `webserver.whzco.com`. (This is the Web server that is a member of the `whzco.com` domain.) DNS is responsible for resolving this name into its actual IP address. This is done by searching for a DNS server that is authoritative for the domain of interest. In the case of top-level Internet domains, these servers are maintained by an assigned authority—the *Internet Network Information Center* (InterNIC). You must apply to the InterNIC for your IP address i f you ever want to connect machines with this addressing scheme to the public Internet. It is also possible to have a local domain hierarchy strictly within a company.

For the most authoritative and thorough treatment of DNS, you should read *DNS and Bind* by Albitz and Liu, O'Reilly and Associates, ISBN: 1-5659-2512-2.

Address Resolution

The *Address Resolution Protocol* (ARP) is used to determine the physical address of a host from its IP address. In a Token Ring or Ethernet network, that is its adapter address. This is normally called its *MAC* (Media Access Control) address. The *Reverse Address Resolution Protocol* (RARP) allows a host to determine its own IP address from its physical address.

Routing

In a TCP/IP network, a message from one host to another is often routed through many intermediate host nodes. The protocols that govern how this is managed are called routing protocols. A router or host computer acting in this capacity will run a gateway protocol such as the *Routing Information Protocol* (RIP) or *Border Gateway Protocol* (BGP). You will typically find specialized devices called routers dedicated to this function from vendors such as Cisco.

Subnetting

A distributed TCP/IP network will normally be broken down into a collection of subnets. This is often done to improve performance by minimizing data traffic to remote sites. As indicated in Chapter 10, this is also done to allow the selection of a local domain controller in the same site to authenticate a use when he logs on. (You will remember from Chapter 10 that a site is a collection of well-connected IP subnets.) Subnets are implemented by using a subnet mask to assign parts of the IP address to different subnets. This effectively breaks up the IP address into a network ID, a subnet ID and a host ID.

There is a lot more to TCP/IP, and this discussion has just scratched the surface. For more information, you can read *Networking with Microsoft TCP/IP*, by Drew Heywood, New Riders Publishing, ISBN: 1-7357-0014-1.

NetBIOS

Prior to Windows 2000, most operating system services were provided natively via NetBIOS. Due to the many limitations of NetBIOS in a distributed network, it was superseded by TCP/IP in Windows 2000. NetBIOS support still exists for legacy Windows NT support. Although TCP/IP is the preferred networking protocol in Windows 2000, a lot of Windows NT system software and other legacy operating systems still use a fair amount of NetBIOS. Some of the terminology of NetBIOS can be confusing. NetBIOS is an API. It defines the command that a program can issue to make network requests. NetBUI is the protocol used to satisfy these API requests. Microsoft's latest implementation of NetBUI is also called *NBF* (NetBIOS Frame).

To map NetBIOS names into friendly names, static files (called LMHOSTS files) had to be set up, or servers running a NetBIOS name-resolution service similar to DNS were required. The *Windows Internet Naming Service* (WINS) servers provided this name-resolution function. WINS servers are still required if you have to support legacy Windows NT systems that use NetBIOS. Because Windows 2000 services are TCP/IP-based, WINS will not be required after these legacy systems have been converted to Windows 2000.

For more information on NetBIOS, you can refer to the IBM publication "IBM LAN Technical Reference, " SC30-3587.

Security Considerations

Chapter 13 discussed Windows 2000 security. Suffice it to say that redirected network resources are also covered by the extensive Windows 2000 security model. When you share a directory or file, you can specify users and groups that can access it. You can also specify access permissions to govern the actions of those users and groups.

Operations

Networking is an integral part of Windows 2000. When the operating system starts, the services that were configured to provide networking support also start automatically. Nevertheless, monitoring is sometimes required. The TCP/IP Ping utility can be used to determine whether a given TCP/IP host can be reached from another host. You can ping a host either by its DNS name or by its IP address. The following example shows the results of pinging a remote host using its IP address. (If you can ping a host by its IP address and not its DNS name, you know that you are having a DNS problem and not a connectivity problem.)

```
1 C:\>ping 192.128.2.245
2
3 Pinging 192.128.3.245 with 32 bytes of data:
4
5 Reply from 192.128.3.245: bytes=32 time<10ms TTL=128
6 Reply from 192.128.3.245: bytes=32 time<10ms TTL=128
7 Reply from 192.128.3.245: bytes=32 time<10ms TTL=128
8 Reply from 192.128.3.245: bytes=32 time<10ms TTL=128
```

To determine whether TCP/IP is correctly installed on your computer, you can use the `ipconfig` command to list your TCP/IP parameters, as follows:

```
1 C:\>ipconfig
2
3 Windows NT IP Configuration
4
5 Token Ring adapter 3COMPORT1:
6
7   IP Address. . . . . . . . . : 192.128.3.10
8   Subnet Mask . . . . . . . . : 255.255.255.0
9   Default Gateway . . . . . . : 192.128.3.1
10
11 Ethernet adapter NdisWan1:
12
13   IP Address. . . . . . . . . : 203.175.98.44
14   Subnet Mask . . . . . . . . : 255.255.255.0
15   Default Gateway . . . . . . : 203.175.98.44
```

Other TCP/IP commands, such as `Tracert.exe` and `Routed`, can be used to trace the route from one host to another. The Windows 2000 *Performance Monitor* (Perfmon) also has counters for network monitoring and can be configured to send alerts if these counters exceed a prespecified value.

Many Windows 2000 shops also find that a hardware monitor is a useful troubleshooting tool. (The most popular one is the Network Sniffer from Network Associates.) Windows 2000 Server also has a software Network Monitor that performs a similar function. It can be used on a single server to monitor network traffic at that server. A more capable version of this monitor also comes with Microsoft's *Systems Management Server* (SMS). The SMS version can be used to monitor traffic at remote computers as well.

This chapter has discussed how OS/390 and Windows 2000 handle networking. You have seen that OS/390 networking is heavily influenced by the hierarchical nature of early SNA networks. Windows 2000 networks, in comparison, owe most of their architecture to originating in the distributed peer-to-peer networking environment.

This chapter has covered OS/390 and Windows 2000 networking. The next chapter discusses the transaction, database, and message processing that make extensive use of this networking support.

15

Transaction, Database, and Message Processing

This chapter examines the subsystems that each operating system provides for implementing interactive transaction-oriented database and data-communications applications. First, the discussion examines the operating system subsystems that support transaction processing. Next, the focus turns to database management systems. Finally, the chapter takes a look at the operating system subsystems that support deferred message processing and message routing between applications.

You will also learn about some of the crossover products that can be used to integrate OS/390 and Windows 2000.

OS/390 Transaction, Database, and Message Processing

This section covers OS/390 transaction processing, database management, and message processing. In the mainframe world, transaction processing over the last 30 years or so has involved the use of the *IBM Customer Information Control System* (CICS).

In the mainframe world, database management primarily involves the use of an IBM database management system, such as DB/2 and IMS.

Also, in the mainframe world, most interapplication and intersystem messaging uses IBM's MQSeries message-oriented middleware.

Application Architecture

CICS applications are normally built on a two-tier architectural model involving dumb terminals and a mainframe running CICS. All processing is performed on the mainframe. The terminals just act as a presentation interface to the applications. Later, when the discuss turns to Windows 2000 applications, you will see that Windows 2000 supports a more complex distributed application architecture.

CICS

CICS is a product that was originally sold separately by IBM. When OS/390 was released, it was bundled into that product and renamed CICS Transaction Server.

As mentioned earlier, CICS applications are normally built on a two-tier architectural model involving dumb terminals and a single mainframe CICS server. CICS has, for years, also supported the development of multitier applications with its *Distributed Program Link* feature. Nevertheless, the majority of the applications running under CICS today are still strictly two-tier. (Later in this chapter, this is contrasted with the multitier architecture favored by developers of Windows 2000 applications.)

The Origin of CICS

In the early 1970s, IBM determined that it had developed more than 20 different transaction-processing monitors for use on various development projects. After reviewing all these packages, it chose CICS as its mainline transaction-processing product. The original version of CICS was developed on a project to build a customer information system for an electric power company. That is why it has that somewhat non-descriptive name. ♦

As mentioned in Chapter 1, "Origins and Evolution of OS/390 and Windows 2000," IBM hardware and software is now essentially the same as it was when the System/360 product line was announced in the mid-1960s. At that time, there was little call for processing business transactions interactively. The hardware interrupt structure and operating systems architecture of System/390 and OS/390 are still designed to optimize batch processing throughput.

When a batch program runs, it requests operating system services. When a program cannot continue for any reason (such as waiting for the completion of an I/O request), it must wait. When it does this, the operating system places the entire region in a wait state. It then dispatches the next-highest priority task, which would probably be in a different region. The completion of the previously scheduled I/O operation eventually causes an interrupt that results in a re-evaluation of the priorities of all tasks that are ready to run, including the one for which the I/O operation was originally scheduled.

This process is optimal where total throughput is more important than response time. In transaction processing, however, response time is normally more important than throughput. A system that supports transaction processing normally needs to achieve an average response time of three to five seconds to satisfy the psychological pacing needs of a human operator.

Maximizing response time rather than batch throughput requires different scheduling algorithms.

The need to support both batch and transaction processing under IBM's predominantly batch-oriented operating systems gave birth to teleprocessing monitors such as CICS. CICS filters requests to the operating system and tailors operating system processing to the requirements of transaction-oriented application programs.

CICS Components

As explained in Chapter 2, "Operating System Architecture," CICS runs in a single region of the operating system. It handles all terminal, file, program, and storage requests issued by transaction-processing application programs. CICS, in turn, makes use of underlying operating system service to satisfy the functional and performance requirements of these transaction-processing programs.

CICS is made up of a nucleus of control programs and associated tables that operate in concert to provide services to applications (see Figure 15.1).

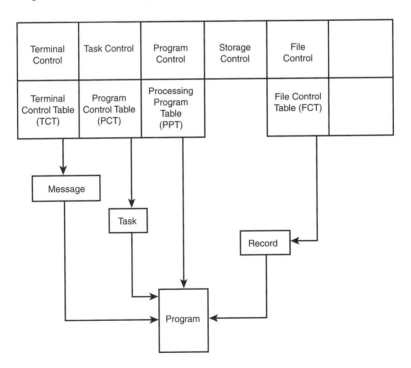

Figure 15.1 *CICS components.*

The CICS nucleus is configured and loaded dynamically when CICS is started as a single job step under the operating system. When a nucleus program needs a service (for instance, when CICS Terminal Control needs storage for a message input area), it issues a request to other components of CICS. User application programs also make requests to these CICS components. The major components of CICS are as follows:

- Terminal Control
- Task Control
- Program Control
- Storage Control
- File Control
- Transient Data Control
- Temporary Storage
- Interval Control

Most of these components work in conjunction with a table that is used to define and control associated resources.

Terminal Control

CICS *Terminal Control* processes all terminal input messages as they are received from the Virtual Telecommunications Access Method (VTAM). When a message arrives, CICS identifies the terminal that it is coming from by looking up its terminal identifier in the *CICS Terminal Control Table* (TCT). This nucleus-resident table is the only thing that needs to be changed when the network changes. (In addition to supporting terminals statically defined in the TCT, CICS can also *autoinstall* new terminals when they connect from VTAM.)

To determine the action required upon receipt of a terminal input message, CICS uses the following algorithm. If no task is currently active on the originating terminal, CICS examines the first one to four characters in the input message. It then treats this as *a transaction identifier* (Transid). It then passes this information, together with a request to start a new CICS task, to CICS Task Control. If there is already a task running on the terminal, Terminal Control just passes the message to the active task.

Prior to the deployment of the 3270 family of terminals, message datastreams were in a simple format. In that case, sending and receiving data from terminals was done one character at a time. The 3270 terminal (with its block-mode, field—oriented mode of operation), required the programmer to build complex output datastreams and parse response data from and to complex message formats (see Chapter 14, "Networking").

To simplify this process, a higher-level presentation interface was developed called *basic mapping support* (BMS). BMS enables the programmer to define input and output terminal maps symbolically, in terms of screen fields and their attributes such as protected and high intensity. It then provides simpler table-oriented definitions that can be used to refer to these fields in CICS application programs. (CICS also provides a screen-painting utility called the *Screen Definition Facility* [SDF] that can be used to generate BMS maps.) When a BMS SEND MAP or RECEIVE MAP request is issued by an application program, BMS is used to present the message in a table format that the program can deal with easily.

Task Control
As discussed in the introduction to this section, CICS is designed to process multiple transactions simultaneously. It attempts to maximize its use of operating system resources and gives up control to the operating system only when it has no other work to do. This requires that CICS handle its own internal multitasking of transaction-processing applications.

The primary component of CICS used to manage CICS tasks is *Task Control*. Information on all possible CICS tasks is stored in the CICS *Program Control Table* (PCT). (It probably should have been called the Task Control Table, but the acronym TCT was already chosen for the Terminal Control Table.) The PCT contains one entry for all possible CICS tasks that can be started by Task Control.

When Terminal Control requests the starting of a new task, Task Control looks up the input Transid in the PCT to determine task-related information such as the name of the program required to begin processing the message, the priority of the transaction, and other associated parameters. It also requests storage from CICS Storage Control to construct task-related control blocks and to chain them to a list of active tasks. Task Control's final step is to make a request to Program Control to invoke the application program specified in the PCT.

CICS programs can be written using one of two techniques. Conversational programs are started from a terminal, send data to the terminal, and wait for an operator response. While they are waiting, the program and its resources are kept in memory, where they tie up program and CICS control block storage resources. *Pseudo-conversational* programs, on the other hand, are written in a different style. In a pseudo-conversational program, the program sends the data to the terminal and then terminates after arranging some way to find out where it left off when it is restarted again by the operator's reply.

Over the years, CICS programmers have used several methods to indicate the progress of a transaction to pseudo-conversational programs. In some of the earliest CICS applications, the programmer just put a new Transid and a progress indicator in a hidden (invisible) field in the upper-left corner of the screen so that it would be received and interpreted as a new Transid in the next input message. (Note that this is how many Internet and intranet applications work. Data to be preserved between Web browser requests is often sent to the browser with the reply so that it will be retransmitted to the Web server with the next browser request.)

To support the preservation of a limited amount of data across transaction boundaries, CICS provides a special save area called the CICS *Commarea*. The Commarea is a special save area preserved across transaction boundaries. It is available to all transactions running on a given terminal. The Commarea can be used by the programmer to pass working storage program state data from one phase of a pseudo-conversational program to another. The data area to be saved is specified when the program issues a CICS RETURN command, specifying the Commarea and (optionally) the Transid of the next transaction to be given control when a new input message arrives from the same terminal. The amount of application data that can be stored in a CICS Commarea is limited to about 32,000 bytes. Larger amounts of data must be preserved by other means, such as CICS Temporary Storage (as discussed later).

Program Control

CICS Program Control is responsible for loading and deleting user application programs and CICS nonresident support programs from memory on an "as-needed" basis. To support simultaneous (multithread) processing of messages, programs must be shared by multiple simultaneously active users.

The method of program sharing used by CICS is as follows. An active CICS program runs until it needs to request a CICS service such as a file read or other operation that would normally result in the suspension of region activity. After CICS initiates this type of request, control is given to CICS Task Control to see whether another CICS task can be dispatched.

In this way, CICS uses as much CPU time itself as it can to favor transaction processing, even at the expense of batch. CICS Program Control also works with an associated table, the *Processing Program Table* (PPT). The PPT contains information on every CICS and user-written application program that can be used under CICS. It contains such information as the name of the program, whether it is in memory, its disk address, its language, and its current use count. (A program's use count is used for sharing the program between tasks, as discussed later.)

As indicated earlier in this section, transaction-processing programs need different handling than batch programs. Batch programs are loaded at the start of a job step, run to completion (subject to I/O interrupts and priority scheduling, as previously discussed), and are deleted from memory. When processing transactions, however, a program is needed in memory only for the time it takes to process the single transaction from a single terminal. Although batch programs are deleted from memory after they complete processing, CICS programs are kept in memory so that they can be used again quickly, if needed.

Program Control also services Program Control requests from the application program. These requests are as follows:

- LINK
- RETURN
- XCTL
- LOAD
- RELEASE

The best way to understand program linkage in CICS is to imagine that programs run at several levels (see Figure 15.2).

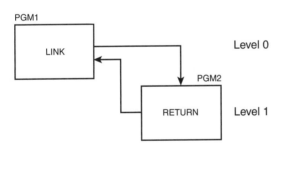

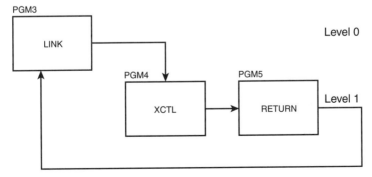

Figure 15.2 *CICS program levels.*

The initial program started by CICS runs at Level 0. A program can issue a CICS LINK request. This causes CICS to look up the name of the LINKed to program in the PPT and pass control to it at a lower program level. When the program issues a CICS RETURN, control returns to the linking program at the instruction following the LINK request. When a program issues an *XCTL* (Transfer of Control) request, the new program replaces the original program at the same level (refer to the top of Figure 15.2). Thus, the originating program can never get control back on a RETURN. When the top-level program issues a CICS RETURN, control returns to CICS and the task is terminated. This return to CICS can also specify the Transid and Commarea, discussed previously, to support pseudo-conversational programming (refer to the bottom of Figure 15.2).

LOAD and RELEASE are used less frequently by CICS applications programs, although they are often used by CICS itself. Their purpose is to allow the loading and unloading of shared data tables.

One feature of CICS that has not been used very often is the *Distributed Processing Link* (DPL) feature of program control. As indicated earlier, a LINK request is serviced by Program Control using the PPT. The PPT entry for the LINKed to program can indicate that the program is in a different region or even on a different computer system. If this is the case, CICS converts the request to a message and transmits it to the remote CICS system. On the remote CICS system, a "mirror transaction" acts as a proxy to issue the request. Then, the result of the request is turned into a communications reply and returned to the original system. Finally, the originating CICS system turns the message into a local CICS RETURN as if the LINKed to program were located on the same CICS system. (Incidentally, files specified in File Control requests can also be located on other systems using a similar mechanism involving the CICS File Control Table.)

Although this DPL feature is not used very much in CICS applications, it is like the *Remote Procedure Call* (RPC) method used by Windows 2000 *distributed component architecture* (DCOM), discussed in the Windows 2000 section of this chapter.

CICS Distributed Program Link and Performance

When I first discovered the DPL feature of CICS, I tried to use it to build a multi-tier, distributed transaction-processing application using two computers running CICS in two cities. Unfortunately, the remote program that I was invoking was located thousands of miles away over a relatively slow (4800bps) communications line. This caused a response time measured in minutes rather than seconds! Today's faster communications circuits make distributed applications more feasible. Nevertheless, the design of distributed applications must factor in the speed of communications lines. ◆

Storage Control

All programs require main storage during operation. The component of CICS responsible for allocating and releasing storage is *Storage Control*. Storage Control maintains several pools of storage for different purposes, and allocates and releases data from them to service requests from CICS applications and other CICS components.

Both batch and transaction programs use main storage. The result of running out of main storage in a batch environment is the termination of the entire processing region. A major contribution of CICS Storage Control is to provide a form of graceful degradation that allows out-of-storage conditions to be handled without region termination. To prevent a lack of storage from abending the entire CICS region, a portion of the region is reserved for use as a "storage cushion" to be released and used to satisfy a temporary storage shortage.

File Control

Batch jobs normally allocate a fixed set of input and output files for each job step. The program running in the job step normally has exclusive use of these files while they are executing. If any other running jobs need the same files, they have to wait for the prior job step to complete. In a transaction-processing application, however, files must be available all the time and sharable by all CICS programs.

The CICS *File Control component* supports shared access to disk files. Normal batch I/O statements are not allowed in a CICS program. Instead, all requests for file services are made via CICS File Control requests. All file control blocks and buffers are defined in the CICS *File Control Table* (FCT). The FCT includes an entry for each CICS-accessible file. This entry describes the attributes of the file such as its dataset name, type, and how it can be accessed. All CICS files are available to all CICS application programs concurrently subject to security authorization. CICS File Control also provides extended record-sharing capabilities to allow applications to perform multiple simultaneous read and update requests without conflicts. When a File Control request is issued, CICS ensures that no two users will get simultaneous access to update the same record. CICS File Control also works in conjunction with CICS Recovery to ensure file and database update integrity (see "CICS Recovery," later in this chapter).

CICS File Control supports access to *direct access storage device* (DASD) files only. Its main purpose is to allow access to VSAM and BDAM files. In addition, it does support the random and skip-sequential processing of DASD files offered by VSAM. When an application program must wait for I/O to complete, CICS Task Control suspends the task and dispatches another ready CICS task.

Note that access to databases is supported outside of CICS. CICS programs, however, can include database access calls. IBM provides support to allow CICS programs to access IBM databases such as DB/2 and IMS. Some third-party vendors also provide the support necessary to access their database management systems from CICS applications. For instance, Computer Associates provides this for their IDMS database management system. Even though these databases are not directly managed by CICS, they still participate in CICS transaction recovery.

Transient Data

CICS Transient Data Control supports two types of services: *Intrapartition Transient Data* and *Extrapartition Transient Data*. Because CICS applications typically make more use of Intrapartition Transient Data services, that facility is discussed here first.

Intrapartition Transient Data

Under CICS, a task is attached to the terminal that created it. It can communicate directly only with this terminal. CICS does not allow the sending of messages directly to other terminals. To send a message to another terminal, the application must cause a new task to be initiated on that terminal. Then, the program related to this new task can send data to the associated terminal. One facility that CICS provides to allow a program to do this is *Intrapartition Transient Data*.

Intrapartition Transient Data Control works with a table, the *Destination Control Table* (DCT). It is used to define a series of named logical files called queues. Multiple records can be stored in a queue, and retrieved either randomly or sequentially from this queue. Each queue has associated with it a "trigger level" or record-count threshold, a transaction identifier, and a terminal identifier. When the number of records inserted into a queue reaches a preset threshold, assuming that the specified terminal is free, the required transaction is started on the specified terminal. After the transaction-processing program is started, it can retrieve the record (or records) from the queue and send them to the terminal. Figure 15.3 shows an example of how this might be useful.

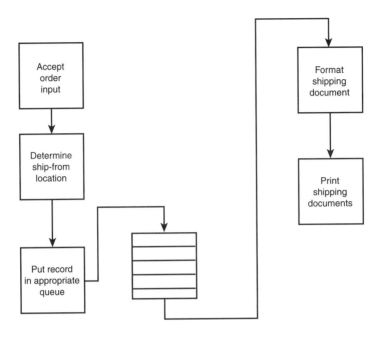

Figure 15.3 *CICS interterminal messaging.*

In this example, an order entry clerk enters an order on a terminal. The transaction-processing program needs to print a copy of the completed order on a printer terminal located at a remote warehouse. Under CICS, this cannot be done directly. Instead, the program writes a record into a transient data queue associated with the appropriate warehouse printer. This record contains the data necessary to perform the desired operation. (For instance, it might contain the key of the order in the order file.) When the queue trigger level is reached and the specified terminal printer is available, the transaction is started. When the program associated with the transaction is started, it can read the record from the queue, read the order from the order file, and print it on the warehouse printer.

Intrapartition Transient Data can also be used to detach a terminal from a lengthy process. In the case of the order entry example, assume that the entry of an order results in a time-consuming database update process that does not require any intervention from the terminal operator. In this case, the actual update could be performed by a new transaction, not attached to the terminal. After writing the update data to the queue, the terminal would then be free to do other processing and the database update would proceed asynchronously.

Note that both of the former examples involve deferred interapplication messaging, where processing is split between two programs in a noninteractive fashion. This type of CICS messaging was (and still is) appropriate where all the programs are CICS programs running on a single CPU. If multiple CICS systems, other (non-CICS) applications, or other operating systems are involved, there is a more industrial-strength method of interapplication messaging available. This is provided by IBM's MQSeries messaging middleware product. (The MQSeries is discussed in more detail later in this chapter.)

Extrapartition Transient Data
Intrapartition Transient Data involved routing data between transactions running under control of CICS. *Extrapartition Transient Data*, on the other hand, involves routing data into and out of the CICS region. There are two major application uses for Extrapartition Transient Data:

- Reading and writing sequential datasets
- Sending jobs to the JES2 Internal Reader

As indicated earlier, CICS file control supports only VSAM and BDAM direct access files. This would leave CICS without any support for reading from and writing to sequential datasets located external to CICS. To allow limited sequential file support, CICS provides Extrapartition Transient Data Control services. For example, this could be used by transaction-processing programs to send update transactions to a file to be used as input to later batch processing.

Chapter 9, "Job and Task Management," discussed how JES2 will allow a program to open and write JCL records to a specially named file that is actually a portal to submit new jobs to the operating system. CICS Extrapartition Transient Data supports this facility. For instance, a CICS program can request exclusive access of just such a transient data destination, and then write the JCL for a new job to it. When it does this, the job will go right into the JES2 input queue for later execution. (Several applications that I have developed make use of this feature.)

Temporary Storage
From the earlier discussion, you will recall that a CICS Commarea is limited to a single record with a maximum of approximately 32,000 characters of data. If an application design requires the storage of more data than that, or if storing multiple records is required, CICS *Temporary Storage Control* provides a fast scratch-pad mechanism. Using this facility, larger amounts of data can be preserved across transaction boundaries. (This is typically used

to pass working storage data across pseudo-conversational boundaries.) CICS supports fast (but nonrecoverable) Temporary Storage in main memory and slower (but recoverable) Temporary Storage on disk.

Interval Control

The Interval Control facility of CICS provides support for time-initiated tasks. Using this facility, you can automatically initiate a task at a specific time of the day or after a specified time interval. For instance, an application program can be initiated at 4:45 p.m. daily to warn users that a particular file will be closed and taken offline. Another use for this facility is a system status display that is refreshed every 30 seconds. Interval Control can also be used to start a time-initiated task on a different terminal, thus providing an alternative to Intrapartition Transient Data for communicating between terminals.

Putting It All Together

At this point, a basic subset of CICS services has been discussed. Now, this section illustrates the "life and death" of a typical CICS transaction. This discussion will act as a recap and a summary of the previous discussion of these facilities.

All CICS application programs are written in a CICS-supported programming language such as COBOL, Assembly Language, PL/1, RPG, or C. The majority of CICS application programs are written in COBOL, using normal COBOL statements to manipulate internal program data and to control execution flow within the program. CICS service requests (called Commands) are coded in-line in the programs to make requests for operating system services.

A simple CICS program is shown in the following example. Note that the line numbers in the code are to simplify text referencing; they are not part of the actual code. (As you probably know, COBOL programs sometimes do have line numbers in columns 1–6.)

```
1       IDENTIFICATION DIVISION.
2       PROGRAM-ID. ARPROG.
3
4       ENVIRONMENT DIVISION.
5       DATA DIVISION.
6
7       WORKING-STORAGE SECTION.
8
9       01 INPUT-LINE.
10          05 CICS-TRANSID        PIC X(4).
11          05 FILLER              PIC X.
12          05 RECORD-KEY          PIC X(5).
13       01 INPUT-LINE-LENGTH      PIC S9(4) COMP VALUE 10.
```

continues ▶

▶ *continued*

```
14
15    01 MASTER-RECORD            PIC X(80).
16    01 MASTER-RECORD-LENGTH     PIC S9(4) COMP VALUE 80.
17
18    01 OUTPUT-LINE.
19        05 FILLER               PIC X(15) VALUE 'For the key: '.
20        05 OUTPUT-LINE-KEY       PIC X(5).
21        05 FILLER               PIC X(21)
22              VALUE 'The data record is: '.
23        05 OUTPUT-LINE-RECORD    PIC X(80).
24    01 OUTPUT-LINE-LENGTH        PIC S9(4) COMP VALUE 121.
25
26    PROCEDURE DIVISION.
27
28        EXEC CICS RECEIVE INTO(INPUT-LINE)
29                  LENGTH(INPUT-LINE-LENGTH)
30        END-EXEC.
31
32
33        EXEC CICS READ DATASET('CMASTER')
34            INTO(MASTER-RECORD)
35            RIDFLD(RECORD-KEY)
36        END-EXEC.
37
38        MOVE RECORD-KEY TO OUTPUT-LINE-KEY.
39        MOVE MASTER-RECORD TO OUTPUT-LINE-RECORD.
40
41        EXEC CICS SEND FROM(OUTPUT-LINE)
42                  LENGTH(OUTPUT-LINE-LENGTH)
43        END-EXEC
44
45        EXEC CICS RETURN
46        END-EXEC.
```

Initially, no CICS tasks are active. Terminal Control is waiting for an input message from VTAM. A terminal operator enters a one- to four-letter transaction code, such as INQY, followed by a space and a five-character record key on a blank screen, and presses the Enter key. For instance, the request might look like this:

```
INQY 23718
```

Terminal Control receives the input message from VTAM. It identifies the source of the message by looking up the terminal ID in the TCT. Because there is no task currently active on the terminal, Terminal Control will treat the first one to four characters as a transaction code and will request initiation of the task via a request to Task Control.

Task Control, in turn, looks up the transaction identifier in the PCT. If found, the name of the application program required and operator security level are extracted from the table and verified. Task Control then passes control to Program Control.

Next, Program Control looks up the program to be invoked in the PPT. This table contains the current main storage and/or disk address of the program. It also contains a program use count, which keeps track of the current number of tasks using the program. This is used to determine when it can be removed from memory, if required. In addition, it also includes the language that the program is written in.

Program Control determines whether the requested application program is currently loaded in main storage. (Remember that only one copy of a program is loaded and shared by all tasks.) If so, it is shared, as discussed earlier. If not, it must be loaded from disk. (For the purposes of this example, assume that it is not currently in main storage.)

Program Control next issues a request to the operating system to load the application program. Instead of an operating system wait at this point, a CICS wait is issued. This allows Task Control to dispatch another ready CICS task.

When the program load is complete and the task is again dispatched, control at last passes to the application program. The application program, in this case a simple record display program, receives control.

In this example, the Working Storage section of the program holds storage definitions for the input line (9–13), the file master record (15–16), and the output screen display (18–24).

When the application program receives control, it issues a Terminal Control RECEIVE command, which stores the input message that started the transaction in the input line area (9–12).

The application program next uses the record key from the input message to execute a File Control read request to read the record. The File Control READ command (33–36) reads the record and stores it in the master record area (15). Because this read would normally result in an operating system wait, CICS again dispatches another ready CICS task.

When the read is completed, the application task is again dispatched, and the program receives control again. Next, the program formats an output display (18–23) and issues a command to Terminal Control to send the reply to the terminal. In this example, a simple terminal Control SEND command (41–43) is used to send the output. In a more practical example, BMS would probably be used to format a neater response. The result of this request might look like this:

```
For the key 23718 the data record is: Jones 125 Elm Street Boston Mass
```

Finally, the program terminates with a CICS RETURN (45–46). This causes CICS Program Control to reduce the program use count so that the program can be removed from memory, if necessary. Task Control then directs Storage Control to release all storage areas related to the task, and the task ends.

CICS/ESA

I have a confession to make here. This section of the chapter is based on an article on CICS that I wrote over 10 years ago. It is a testament to the durability of CICS that most of CICS still works the same way as it did back then. IBM did make several major internal changes to CICS when it developed the version known as CICS/ESA a few years ago. Nevertheless, the programmer, operator, and end user's view of CICS is essentially unchanged.

More recently, IBM has added features to CICS to allow it to optimize application execution on multiprocessor and cluster versions of System/390. Because these aspects of CICS architecture are mainly of interest to systems programmers, this chapter doesn't go into any detail on that. For more information, you can refer to CICS, A Guide to Internal Structure, by Eugene S. Hudders, Wiley-QED, ISBN: 0-4715-2172-8. ✦

CICS Security

CICS is a full participant in OS/390 security as managed by RACF and ACF/2 (see Chapter 13, "Security"). Security controls can be applied to CICS transactions, programs, files, and other CICS resources. To provide this level of security, CICS has a direct interface to the OS/390 System Authorization Facility discussed in Chapter 13.

CICS Recovery/Restart

Normally, the result of transaction processing is to update one or more files or databases. To preserve the integrity of these files and database, CICS provides support for recoverable transactions.

Transactions have four properties, called the ACID properties:

- *Atomicity*—A transaction that updates multiple resources must be atomic. It must appear to execute completely or not at all. If a transaction attempts to update multiple resources but it fails in mid-execution, the results of any partial updates must be reversed by the transaction-management software.

- *Consistency*—A transaction must provide consistent and correct results. It cannot produce a different effect, based on other events or influences that are not supposed to be part of the same transaction.

- *Isolation*—This means that concurrent transactions may not influence each other, and the result of a transaction may not be affected by the order in which these concurrent transactions are executed.

- *Durability*—This means that the user should always know whether a transaction has been applied successfully. This means that the user should not be notified that the transaction is complete until that state of completion is guaranteed.

To support ACID transactions, CICS uses a special journal file and a disk-based recovery dataset. CICS allows the programmer to define a *logical unit of work* (LUW), which can involve multiple file and database updates. During an LUW, all updates to resources are considered to be atomic. If an application program fails to complete all its updates successfully, the results of processing are automatically rolled back. CICS provides the SYNC-POINT request, so that applications can notify CICS that the program is at the end of an LUW and that its updates can be committed. It also provides the SYNCPOINT ROLLBACK command, so that a program can request that its updates be reversed, if necessary. If a CICS program, or all of CICS, fails for any reason, CICS *Emergency Restart* will perform the necessary rollback for transactions that were in progress at the time of the failure.

CICS recovery also supports an industry-standard, two-phase commit protocol used to ensure atomic transactions across multiple distributed databases. In this protocol, multiple database updates are synchronized so that the updates to both databases are either successfully completed or completely rolled back. This protocol gets its name from the fact that one side of the transaction notifies the other side that it is about to commit all changes. The other side replies as to whether it can also commit changes. Then, in the second phase, the two parties commit their changes and notify each other of that fact. If for any reason they cannot perform both phases successfully, they notify each other to back out of all the changes made on both sides. Many vendors support this two-phase commit protocol. In the section on Windows 2000, you will see how Windows 2000 handles transactions and transaction recovery using the *Microsoft Transaction Server* (MTS).

CICS Startup and Shutdown
As indicated previously, CICS runs as a single job step under OS/390. The CICS *Systems Initialization Program* (SIP) loads and initializes all nucleus programs and associated tables based on parameters specified in the *CICS System Initialization Table* (SIT).

CICS can be restarted in one of two modes: *auto* or *cold*.

Cold restart does not preserve the contents of CICS recovery/restart information. For that reason, it is rarely used. What happens on an auto restart depends on whether CICS was previously shut down normally or abnormally. If CICS was shut down normally, it will perform a *warm* restart. This means that the status of CICS resources at the time that CICS was shut down will be preserved. This includes any prescheduled time-initiated tasks, the contents of transient data queues, trigger levels, and so on.

If CICS was not normally shut down, an emergency restart will occur. In this case, CICS will attempt to bring all files, databases, and queues to a logically consistent state. For each in-process LUW, CICS will determine the status of any incomplete changes. Then, it will undo the effect of the change using before-images of update records from the CICS System Journal. This will bring all related files, databases, and recoverable queues back to a consistent state.

To shut CICS down, an operator with the appropriate CICS security level can issue the CICS *Master Terminal* (CEMT) command, CEMT PERFORM SHUTDOWN. This will quiesce all CICS processing and prepare CICS for a warm restart. (CICS Master Terminal commands can also be issued by a console operator as part of quiescing the entire operating system during a planned OS/390 shutdown.)

CICS Administration

Originally, all terminals, files, and other CICS resources had to be defined in static tables that were loaded at CICS startup. Changes to most of these tables required that CICS be stopped and restarted for the changes to take effect. About the time that data centers began to require round-the-clock 24-hour-a-day, seven-days-a-week (24 × 7) operation, IBM added the *Resource Definition Online* (RDO) feature to CICS. RDO allows changes to CICS tables to be made dynamically while CICS is still in operation. RDO changes take effect immediately.

Also, to support 24 × 7 operation and to accommodate frequent network changes, CICS supports a terminal *Autoinstall* feature. This feature elimi-nates the need to define all possible terminals in the static CICS TCT. When a VTAM message arrives from a new terminal, CICS dynamically creates a new TCT entry for the terminal.

CICS Operation

The CICS Master Terminal program can also be used to monitor the status of CICS and the resources that it manages. The command CEMT INQUIRE, for example, has many options to display the status of resources, such as the number of active tasks, status of open files, program use counts, and the state of program storage. The operator can also enable or disable these resources using other CEMT commands.

If you are interested in knowing more about CICS application programming, you should read the IBM "CICS Reference Guide SC33-0077."

Database Management

OS/390 supports *database management systems* (DBMS) in both batch and transaction-processing mode. IBM provides two DBMS products: the legacy hierarchical *Information Management System* (IMS) and the newer relational DB/2. Other vendors also offer DBMS that work under OS/390. IBM's DBMS are the most popular products used today. Computer Associates' IDMS DBMS is also still quite popular. Other companies, such as Oracle and Software AG, also sell DBMS for OS/390.

All these DBMS products support the ACID model and two-phase commit protocol that was previously discussed. When used in conjunction with CICS, they are also protected by CICS recovery/restart. When they are accessed from a batch program, they use similar recovery capabilities built in to the DBMS itself.

The Windows 2000 section of this chapter talks about Microsoft's *Open Database Connectivity* (ODBC) Architecture, which defines a common interface for access to databases from Windows applications. For now, you should be aware that there are also ODBC drivers for mainframe databases such as DB/2 and IDMS. This makes it possible to use mainframes as servers in a Windows 2000-distributed application architecture.

For more information on specific DBMS, you should consult the documentation provided by the vendor of your particular DBMS.

Messaging and IBM MQSeries

As discussed earlier in this chapter, CICS provides rudimentary message-queuing facilities that support the development of transaction-processing applications. In building CICS (and other) applications, it is often useful to have one program send a message to another program. The rules of ACID transactions discussed earlier require that the delivery of the message be guaranteed, in that the sender can assume that the transaction is complete (even if it has not yet been processed by the recipient).

Over the past few years, a number of middleware products that allow applications to pass messages between each other with just such a guarantee of delivery have evolved. These products can be specific to a single vendor, such as Microsoft's MSMQ product that is discussed in the Windows 2000 part of this chapter. Other products can be more generalized cross-platform products. For deferred message processing involving OS/390 and other vendors' platforms, the industry leader is IBM's *MQSeries message-oriented middleware* (MOM).

MOM and RPC

There are two kinds of middleware products: message-oriented middleware (MOM) and Remote Procedure Call (RPC) middleware; and, because they are used for quite different purposes, it is important not to confuse the two.

RPC middleware is transactional in nature and normally synchronous. When a program issues an RPC call, it usually waits for a response before proceeding. This means that RPC middleware must operate quickly to satisfy the three- to five-second interactive response-time requirements.

MOM, on the other hand, is used for more loosely coupled situations. It does not usually provide a synchronous response. Instead ,it is used to send data to another program and guarantee the delivery of that data to the remote program.

Examples of MOM include IBM's MQSeries and Microsoft's Microsoft Message Queuing (MSMQ) products. An example of an RPC middleware product for OS/390 is the Application-to-Application Interface (AAI) from MicroFocus/ Merant and DCOM from Microsoft. Many middleware products are also available on multiple platforms. ◆

Conceptually, what MQSeries does for application messaging is quite simple. Each system that supports MQSeries runs a local queue manager program called an agent. Programs in the local system post messages to other destinations by issuing an MQPUT procedure call. The local agent stores the message in the local queue. The local agent then forwards the message to the agent on the remote system, where it is stored in that system's local queue. At the remote system, the receiving application issues an MGET procedure call to retrieve the message from the local queue. Because message delivery is guaranteed, the sending system can assume that the message will be delivered and can commit other resources that are part of the transaction, even before the receiving application processes the message.

To find out more about IBM's MQSeries, you can read the IBM publication "MQSeries: An Introduction to Messaging and Queuing" (GC33-0805).

Windows 2000 Transaction, Database, and Message Processing

This section covers the Windows 2000 equivalents for transaction, database, and message processing. In the Windows 2000 world, client/ server applications have been implemented with both client/server and intranet architectures. Although client/server is the "legacy" architecture of the Windows world, it currently seems to be losing ground to the intranet style of architecture. The intranet architecture uses Internet-style products (such as Web browsers and Web servers) to implement a private company intranet.

This section discusses a set of technologies built around Microsoft *Active Server Pages* (ASP). ASP is currently being used to develop a large number of intranet-style, transaction-processing applications. As a result, it is the nearest thing in the Microsoft world comparable to CICS.

Application Architecture

Distributed information systems can be built using a monolithic design or using a layered multitier model. (Note that this parallels the development of early communications software prior to the introduction of layered models such as the OSI, SNA, and TCP/IP models that were discussed in Chapter 14). One quite useful technique is to partition an application into layers. As discussed in the preceding chapter, CICS primarily supports a two-layer architecture with CICS running on the host supporting dumb terminals. The intranet architecture, on the other hand, normally uses a three-layer approach.

These layers are as follows:

- User Interface
- Business Objects
- Data Access

User Interface Layer

The User Interface layer (UI) corresponds loosely to the presentation layer of the OSI model (see Chapter 14). It is where all formatting of human-readable data should be done. It should not contain any business logic because that should be relegated to the Business Object layer. (Simple local field validations are an exception to this rule. They may exist in the UI layer to provide a responsive error-correction interface to the user.) The UI should also not normally contain any database access logic. All database access should be done from the Business Object layer.

Business Object Layer

Business objects typically contain all the business rules and calculations of an application. The may also contain code to perform any necessary database accesses needed to execute these business rules and return data to the UI layer. Business objects are typically invoked from the UI layer. In a fat-client, client/server application implementation, the User Interface and Business Object layers can reside on the same computer. In a thin-client, intranet-style implementation, the Business objects typically run on a separate system, such as a Web server.

Data Access Layer

The Data Access layer provides access to databases, files, and other persistent resources. In the case of a relational database (such as SQL Server or DB/2), this means using SQL queries. In the case of a file, it means using an API provided by the local programming environment.

The Data Access layer is normally located on a separate computer so that it can be close to the data that it is accessing for maximum performance. (In fact, it is often implemented in the form of stored procedures that execute under the database management system itself.

Two-Layer Windows 2000 Applications

Windows 2000 also supports a purely two-layer nondistributed approach to applications using the Terminal Server option of Windows 2000. The Windows 2000 Terminal Server option runs all applications on the server, and just remotes the GUI interface to a client system. In this respect, it is a lot like remote-control software such as pcAnywhere and Remotely Possible. In addition to remoting the interface, it also allows each remote client to run applications in its own session as if it has exclusive use of the machine. Note that this is a lot like the environment provided by TSO under OS/390. As a result, it is better suited for running applications such as Word or Excel, as opposed to the type of transaction-processing applications considered in this chapter.

The advantage of this technique is that client workstations do not have to be powerful enough to run Windows 2000 Professional by themselves. For instance, these could be legacy 386 and 486 PCs. A number of devices on the market, called Windows terminals, run only the software and/or ROM-based microcode necessary for them to boot up and connect to Terminal Server.

Because this feature of Windows 2000 is not in widespread use at this time, this book does not cover it in detail. If you want to know more about this feature, you can read Windows NT Thin Client Solutions: Implementing Terminal Server and Citrix MetaFrame, by Mathers and Genoway, Macmillan Technical Publishing, ISBN: 1-5787-0065-5. ◆

Windows 2000 Intranet Implementation

The Windows 2000 implementation of the three-layer architecture presented in this book uses a set of Microsoft products and technologies that have been integrated into Windows 2000. These products form the basis for widespread development of intranet and Internet applications. They are as follows:

- Internet Explorer
- Internet Information Server
- Active Server Pages
- ActiveX Business objects
- Microsoft Transaction Server
- Microsoft Message-Queuing System

Internet Explorer

Microsoft's *Internet Explorer* (IE) is one of the two most popular Web browsers in use today. (The other one is Netscape.) IE is free with Windows 2000 and other Microsoft operating systems

If you use a single Web browser in an intranet application, you can make use of browser-specific features of your chosen browser, such as Style Sheets, to achieve finer control of your application presentation. If not, you have to use a dumbed-down subset of features supported by all the browser types that you need to support. This chapter assumes that you are building an intranet application, and that you can standardize on IE; however, the information here is generally applicable to other Web browsers as well.

A Web browser provides the *user interface* (UI) of an intranet application. It runs a software engine that can receive, interpret, and display datastreams containing data encoded in the *Hypertext Markup Language* (HTML). One way to look at these datastreams is to compare the HTML datastream with the 3270 datastream that were discussed in Chapter 14. You will remember that the 3270 datastream contains data and instructions on how to display the data. This includes commands and orders that define fields in the data as protected, high intensity, and so on. HTML uses a predefined tag language to perform a similar function. In HTML, these tags are surrounded by delimiters with the format <tag> and </tag> to indicate the beginning and end of an HTML tag. (There is an example of this later in this chapter.)

An HTML document begins and ends with <HTML> and </HTML> tags. Every HTML document has a heading section bracketed with <HEAD> and </HEAD> tags. The heading section normally contains a title set off by <TITLE> and </TITLE> tags.

Following the heading, there is a body section delimited by <BODY> and </BODY> tags that define the actual content of the page. In the body, the programmer can define tables, image references, line breaks, and many other HTML constructs. They can also code ASP scripting statements, as shown in the example later in this chapter.

HTML is a big subject and beyond the scope of this book. If you want to know more about HTML, you can read *Raggett on HTML 4* by Dave Raggett, Addison Wesley Publishing Company, ISBN: 0-2011-7805-2.

Unlike the IBM 3270 terminal, the Web browser can also execute local scripts and small programs sent to it from the Web server. Scripts can take the form of statements in VBScript or JavaScript. These programs can be in the form of downloaded objects such as ActiveX components and/or Java applets. (The next section shows that objects and scripts can also be run on the Web server. This can be used to tailor the page presentation before it even reaches the browser.)

Migrating from 3270 Applications

Normally, a company will still have existing legacy CICS 3270 applications in production while it is implementing new intranet applications or converting the legacy applications to Windows 2000. Many vendors, such as Wall Data and Attachmate, make 3270 emulators that are used to provide a standard 3270 window on the client desktop. These windows can coexist with newer intranet applications running in a browser on the same desktop.

Some of these products just display a standard 3270 "green screen" character-mode window on the desktop. Some of them provide a pseudo-GUI user interface by translating 3270 datastreams into GUI objects such as windows, list boxes, and dialog boxes. Some of them also include a 3270 control, which can be used in an intranet application to provide more integrated 3270 access. Others, such as Wall Data's Rumba and Attachmate's Extra!, provide an ActiveX automation model, so that scripts in the Web page can even be used to create one or more 3270 windows dynamically inside the browser window. As you can see, there are lots of migration possibilities. ◆

The HTML datastream is carried to the browser by the HTTP protocol. This is a higher-level protocol carried over TCP/IP (see Chapter 14). HTTP is a *stateless* protocol. When a browser requests a Web page, the Web server sends it the page and then breaks the connection with the browser. When the user requests the next page, the Web browser considers this a brand-new request. This statelessness means that a Web server application must find a place to save any working storage data that must exist across these boundaries. The stateless nature of HTTP makes programming a Web application a lot like programming a pseudo-conversational CICS application, as was discussed in the OS/390 part of this chapter. (The next section shows how ASP provides features analogous to those provided by CICS to perform this function.)

Normal Web pages are stored on the server as files with a file extension of .HTML or .HTM. (Microsoft's Web servers generally use .HTM, so that is what is used in the rest of this chapter.) When the browser receives a page of this type, it knows to render it as HTML. It can also receive other object types from the Web server. For instance, images and links to other documents can be embedded in a Web page. When the browser encounters one of these objects, it knows to make additional requests to the Web server for the object, so that it can add it to the page. If it receives an .IMG file, for example, it knows to fetch and render this as an image on the page.

Pages ending in .ASP can also be requested from the Web server. These requests are for Active Server Pages, which are to be interpreted by the Web server and the result sent to the browser as HTML pages.

Internet Information Server

Internet Information Server (IIS) is a complete Web server that comes bundled with all Windows 2000 Server versions. (A less full-featured version of IIS, called *Personal Web Server,* comes with Windows 2000 Professional. It is mainly useful with Web application development.) IIS handles the server side of the HTTP protocol. It accepts a browser connection request, sends the requested objects to the browser, and then breaks the connection.

Active Server Pages

As indicated earlier, browser requests can be for Web pages that end in .HTM, .HTML, or .ASP. As part of satisfying the request, IIS can also invoke one or more scripting engines that it can use to interpret scripting code embedded in the Web pages that end with an .ASP extension. The standard scripting engines provided with IIS are VBScript and JavaScript. When the browser requests a page ending in .ASP, the Web server scans the page for code surrounded by <% and %> delimiters. The Web server interprets the ASP code contained within these tags, and can perform processing logic or even do database access to add additional HTML data to the page before it is transmitted to the browser. It then sends the completed page to the browser.

The following example illustrates a simplified ASP implementation of the record retrieval and display application that was used in the CICS section of this chapter.

Browser requests normally take the form of a *universal resource locator* (URL) string. A URL starts with //http (which identifies the request as an http request). Following that, it specifies the Web site and page to be retrieved. It can also include optional input data to be received by the Web page.

The URL might look like this, for example:

```
//http: webserver.whzco.com/INQY.asp?recordkey=23718
```

In this URL, the Web site is `webserver.whzco.com`. The page to be retrieved and interpreted by ASP is INQY.asp (INQY in this request is analogous to the INQY Transid used in our CICS example.) The data following the question mark (?) in the URL is a keywork=value pair that defines the key of the record to be retrieved.

When IIS receives this request, it retrieves the .ASP page, processes it (as discussed later), and sends it to the browser. (In the following example, the line numbers are for reference.)

Example:

```
 1   <HTML>
 2   <HEAD>
 3      <TITLE>Record Display Application</TITLE>
 4   </HEAD>
 5
 6   <BODY>
 7   <%
 8    set VBObject=Server.CreateObject(Whzco.OEApplicaton)
 9    key= Request.Querystring("recordkey")
10    record=VBObject.GetRec(key)
11   %>
12 For the key <%=key%> the data record is: <%=record%>
13 </BODY>
14
15 </HTML>
```

This page is interpreted as follows:

Lines 1 to 4 define the start of the page and its title. Line 6 indicates the beginning of the body of the Web page.

Lines 7 through 11 define a block of ASP code written in VBScript, the default ASP scripting language. These lines will be interpreted by the ASP scripting engine, and will result in data being added to the ASP page.

Line 8 creates an instance of an ActiveX Business object that I previously developed in Visual Basic. (I use Visual Basic and VBScript for all the examples in this book because Visual Basic is the most popular programming language for developing Windows 2000 applications. I like to think of it as the "COBOL" of Windows 2000.) This object takes a record key as an input argument and returns a record from the Customer file, just as it did in our CICS example. After you create an object such as this in an ASP page and set it equal to a variable, you can call functions in the object using the name of the variable and the name of a function in the object, as shown in line 10.

Line 9 uses the ASP built-in Request object to retrieve the data following the question mark in the input request. When the keyword "key" is specified, the associated value 23718 is returned and placed in the variable *recordkey*.

Line 10 invokes the GetRec function in the ActiveX Business object and places the result in the variable *record*.

Line 11 marks the end of the open block of ASP code, so the following line is just sent to the browser as normal HTML. Note, however, that two small snippets of ASP code are buried in this line (`<%=key%>` and `<%=record%>`). In an ASP assignment, if there is no variable on the left side of the assignment statement, the result of evaluating the expression is to emit the result into the generated HTML page. This causes the text line to include the key and record values in the page. It might look like this, for instance:

```
For the key 23718 the data record is: Jones 125 Elm Street Boston Mass
```

Naturally, a real Web page would be prettied up with graphics, tables, and other formatting to give a pleasing presentation. I have tried to keep this example as simple as possible to concentrate on the basics. It is interesting, however, to contrast the role of basic mapping support used under CICS with the HTML data tags used to format a pretty Web page.

Managing ASP State

As explained earlier, HTTP is a stateless protocol. This makes developing ASP applications similar to developing pseudo-conversational CICS applications.

After the page is interpreted, it is sent to the browser, and the Web server breaks the connection. Note that if the next input request from the browser were to be a continuation of a transaction (for instance, an update to the retrieved record), some temporary data (such as the record key and data) would have to be preserved across this disconnect boundary. This is very much like the situation in programming pseudo-conversational CICS applications. The data must be preserved somewhere. ASP provides a *Session* object that can be used to store data across a connection boundary, much as CICS temporary storage was used to preserve data earlier in this chapter. Data, such as the record key, could have been preserved with a statement of the following form:

```
<%Session("SavedKey")=key %>
```

It could then be retrieved later with an expression of the following form:

```
<% NextKey=Session("SavedKey") %>
```

The former saves the current value of the variable key. The latter retrieves it by name and stores it into the *Nextkey* variable.

ASP Database Access

ASP also supports direct access to databases and files to satisfy processing requests. In general, however, you should not use database access requests directly from ASP. It is much better to do your database access from a Business object that you call from ASP.

Useful Built-in ASP Objects

In addition to the Session and Response objects, ASP also includes several other useful objects. Additional objects can be acquired from third parties and/or developed by yourself in Visual Basic, C++, or any other language that supports the development of ActiveX components.

Some of the other objects that ASP comes with include the following:

- The Response object provides an alternative way to emit HTML code into a generated page. For instance, you could have coded the result line in the example, as follows:

```
<% Response.write("For the key: ") %>
<% Response.writeA(key) %>
<% Response.write("the data record is: " %>
<% Response.write(record) %>
```

- The Application object is similar to the session object; however, it can be used to preserve data that needs to be shared by all sessions.

- The FileSystem object is used to provide basic access to local Windows 2000 files.

Many other useful objects are included with ASP and, in fact, many more features are also provided by the objects that have been discussed in this section. Many third-party ASP-callable components are available from Microsoft and other third parties free, or for a nominal cost. For an excellent introduction to ASP, you can read *Beginning Active Server Pages 2.0*, by Brian Frances, Wrox Press, ISBN: 1-8610-0134-7.

ActiveX Business Objects

Chapter 9 discussed ActiveX Business objects. That chapter covered the use of built-in ActiveX objects that enabled you to access Windows 2000 resources from the Windows Scripting Host.

As you will recall from that chapter, there are ActiveX servers and ActiveX clients. An ActiveX client can use the internal resources of an ActiveX server by setting and retrieving its *properties* and by calling *methods* that it supports internally. ActiveX objects can be used to encapsulate business logic so that it can be shared by multiple clients.

When you build applications to run in a Windows 2000 distributed processing architecture, you are not restricted to using only the ActiveX components provided by Microsoft. You can buy ActiveX components from third-party vendors or develop them yourself using a language such as Visual Basic or C++. In the case of internal application development, you will most likely use ActiveX components to encapsulate the business rules that were covered in the discussion of the layered Windows 2000 application model. Because these applications hold only business logic and include no user interface, they can be written to be used by both client/server and intranet/Internet user interfaces. (An excellent treatment of how to do this is described in *Professional Visual Basic 6 Business Objects*, by Rockford Lhotka, Wrox Press, ISBN: 1-861000-43-X.)

You can find out more about programming ActiveX component by reading *Developing COM/ActiveX Components in Visual Basic 6*, by Dan Appleman, SAMS, ISBN:1-5627-6576-0.

Microsoft Transaction Server

CICS, which was discussed in the opening part of this chapter, provides a large number of services to support transaction-processing applications. CICS manages the shared use of application programs. It also provides services to define and control the update of multiple resources so that a transaction can adhere to the ACID model. In the Windows 2000 world, these two services are provided by a component of Windows 2000 that was previously named the *Microsoft Transaction Server* (MTS). These services have been integrated into the COM+ components of Windows 2000. (Out of familiarity, we will continue to call it MTS in this chapter.)

MTS provides two functions:

- Brokering ActiveX objects
- Coordinating transactions

Brokering ActiveX Objects

As discussed earlier in this chapter, CICS loads and shares a single copy of an application program for all concurrent transactions that need to use it. In modern terminology, CICS is acting as a program *broker* for requesting clients.

In Windows 2000, programs acting as servers to remote clients are normally written as ActiveX components. Normally, they are running on a Web server or an application server located remotely. The Windows 2000 *Component Object Model* (COM+) supports the loading and sharing of multiple copies of a component, so that a small number of copies of the component can satisfy a large number of users. In keeping with the terminology used earlier, this is acting as an *object request broker* (ORB).

The MTS service of Windows 2000 handles the loading and sharing of these components. In Windows 2000, the MTS service creates a pool of objects as they are requested. Then, it allocates objects from this pool instead of creating new objects for each new incoming request. (Note that Windows NT did not handle the pooling of objects. This feature was added in Windows 2000.) This object pooling is designed to make use of just-in-time activation and early deactivation of objects to maximize performance.

Coordinating Transactions

The second function that MTS provides is to coordinate the execution of transactions implemented by distributed components. The *Distributed Transaction Coordinator* in MTS provides ACID transaction integrity, just as CICS recovery/restart does. By running transactions under MTS, different components at different locations can update resources, so that all updates occur successfully or the results of partial updates at all locations are backed out.

To make use of MTS components that execute as part of a distributed application, their components must be installed as part of an MTS *package*. They must also issue API calls to indicate whether they are part of an MTS transaction. For instance, a component can be marked as follows:

- *Requires a transaction*—A component that requires a transaction is created within the context of a transaction started by the object's creator. Then, it runs within the scope of an existing transaction. If there is no transaction currently in effect, a new one will be created.

- *Requires a new transaction*—A component that is marked as "requires a new transaction" forces the creation of a new transaction when the object is invoked.

- *Supports transaction*—Indicating that a component supports a transaction depends on the context of the creator. If a transaction already exists, the component is enlisted in the current transaction. If not, no new transaction is created.

- *Doesn't support transactions*—A component that "doesn't support transactions" will not take part in any transaction.

By defining transaction participation in this way, programmers have a lot of flexibility in how they use components that take part in transactions. When multiple objects are required, the sum total of transaction specifications is considered. Unlike CICS, MTS transactions can be nested within each other. (In CICS, the level 0 program in a transaction normally defines the start and end of a CICS transaction.)

Controlling Transactions
Components that run under MTS, should notify MTS when the results of their processing can be committed. API verbs are used to indicate that a transaction is starting and when it is ending. At the end of a transaction, the application can indicate whether the results of its processing should be committed or rolled back. In addition, if the transaction fails for any reason, the partial results of the transaction will be automatically rolled back.

As soon as the application reaches a state where the results of its processing can be committed, it should issue the SetComplete API call. (Although this will be done automatically at the end of the component's processing, it should be done as soon as possible to allow MTS to reuse the component as quickly as possible.) This is analogous to the SYNCPOINT command in CICS.

If the component determines that it should not commit any changes that it has made to resources, it can issue the SetAbort API call. MTS will supervise the automatic reversal of its partially completed updates. This is analogous to the SYNCPOINT ROLLBACK command in a CICS application.

Database Management
Windows 2000 supports DBMS from Microsoft and other third-party vendors. Microsoft's Premier transaction-processing DBMS is SQL Server. SQL Server comes bundled with the Microsoft BackOffice suite of applications. (BackOffice also contains many other useful products, including SNA Server, which is discussed in Chapter 17, "Integrating with Legacy Mainframe Applications and Data"). SQL Server runs only on Windows 2000.

Companies such as IBM, Oracle, and Sybase also sell DBMS software to run on Windows 2000. Because these vendors also sell products to run on other platforms, they can form the basis for multiplatform application solutions. A natural interoperability design might involve building a distributed database application with IBM's DB/2 on the mainframe and the Windows 2000 version of DB/2 on a database server. Microsoft itself also provides a SQL Server–to–DB/2 replication product that can be used to keep distributed databases synchronized.

All these DBMS products work with Windows 2000 to support the ACID model and two-phase commit protocol. They are also protected by MTS distributed transaction coordination and two-phase commit support.

To support a wide range of DBMS, Microsoft supports a general DBMS interface model: *Open Database Connectivity* (ODBC). ODBC provides a standard interface for accessing relational and nonrelational databases and files under Windows 2000. Although it is a Microsoft-developed standard, it has been adopted by many other vendors. It provides a generic vendor-neutral API based on the X/Open standard SQL Call Interface. Use of this common interface insulates applications from differences due to different underlying databases and changes in the underlying database structure.

In addition to the ODBC driver for DBMS running on Windows platforms, there are also ODBC drivers for mainframe databases such as DB/2 and IDMS. This makes it possible to use mainframes as big database servers in a Windows 2000 distributed application architecture.

ODBC Driver Differences

As with any "standard," there can be differences in how the standard is implemented. Not all ODBC drivers for all DBMS implement all the possible features defined in the ODBC standard. In practice, this makes for minor differences when writing programs that access different vendors' DBMS products using ODBC. In particular, the database connection string used to establish a connection to an ODBC database often has a slightly different format, depending on whether the database is Oracle or SQL Server. In addition, some DBMS support data types and navigation methods are not supported by other database types.

ODBC defines a layered model. The client application accesses the database via an industry-standard SQL call interface. This request is passed to a driver manager that loads the appropriate ODBC-compliant database driver (because multiple database types may be accessed in the same application). The loaded database driver, in turn, executes the application request, performing any request and response translation required by the underlying database.

Again, for more information on specific DBMS, you should consult the documentation provided by the vendor of your particular DBMS.

One of the useful features of the ODBC standard is that it supports database connection pooling. Opening a connection to an ODBC database involved a degree of processing overhead. Connection pooling improves the performance of applications by keeping a pool of resources allocated and available to satisfy application requests. ◆

Microsoft Message Queuing System

Like IBM's MQSeries, *Microsoft Message-Queuing System* (MSMQ) is message-oriented middleware that can be used to pass messages between application components with guaranteed delivery. MSMQ provides an administrative MMC snap-in that can be used to define message queues, as well as ActiveX (COM) objects to locate queues, and send and receive queued messages.

MSMQ COM objects are provided and can be invoked from Visual Basic and C++ programs. Functional APIs can be invoked from C programs. Using either of these approaches, applications can locate a named message queue, open the queue, send a message, check for and receive messages, and close the queue.

Unlike MQSeries, MSMQ runs only on Microsoft platforms. However, third-party products provide interfaces between MSMQ and MQSeries. The Level 8 Falcon MSMQ-MQSeries bridge is currently included with Microsoft's SNA Server product. This bridge allows integration of MSMQ with MQSeries on different platforms such as OS/390 and the AS/400. Level 8 also makes products that can tie MSMQ to messaging systems on other platforms such as UNIX, Tandem, Compaq/Digital VMS, and Unisys.

There is another major difference between MQSeries and MSMQ. MQSeries is quite expensive, costing thousands of dollars. MSMQ is built into Windows 2000 and is effectively free!

CICS/NT

As indicated in the OS/390 part of this chapter, CICS is available on a wide variety of platforms. One of these platforms is Windows NT. Because Windows 2000 is the successor to Windows NT, I expect IBM to provide a version for Windows 2000 by the time that you read this. This provides an interesting and useful vehicle for interoperability. Because CICS has always supported distributed transaction processing via its Distributed Program Link feature, you can build distributed applications that include mainframe and Windows NT processing components running under CICS. In fact, IBM has recently added features to CICS to allow Internet and intranet applications to be built with CICS as well.

Bridging DCOM and CORBA

The Windows 2000 part of this chapter has concentrated on Microsoft technologies. Most of these technologies fall under the general heading of Microsoft's *Distributed Component Object Model* (COM+). You should be aware that there is a competing standard, the Common Object Request

Broker model (CORBA). These two models are different and do not inter-operate with each other directly. Bridges are available, however, from companies such as Iona; these bridges can be used to interconnect DCOM and CORBA applications.

This chapter has covered transaction, database, and message-processing alternatives for building applications under OS/390 and Windows 2000. The following chapter covers the way Windows 2000 systems can communicate with OS/390. This includes using Windows 2000 systems to emulate mainframe terminals and transfer files between Windows 2000 and OS/390. The following chapter also discusses Microsoft's SNA Server SNA gateway, the premier product used to interconnect Windows systems with IBM mainframes.

16

Communicating with OS/390

The original proponents of client/server computing fully expected mainframes to go the way of the dinosaur. Instead, mainframe computing is more widespread than ever. What companies have today is a major need to interconnect mainframes with other types of computer systems and provide infrastructures that support the interoperation of these systems. This chapter is dedicated to that need.

A wide variety of methods are used to communicate between a Windows 2000 system and an OS/390 system. This chapter describes the use of the following:

- Terminal emulation
- File transfer
- SNA gateways

Because this chapter focuses on communications between Windows 2000 and OS/390, it does not cover the use of mainframe-based Web servers. You should be aware, however, that OS/390 does support the Lotus Domino Web Server that can be used to build e-commerce applications on mainframes.

Terminal Emulation

Perhaps the simplest and most pervasive way to use Windows 2000 systems to communicate with mainframes is 3270 terminal emulation. Since the 1980s, many products such as Wall Data's Rumba and Attachmate's Extra! have been used to turn an x85 system into a substitute for an IBM 3270 terminal. In addition, these emulator packages also provide file transfer capabilities and often provide additional services, as discussed in the following section.

Emulator Types

There are two basic types of terminal emulators. The oldest type runs completely on the workstation and adds a full SNA protocol stack to the operating system (see Chapter 14, "Networking"). This form of emulator communicates directly with the host or a *front-end processor* (FEP) over a LAN or WAN connection.

The second type of emulator uses an SNA gateway system (such as Microsoft's SNA Server) to implement a host connection. Typically, these emulators place only part of the SNA protocol stack on the workstation and the rest on the gateway system. Normally, these "light" emulators use TCP/IP or a proprietary protocol to communicate from the client to the gateway and do the actual conversion to the SNA protocol on the gateway.

The SNA Protocol Stack Revisited

As discussed in Chapter 14, the layers of the SNA model are as follows:

- Application
- Presentation
- Data flow control
- Transmission control
- Path control
- Data link control

All emulators provide at least the top two layers. "Thin client" emulators that work with SNA gateways normally relocate the lower layers to a gateway system that sits between the clients and the host. Clients communicate with the gateway using a non-SNA protocol (such as TCP/IP) or a proprietary protocol.

The following section discusses the features of a typical "fat client" emulator, Rumba. Rumba is one of the two most popular terminal-emulator packages in use today. (The other one is Extra!.) This section uses Rumba to explain terminal emulation and file transfer between a PC running Windows 2000 and an OS/390 system.

3270 Emulation

Terminal-emulation packages essentially turn your Windows 2000 system into a glorified 3270 terminal, capable of providing one or more 3270 terminal windows into your mainframe.

Figure 16.1 shows a typical 3270 window, as displayed by Rumba 95/NT. If this figure were in color, you would see that Rumba displays protected, unprotected, normal, and high-intensity fields in different colors. (The default text color of purple on black is not very clear on most monitors. Fortunately, you can select your own color scheme easily.)

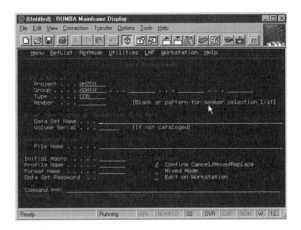

Figure 16.1 *3270 emulator terminal window.*

Rumba provides a menu bar and an icon bar for common functions. The Status area at the bottom of the screen also shows session status just as the *Operator Information Display* (OID) area does on a real 3270 display.

File Transfer

Most commercial terminal emulators can also transfer files from the workstation to the mainframe and from the mainframe to the workstation. The type of file transfer service provided depends on whether the file being transferred is text or binary data. The type of file is specified in the file transfer dialog box of the emulator.

When a text file is transferred to or from the host, it must be converted to or from ASII and EBCDIC. Text-line delimiters will also have to be converted from the PC convention to the mainframe convention.

File transfer from a workstation to an IBM mainframe requires software at both ends. Originally, PC file transfer involved the execution of a SEND or RECEIVE command at the PC. The program executed by this command handled the PC end of the file transfer protocol. The mainframe end of the process was normally supported under TSO by the IND$FILE program. (There is also a component of CICS that supports file transfers to a CICS system.) Although the PC end of the protocol has been absorbed into the emulator products that provide this feature, IND$FILE is still used on the TSO side for file transfer. IND$FILE is normally invoked from a bare TSO screen or from the TSO command panel of SPF.

When a binary file is transmitted, no data conversion is performed. The file is just transferred intact.

Selecting *Transfer* from the display window brings up the Copy From PC To TSO Host dialog box (see Figure 16.2).

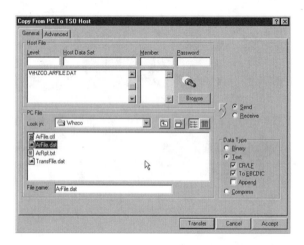

Figure 16.2 *Rumba file transfer.*

This dialog box has two pages: *General* for the most commonly used options, and *Advanced* for less commonly used ones.

The General page lists both the files in the current Windows directory and the files cataloged under the user's ID on the mainframe. To transfer a file, you just need to select a local file to transmit and select a mainframe file to receive the data. (The Advanced page has parameters that enable you to allocate a new mainframe dataset to receive the uploaded data. My experience, however, has shown that it is better to upload data to a pre-allocated file on the mainframe.)

Also, note that you must specify the data type (binary or text). For text files, you must also indicate the end-of-line conversion convention (CR/LF). You also need to specify whether ASCII data in the file is to be converted to EDCBIC during the transfer. If the host program (IND$FILE) can receive compressed data, you can specify that option as well. Rumba also enables you to write macros to automate file transfer.

IND$FILE has been around forever, and it is often used to transfer files between PCs and hosts. It is not terribly efficient because it runs under control of TSO, and TSO was designed to optimize interactive traffic and not bulk data transfer. Other third-party options, such as IND$FILE Plus from Proginet, are available. IND$FILE Plus uses a fast VTAM application rather than TSO on the host end. This avoids the overhead of passing the data through TSO.

SNA Gateways

On a LAN, a 3270 emulator is frequently used to connect a client directly to a remote SNA host. In many cases, however, an SNA gateway is used. This discussion covers the use of Microsoft's SNA Server Gateway product. This product is the centerpiece of Microsoft's *SNA Open Gateway Architecture* (SOGA). SNA Server is the most popular product used to provide SNA access from Windows systems. SNA Server is a component of Microsoft BackOffice. SNA Server consists of two components: client software that sits on the workstation and server software that resides on a server.

As discussed in Chapter 14, a mainframe-based SNA network is hierarchical in nature. In this architecture, SNA Server acts as a cluster controller (PU 2) node. As a cluster controller, it relieves attached workstations of the need to have a full SNA protocol stack installed on them.

This section focuses on SNA Server, and discusses how it can be used to support two of the most common client communication requirements— providing 3270 terminal emulation without having a full 3270 emulator on the client, and providing APPC communications between a program running on the client and one running on the host under CICS.

Hardware Requirements

SNA Server has quite modest hardware requirements. Microsoft recommends at least an Intel 80486 computer with at least 32MB RAM. Based on the complexity of your network and the services of SNA Server that you want to host on the box, 64MB or even 128MB would be better. (SNA Server has a lot of optional services that are discussed later in this chapter.)

Microsoft also recommends a minimum of 50MB of disk storage. Again, the actual amount of disk space that you will need depends on what you plan to run on the machine. In any case, this is a good use for those obsolete 486 and 100MHz Pentiums that you are replacing with newer, more powerful machines.

SNA Server also requires a method of communicating with remote clients and with the host computer. This could be a Token Ring or Ethernet LAN *network interface card* (NIC), a serial port or SDLC adapter and modem, an X.25 interface card, a DFT interface card, or a channel adapter. It also supports hardware that provides data-link switching, Frame Relay, *asynchronous transfer mode* (ATM), and fiber-optic connections.

In the case of an AS/400, it could also be a Twinax adapter. Although SNA Server also provides access to AS/400s, this book concentrates on mainframe access to System/390 hosts running OS/390. Therefore, this chapter ignores any AS/400 considerations.

Software Requirements

SNA Server 4.0 also requires at least Windows NT 4.0 with Service Pack 3. If you are running Windows NT 4.0, the Windows NT option pack is required for some SNA Server features.

It also requires that you have installed the appropriate networking protocol at the time that you installed Windows NT or Windows 2000. If you are going to use TCP/IP over a Token Ring network, for example, you must have installed TCP/IP and the DLC 802.2 network support in the base operating system.

SNA Server Functions

SNA Server provides the following functions:

- Terminal access
- File transfer
- Network printing
- Security integration
- Database integration
- Transaction integration
- Centralized or decentralized management and control
- Security

The remainder of this chapter discusses most of these features. First, however, a review of the software architecture of SNA Server is in order.

Software Architecture

SNA Server itself is built with a client/server architecture. There are two components to this architecture: the server software, which runs on the server to provide the SNA gateway functionality; and the client software, which runs on the client to provide client access to the host via the server (see Figure 16.3).

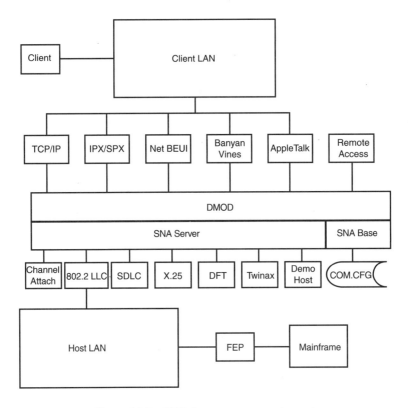

Figure 16.3 *SNA Server server component.*

SNA Server Server

The SNA Server server component consists primarily of the following components:

- SNASERVER
- SNABASE
- SNADMOD

SNASERVER runs as a service. It is the protocol conversion engine of SNA Server. It provides physical unit (PU) 2.0 and 2.1 node emulation on the server. It communicates with clients, other SNA Servers in the network, and the host computer (or FEP). It also provides information to allow SNA Manager to display real-time status of servers, links, connections, and LUs.

SNABASE also runs as a Windows 2000 service. It actually runs on both the client and the server, although it serves a slightly different purpose on each. On the server, it builds and broadcasts a service table containing a list of available SNA Server computers, links, and invokable *transaction programs* (TPs) that are available in the subdomain. (A subdomain is a collection of SNA Servers that share a common network configuration. See the section titled "Domains and Subdomains," later in this chapter.)

SNABASE responds to client connection requests by sending the list of available SNA Servers to the client when it connects with the server. (This connection is called a client-sponsor connection.) The configuration of all servers, connections, and LUs is maintained in a configuration file with the name COM.CFG. It is normally located in the \SNA\SYSTEM\CONFIG directory on the server.

After the initial connection, SNABASE is also used to tell the client where to find a specific LU or LU pool. If the request is for a specific LU, for example, the server can tell the client the name of the SNA Server that has that LU defined on it. If the request is for an LU from a pool, the server can tell the client the names of all the servers that own LUs in the pool. SNABASE uses the DMOD protocol provided by SNADMOD to send messages to other SNA Server components.

SNADMOD is a supporting DLL that provides the DMOD proprietary protocol used to communicate between SNA Server client and server components. DMOD uses the underlying client/server protocols to provide a proprietary *Remote Procedure Call* (RPC) service that supports multiple simultaneous links between components, can send and receive variable-sized messages, and is essentially non-blocking in nature. Although Figure 16.3 shows a whole range of possible client/server protocols, in general there would be only one protocol used to communicate between a given SNA Server and a given host. For purposes of the examples in this chapter, the SNA Server is located at the data center and it uses the 802.2 protocol to communicate with a FEP via a Token Ring attachment.

SNA Server Client

The client component of SNA Server runs on the client computer. It provides the APIs and the top layers of the SNA protocol stack on the client. It communicates with the SNA Server server, which performs the actual protocol conversion from the selected client/server protocol to SNA.

In Figure 16.4, the boxes at the top of the diagram represent all the various APIs and client-side interfaces provided on the client. Note that there are quite a few of them, and that some of them support AS/400 protocols such as CA/400 and 5250 terminal emulation. Others are common to both AS/400 and mainframe access. You should also note that some of these APIs make use of lower-level APIs, as shown in the diagram.

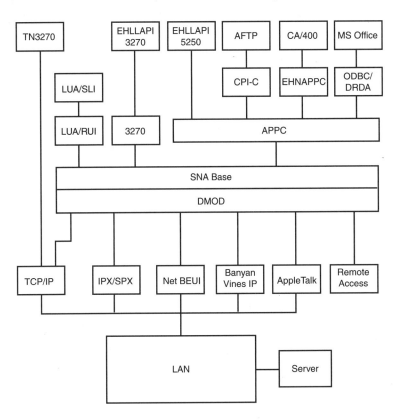

Figure 16.4 *SNA Server client component.*

In the interest of simplicity, this chapter concentrates on two of these client-side protocols: 3270 datastream and APPC. This discussion also assumes an 802.2 LAN connected to the FEP at the data center.

The SNA Server client uses the following components in addition to the API modules shown in Figure 16.5:

- SNABASE
- SNADMOD

SNABASE, which runs as a service on the client as well as on the server, is used at connect time to respond to requests for a sponsor server. After the initial connection, SNABASE is used by the client to request the location of a specific LU or an LU pool. If the request is for a specific LU, for example, the server can tell the client the name of the SNA Server that has that LU defined on it. If the request is for an LU from a pool of LUs, the server can tell the client the names of all the servers that own LUs in the pool. If the request is for an LU that is part of a pool of LUs defined across multiple servers, the client will try the servers in random order until it finds a free LU from the pool. (See the discussion of LU pools later in this section.) SNABASE on the client also uses the DMOD protocol provided by SNADMOD to communicate with SNABASE on servers.

As in the case of the server, **SNADMOD** is used to support the DMOD proprietary protocol used to communicate between the client and the server.

Domains and Subdomains

SNA servers are located in an SNA subdomain. SNA subdomains really have nothing to do with Windows 2000 domains (although an SNA Server is normally located in a Windows 2000 domain). An SNA Server subdomain is a collection of up to 15 SNA Servers that share a common network configuration file describing the SNA resources in the subdomain. Although you are limited to 15 SNA Servers in a subdomain, there can be any number of subdomains in a network. Normally, however, you need only to have more than one domain when you have different configuration files for different locations in your network. You may also want to set up separate subdomains for servers that are connected to a single LAN to keep interserver broadcast traffic from being transmitted to other servers across a WAN.

Server Roles

Configuration files are managed through the use of SNA Servers with specific roles in the subdomain. It is unfortunate that Microsoft chose to use the terms *primary, backup,* and *member* server to define the roles of SNA Servers because that causes confusion with Windows NT and Windows 2000 terminology.

In Windows NT, the primary domain controller manages the security database for the NT domain (see Chapter 13, "Security"). Backup domain controllers maintain a read-only copy of the security database to allow logons if the primary domain controller is down. Member servers just host resources. Windows 2000 simplified this model by eliminating the distinction between primary and backup domain controllers.

The machines on which SNA Server subdomain controllers are located do not have to be Windows 2000 domain controllers, although they could be. Often they will be dedicated systems. In small locations, however, they could be on the same system as one of the domain controllers (see the description of the branch deployment model, later in this chapter).

All SNA Servers can provide connectivity to network resources for clients. SNA Server roles define how SNA Servers maintain and manage the subdomain configuration files. These roles are Primary SNA Servers, Backup SNA Servers, and Member SNA Servers.

Primary SNA Server

The Primary SNA Server in a subdomain provides connectivity to clients in the subdomain. It contains the master copy of the configuration file COM.CFG. There can be only one Primary SNA Server in a subdomain (although a Backup can be promoted if the Primary fails). The first server installed in a subdomain should be defined as the Primary.

Backup SNA Servers

Backup SNA Servers contain a read-only copy of the configuration file. They can be promoted to Primary if the Primary fails. There can be a total of 14 Backup and Member Servers defined in a subdomain.

Member SNA Servers

Member SNA Servers do not contain a copy of the configuration file. There can be up to 14 Member Servers and Backups in a subdomain. Member Servers host SNA resources such as LUs.

Deployment Models

In addition to organizing SNA Servers in the subdomain, you must also choose a deployment model to use for your SNA Servers. These models are centralized, branch, and decentralized.

The Centralized Deployment Model

Traditionally, SNA gateway products were located at the data center. Data-center location provides the advantage that the gateway can be attached to the host directly via direct channel attachment or to an FEP via a high-speed circuit.

In this configuration, all the SNA Servers are located near the host, and can be pooled for load balancing and hot backup. Furthermore, they can be administered by local MIS personnel. A disadvantage of this model is that all the clients must connect to the SNA Servers over a WAN link. Because the SNA stack is split between the client and an SNA Server, there is generally more WAN traffic between the client and the SNA Server than there is between the SNA Server and the host.

Branch Deployment Model

In the branch deployment model, SNA Servers are located in close proximity to the clients that they support. The heavier traffic between the clients and the servers is concentrated on the LAN. WAN traffic between the SNA Server and the data center makes use of SNA protocols, which are generally more efficient than the protocols used to communicate between clients and SNA Servers. This can lead to better overall performance.

Another advantage of this deployment model is that the server can be administered locally by local administrators. (SNA Server can also be managed remotely, as discussed later in this chapter.) In addition, in a small location it can even run on a domain controller or host other services such as IIS or SQL Server. (In general, however, you will want to dedicate a computer to act as an SNA Server.)

One disadvantage of this model is that there is no high-speed connection from the SNA Server to the host. In addition, WAN routers must be smart enough to prioritize traffic over the WAN if the WAN link is also being used for other purposes.

Distributed Deployment Model

The distributed deployment model combines the best of both of the previous models at the expense of some setup and administrative complexity.

It has the advantage that the link between the centralized SNA Server (or server pool) and the host is fast because they can be on a LAN, FEP attached, or channel attached. The link between the remote clients and their local server (or local server pool) is fast because they can be connected via a local LAN. In this configuration, only concentrated server-to-server traffic travels over the WAN connection between sites using the SNA Server Distributed Link Service. SNA Server–to–SNA Server link traffic can be compressed and the data can also be encrypted for added security.

The disadvantage of this deployment model is that there are more SNA Servers to configure and administer. This is not a serious disadvantage, however, because they can be administered remotely from a central site.

Server Installation

SNA Servers are installed and configured in a two-step process. There is plenty of documentation on how to install SNA Server provided on the BackOffice CD. The *Getting Started* Help file on the CD is particularly useful. There is no need to repeat that information here. Instead, this section provides a logical explanation of the configuration process so that you can determine the proper configuration options to use in setting up SNA Server for the most common types of client-to-host communications.

The problem with most of the SNA Server documentation and the few chapters on SNA Server in books on BackOffice is that they tend to describe every setup case that could occur, together with all the possible parameters. SNA Server supports TCP/IP, IPX/SPX, Microsoft Networking (named pipes), Banyan VINES, and AppleTalk.

This chapter concentrates on setting up SNA Server to support two of the most common client protocol requirements: 3270 emulator host access, and APPC. This discussion assumes that the protocol used between clients and the servers is TCP/IP; and also assumes that the SNA Server is located at the host site, and that the link between the SNA Server and the host is a local 802.2 DLC link to the FEP. (This is the centralized deployment model.) It is also assumed that the SNA Servers at the data center control a pool of 3270 LUs and a dedicated LU 6.2 for each connection.

To define the end-to-end connection between LUs at the client and at the host, you must define links, connections, and LUs. (As discussed later in this chapter, you may also have to define other objects associated with these entities.) If you are not the VTAM systems programmer, you will have to get much of the information necessary to complete the configuration of SNA Server from him/her.

This chapter is not a step-by-step guide to configuring SNA Server because the documentation that comes with SNA Server handles that adequately. Instead, this chapter gives you an overview and explains some of the information that you need to specify.

Configuration

Completing the setup of your SNA Server network requires that you configure the server as well as your link services, connections, and LUs.

Server Configuration

You must provide a small amount of data to configure your overall server. This includes the name of the server, and its SNA network and control-point names. (The control-point name is often the same as the server name.) Many companies use a standard naming convention for server names, such as part of the machine's network adapter address. You should check with your local administrator about this. You can also get the network name from your VTAM systems programmer.

The next step in configuring SNA Server is to configure the communications path between the SNA Server and the host. This requires configuring the link services, connections, and LUs.

Link Services

As discussed earlier, the layer directly above the physical layer in the SNA layered model is the data link layer. The data link layer provides the lowest-level protocol that is used to communicate over an SNA network. In particular, it defines the interface between the software and the network adapter.

You must choose and configure the link services to be used for a given link during the configuration process. The data link protocol that you select must have been installed as part of the operating system network protocol installation. It is not installed during the installation of SNA Server. This link service corresponds to the protocol driver for the NIC. In this example, it would be the 802.2 DLC link service.

This takes care of the link from the server to the host. Had this discussion reviewed the actual installation of the client/server software, you would have seen that you specify the protocol used to communicate between the clients and the server at the time that you install the server and client software on the systems.

Assuming that you are configuring an 802.2 DLC connection, you will also have to know the connection name to use. You will also need to specify the remote end type as host system. In addition, you will need to assign a name to the link service and specify other assorted options.

Connections

After defining a link service, you have to configure a *connection* between the SNA Server and the host. A connection corresponds to an SNA PU. As such, the parameters specified for the connection define how communications flow between the PU and the host.

Again, you will have to get some information from your VTAM systems programmer because the information that you specify must match the information used to define your PU node in the VTAM tables. For the 3270 example, this information includes the following:

- Remote network address
- Remote SAP address
- Remote network name

- Remote control-point name
- Remote node ID
- Local network name
- Local control-point name
- Local node ID
- Type of compression
- XID type

When configuring an 802.2 connection, the remote network address is normally the full Token Ring or Ethernet (MAC) address of the FEP.

The remote node ID must agree with the IDBLK and IDNUM parameters in the VTAM PU definition.

The remote SAP address is normally 4, but again you should check with your VTAM systems programmer. The local SAP address is normally also 4.

Other parameters, such as maximum BTU length, as well as the various timeout values and retry limits, should be left at their default values initially.

Logical Units

After defining the link services and connections, you need to define the LUs that the clients will use to communicate with the host via SNA Server.

As stated earlier, LUs are the endpoints in the SNA network. The connection between two LUs is called a session. SNA Server can support up to 30,000 sessions per server. Sessions are created when host software introduces the two LUs to each other, and binds them together so that they can talk to each other using a common subset of a protocol that both endpoints can understand (see chapter 14).

SNA Server supports all the popular LU types used by SNA networks. The following sections show how to configure two types of LUs: LU 2 (3270) and LU 6.2 (APPC). Printer LUs are beyond the scope of this discussion. Be aware, however, that SNA Server can support host-to-workstation printing using LU types 1 and 3 (see Chapter 14).

LU 2 Configuration

LU 2 LUs can be configured individually or by using a base name and a range of numbers normally starting at 3. (LU number 2 is reserved.) The LU number must agree with the VTAM LOCADDR parameter for this LU.

You must also specify the LU name and the name of the connection that you specified when you configured it. (Leave the pool identifier blank. It will be used later to show whether the LU is part of a pool.)

You can also specify *Use Compression* if you know that the remote endpoint can support this feature.

LU 6.2 Configuration

Configuring LU 6.2 LUs is a little more complex than configuring 3270 LUs. Because of this, an APPC/LU 6.2 Mainframe Connection Wizard comes with SNA Server. It is located in the Tools menu in SNA Server Manager.

In addition to the data specified for 3270 LUs, you must specify a mode name to control the number of parallel sessions permitted between the two LUs and the maximum number of parallel sessions that you want this LU to support. (Normally, you will leave the rest of the LU 6.2 parameters at their default values.)

Add Users and Groups

After completing LU definitions, you have a bit of security housekeeping to take care of. SNA Server, like all other Windows 2000 services, is a participant in the Windows 2000 security model. SNA Server uses Windows 2000 users, groups, and access controls to permit or deny access to SNA Server services. Users and groups can be granted access rights to use specific resources such as LUs or LU pools.

All the information about the network configuration is stored in the network configuration file (`COM.CFG`). This file should be on an NTFS drive for maximum security. You can add users and groups and set permissions using the SNA Administrator, or you can use the `SNACFG` command-line program. Of course, the whole purpose of SNA Server is to connect clients to the host. The following sections cover the client side of SNA Server.

Client Configuration

After the server side of SNA Server is configured, you must install the client software on the clients. SNA Server supports a wide range of clients, such as Windows 2000, Windows NT, Windows 95, Windows 3.x, Windows for Workgroups, MS-DOS, Macintosh, and UNIX. It also supports Windows 98 clients if you have SNA Server Service Pack 2 applied.

The client software can be installed from the CD, a disk, or a network share. The client installation process looks like a subset of the server installation process.

SNA Server clients run an abbreviated protocol stack that communicates with the server over DMOD. (The lower layers of the protocol stack and the protocol conversion routines are located on the server.)

One of the things that you will want to install when you are installing the client software components is the 3270 applet. This applet can be used to test end-to-end connectivity with the host after everything is configured properly. (You may also want to install some of the other components, based on your requirements.) The 3270 applet is useful for performing these basic tests, but it is no substitute for a full-featured 3270 emulator such as Rumba or Extra!. For instance, it only supports one 3270 session to the host. Users in a mainframe environment normally need multiple 3270 sessions. For example, a developer may need one session to TSO and one to CICS. (Although mainframe-based multisession managers, such as Teleview from Computer Associates, can also be used to provide multiple sessions using one host connection.)

After installing the client components, you will be asked to specify the client/server protocols used to communicate between the client and the server. (This is TCP/IP in this example.)

Following this, you will be asked to specify how the client will locate a sponsor server (covered in the next section). You can specify that the client is to broadcast a request for a sponsor server list to the subdomain or that it is to request the list from a specific list of servers. In the example case, it is assumed that you have configured it to broadcast a request to the client's subdomain.

Client/Server/Host Operation

When an SNA Server client connects to the network, it broadcasts a request for a sponsor server. A client, such as Windows 2000 Professional, will then select a server at random from the replies. If this fails, other servers that replied will be tried. This provides a degree of fault tolerance controlled by the client.

After setting up a sponsor connection, the sponsor server will send the client a list of network resources such as other servers, LUs, and pools. During the operation, the list will be kept up to date by the sponsor server.

When a client application such as a 3270 emulator needs a connection to the host, it will need to locate an LU to use. At that time, the client will get the name of the server that hosts the individual LU or the name of the servers hosting the LU pool. Using an LU pool spread over multiple servers also provides fault tolerance and load balancing.

SNA Server Management

SNA Server management is performed using the SNA Manager MMC snap-in. (You can also perform SNA Server management from the command line using the SNACFG utility.) Any SNA Server can be controlled from any server or client that is subject to permissions and access controls.

Superimposed over the client/server architecture used to connect clients to the mainframe is another complete client/server management architecture. To keep this chapter from becoming too long, the features of this other architecture are just summarized here.

SNA Server uses a manager agent program (MngAgent) on the server and a client management program (MngCli) to implement this architecture. Management data is transferred between these two programs using the same DMOD protocol used by normal client/server operations. It also uses a set of queues on the client and server to buffer changes.

SNA Servers use this management architecture to trade information on network status changes. During operations, this includes server changes such as LU status changes, the addition of new users, and session status changes. These changes are then sent to the clients using this architecture.

The SNA Manager snap-in follows the standard Windows Explorer-like architecture that you have seen in other chapters. The left-hand pane shows a tree view of all the resources in the domain, including the following:

- SNA Server subdomain
- SNA Servers in the subdomain
- Print servers
- Shared folder servers (AS/400)
- TN3270 servers
- TN5250 servers (AS/400)
- LU pools
- Configured users
- APPC modes
- CPIC symbolic names
- Active users
- Host security domains

The right-hand pane shows icons representing the selected element in the tree. You can view and control the status of all network resources from this display.

To make changes to a resource, you normally right-click on the resource in the left or right pane, or use the menu bar in the window. This enables you to add new resources of a given type or to modify the configuration of an existing resource.

In addition to using the SNA Management snap-in, the administrator can give users read-only access to it so that they can also view the status of network resources.

In addition to the SNA Manager, a few other useful management tools are provided with SNA Server. The Windows 2000 Performance Manager (Perfmon) can also be used to monitor and tune SNA Server. When you install SNA Server on a system, the installation adds specific SNA Server performance counters to the operating system. These counters can be read by Perfmon.

SNA Server also includes software to interface with NetView on the mainframe. This enables a mainframe operator to run NetView commands on the SNA Server and to receive alerts from it. SNA Server also writes error information to the Windows 2000 application event log.

The command-line utility DLSSTAT can also be used to list the names of all remote connections, their remote adapter and SAP addresses, and their Token Ring source-routing information.

Fault Tolerance and Load Balancing

Load balancing distributes client connection requests across multiple servers and host connections in the subdomain. For instance, requests for LUs can be distributed across multiple servers. You can assign LUs or LU pools to individual users or groups. You can even assign specific LUs to workstations.

Fault tolerance is also provided in this architecture. When a resource such as a host connection fails, another resource can automatically take its place. Hot backup can be implemented across multiple connections on a single server or across multiple servers in a subdomain.

Distributed Link Service

The Distributed Link Service is used in the distributed deployment model to connect clients to the host via multiple SNA Servers. The two servers concentrate the connections, and you can use data compression for greater performance and encryption for security.

TN3270 and TN3270E

The full SNA client provides complete 3270 access, plus support for a large number of other protocols. If all you need is 3270 access, however, SNA Server provides a lightweight 3270 client protocol, TN3270. Not all 3270 features are supported by TN3270. It has some weaknesses, specifically in the area of supporting 3270 family printers. If you can live within its limitations, however, it does take less overhead than the full 3270 version.

TN3270 on the client uses Telnet on the client to communicate with Telnet and TN3270 on the server. These two components communicate with each other using the proprietary DMOD protocol supported by SNA Server. SNA Server also comes with an enhanced version of TN3270, TN3270E. This version has some display and printing enhancements.

PU Passthru Service

The PU Passthru service allows a downstream client, such as an IBM Communications Manager/2 (CM/2) system, to access host connections via SNA Server. This may be useful during a conversion from CM/2 to SNA Server. In the distributed deployment model, you can use SNA Server as a PU concentrator to limit the number of connections that you have to define to VTAM.

Access to Other Database Management Systems

SNA Server comes with an ODBC driver and bridge software to allow SQL access to IBM DB/2 databases. It also comes with ODBC drivers for a large number of the database management systems.

SNA Server also includes a data replication service that can replicate changes between SQL Server and IBM's DB/2 database running on OS/390s, OS/400s, and AIX.

Host Security Integration

Users working in a heterogeneous Windows 2000 and mainframe environment are often faced with the chore of remembering multiple sets of user IDs and passwords. (At best, this is often one set for RACF or ACF/2 on the mainframe, and one for their Windows 2000 domain.) To simplify the security process, SNA Server comes with software to help synchronize Windows 2000 and mainframe security information. Because it comes from Microsoft, this software is somewhat useful. If you want to truly implement tight integration between host and Windows 2000 security, however, you must install third-party security integration software on your mainframe. Proginet, the maker of the Single Signon software bundled with SNA Server, sells an add-on product, SecurPass, that provides this function.

Web-to-Host Integration

SNA Server can be integrated with Microsoft's Internet Information Server. This forms a browser to Web server to SNA Server to host connection, which will be used to give browser access to legacy mainframe data over an intranet or the Internet.

SNA Server also comes with a 3270 Web client that can be deployed to the Internet Explorer Web browser as an ActiveX control and used to access the host via SNA Server.

Many third-party utilities convert 3270 character-mode screens to GUI screens. Some of these packages require offline screen format conversion and some of them perform on-the-fly conversion to HTML.

Other third-party packages provide similar plug-ins for other Web browsers such as Netscape Navigator.

Information on SNA Server is pretty hard to find. Your best source of information is the documentation that comes with BackOffice, such as the following:

- "Microsoft SNA Server: Getting Started"
- "Microsoft SNA Server: Planning Guide"
- "Microsoft SNA Server: Administration Guide"
- "Microsoft SNA Server: Reference"

Although there is a lot of documentation on the Microsoft Web site (www.microsoft.com/sna), in the Microsoft Knowledge Base (support .microsoft.com), and in the TechNet CD distribution, most of it seems to be for older versions of SNA Server. There is a set of newsgroups for peer support of SNA Server at msnews.microsoft.com.

This chapter has discussed ways to communicate with the mainframe from clients and other servers. The next chapter adds to this picture by discussing two SNA Server components that provide bridges to legacy data: the *COM Transaction Integrator* (COMTI) and the OLE/DB Provider.

17

Integrating with Legacy Mainframe Applications and Data

There are several methods of integrating Windows 2000 applications with legacy mainframe applications. This chapter discusses some early methods of integration and then spends some time on two features that come with SNA Server to facilitate this integration: the COM Transaction Integrator and the OLE DB Provider, which supports direct access to VSAM files from Windows 2000.

3270 Screen Scraping

Early attempts to integrate mainframe and workstation programs used a technique called "screen scraping." In this technique, terminal-emulator software was used to send mainframe transactions to CICS and intercept the reply sent back by the CICS program. This made it possible to put a prettier GUI front end on a 3270 character-mode transaction. It also made it possible to perform additional processing on the received data before presenting it to the user. Using this technique, a program could be designed to issue several CICS transactions in a row and then present the results to the user in a single display. (Another popular use of this technique was to combine data from multiple mainframes in a single display.)

Some companies even went so far as to try to build whole applications using this technique. This, however, was not successful for two reasons. The first reason was that screen scraping involved a lot of overhead and had to be done in real-time. The second reason was that there was no way to integrate atomic transaction integrity across both platforms (see Chapter 15, "Transaction, Database, and Message Processing").

Distributed Program Link

As indicated in Chapter 15, CICS can be used to build distributed transaction-processing applications involving multiple CICS systems. For a CICS program to be used in this way, however, it must be written without a user interface. Furthermore it must be written in such a way that it can be invoked remotely by a distributed program link (as introduced in Chapter 15).

Using DPL, an originating program can issue a CICS LINK request to invoke a target program. As part of LINK request processing, CICS will look up the location of the program in the CICS PPT (see Chapter 15). If the PPT indicates that the target program is on another system, CICS will change the request into an *Advanced Program-to-Program Communications* (APPC) request to send the LINK request to the target system where the program will actually be executed. When it finishes execution, control will be returned to the LINKing program.

> ### *Advanced Program-to-Program Communications*
>
> *APPC is a protocol developed by IBM to allow two programs running on different computer systems to communicate with each other. Among other things, ACCP supports atomic transactions and a two-phase commit process across both systems. (Chapter 16, "Communicating with OS/390," discusses APPC in more detail.)* ◆

CICS also passes the requester's Commarea across to the target system with the request. This Commarea must contain any input and output parameters for the LINK request. (See Chapter 15 for a discussion of Commareas and how they are used.)

When the target system receives the incoming transaction, it is handled by the local CICS Mirror transaction (CSMI). CSMI, acting as a proxy for the original CICS system, issues the LINK request and passes control to the requested program with the received Commarea.

If the source and target programs are part of the same *logical unit of work* (LUW), the originating system adds an LUW token to the request so that the atomic transaction can be preserved across both systems. If resources are updated on both systems, SYNCPOINT and SYNCPOINT ROLLBACK requests issued on either side will result in the appropriate atomic transaction actions.

Finally, when the target program returns, the results of the LINK are returned back to the originating program.

These programs were not simple to write and so companies began to develop solutions involving middleware that could simplify the details. One such middleware solution is provided by Microsoft's *COM Transaction Integrator* (COMTI), as discussed in the next section.

COMTI

The Microsoft *COM Transaction Integrator* (COMTI) is used to create an MTS-resident COM "wrapper" component that makes a legacy CICS or IMS mainframe application program look like an MTS component at execution time. (See Chapter 15 for a discussion of COM and MTS.) Windows 2000 applications make method calls and pass parameters to what appears to be just another COM MTS component. This call is translated under the covers to the appropriate CICS DPL call and sent to the mainframe via SNA Server and LU 6.2 (see Chapter 14, "Networking").

COMTI comes in two parts: a component builder used to create the COM components, and a runtime component used to execute the created components under MTS. These generated components participate in MTS atomic transactions involving two-phase commits (CICS Syncpoint Level 2). After these components are built, they can be called from ASP, Visual Basic, or any other development environment that supports COM.

These components are easy to work with because they do not require anything on the host end besides the CICS or IMS applications. (As in Chapter 15, this discussion concentrates on CICS because most transaction-processing systems use CICS.) The primary requirement of the original CICS transactions is that they must be written to support invocation via DPL. You build COMTI components using the COMTI GUI that comes with SNA Server. First, of course, you must download your COBOL source code using one of the file transfer methods discussed in the preceding chapter.

Next you will import this code into COMTI using the GUI component builder. After importing the code, the component builder parses the CICS COBOL code and translates it into a COMTI MTS component. This component consists of tables and an interpreter that can be used at runtime to translate calling parameters and "wrap" a call to the mainframe transaction in the MTS component. This call also includes feeding in a token that tells MTS whether this call should be part of an atomic transaction. If it is part of a transaction, the generated component participates in the semantics of MTS atomic transaction recovery, which includes the two-phase commit discussed in Chapter 15.

When the code is translated, the name of the program becomes the callable method of the MTS transaction and the variables passed to the original COBOL program in the Commarea are translated into method parameters.

The COMTI builder does a pretty good job of converting COBOL data types to their COM equivalents, although some esoteric COBOL data-type variations may have to be converted manually.

If the original DPL program participated in a CICS transaction, the DPL interface requires the passing in of a LUW token. The component generated by COMTI supports this feature. This allows CICS DPL programs to support atomic transaction semantics similar to the MTS transaction specifications: Requires a transaction, Requires a new transaction, Supports transaction, and Doesn't support transactions. (Chapter 15 discusses these specifications in more detail.)

OLE DB Provider for AS/400 and VSAM

The Microsoft OLE DB specification defines a standard COM interface for data sources of all kinds. These data sources can be hosted by computers running Microsoft products such as SQL Server. They can also be hosted by non-Microsoft sources such as mainframes.

Using OLE DB providers, data can be requested using SQL from a data source that supports SQL. It can also be requested from non-SQL data sources using other methods described in this section.

Data retrieved from an OLE DB source is in the form of recordsets. In the case of SQL data, a recordset corresponds to the rows in a query results table. In the case of a nonrelational source, the recordset corresponds to a file of records. In either case, a program using OLE DB can move up and down the rows in the recordset to process the data. OLE DB also supports the concept of a *disconnected recordset*. A disconnected recordset is actually cached on the client computer and processed locally without tying up a connection to the data on the actual data source.

The OLE DB Provider for AS/400 and VSAM is an SNA Server component that provides direct access to mainframe VSAM and AS/400 data on OS/390 and AS/400s. (This book considers only mainframe access to VSAM files via OS/390.) It provides this access at the record level without requiring any special software on the host. It does require, however, that the host be running IBM's *Distributed Data Management Services* (DDM). DDM is a multiplatform standard for supporting interoperating system access to VSAM files using simple record-level access. The DDM service of interest here runs on OS/390 and is called DFM/MVS.

The OLE DB Provider supports the following features:

- Define record attributes and fields in a record
- Navigate to the beginning or end of a file
- Move to the next or previous record in a file
- Move to a record based on a symbolic record key
- Lock files and records for update
- Update, insert, and delete records

The OLE DB Provider runs as a service on Windows 2000 and Windows NT. No mainframe software is required beyond IBM's DDM/MVS support.

The OLE DB Provider supports VSAM key- and entry-sequenced datasets (KSDS, ESDS, and RRDS). It also supports both fixed and variable-length records as well as VSAM alternate indexes.

The name *OLE DB Provider for AS/400 and VSAM* is a bit of a misnomer because it also provides support for read/write access to BSAM and QSAM disk datasets as well as full access to PAM (PDS and PDSE) datasets, including their members. Tape datasets, however, are not supported. In addition, all datasets must be cataloged in the ICF catalog (see Chapter 10, "Catalogs and Directories").

To use this feature, a Windows 2000 programmer writes a program in a language such as Visual Basic, VBScript, or C. These languages support both a data model and a manipulation technique called *ActiveX Data Objects* (ADO). ADO defines the concept of a recordset. An ADO application opens a connection to a data provider such as the OLE DB Provider or an ODBC-supported database. Then the application can retrieve and update rows of data from the data source. When the OLE DB Provider is used to access files on MVS, the rows of the recordset correspond to the records in the dataset.

Using this technique, a programmer can write a program that accesses mainframe data just as easily as it accesses SQL Server data, or data from any other ODBC data source (see Chapter 15). Unlike access to an ODBC data source, however, you don't need to formulate a request in SQL. The OLE DB Provider uses simple ADO semantics to position the record pointer at the beginning or end of a file, the next or preceding record in the file, or a specific record as identified by a key to an index. It also allows read, write, and update access to the data in the record. When the ActiveX object is destroyed, the file is closed by DDM.

For more information on the OLE DB Provider, refer to the documentation that comes with the *Microsoft OLE DB 1.5 Software Development Kit*. For more information on DDM, you can read the IBM publication "IBM DDM General Information Manual, (C21-9527)." For more information on the OLE DB Provider, see the documentation that comes with SNA Server, particularly the *Software Developers Kit* (SDK) documentation that is installed in the SNA folder when you install SNA Server.

This chapter has covered two Windows 2000 techniques for integrating Windows 2000 and legacy mainframe applications and data. The next chapter examines how to set up a mainframe-like developement environment on a Windows 2000 Professional Workstation. This technique can help to ease a developer's transition from OS/390 to Windows 2000.

18

Structuring a Mainframe-like Development Environment

This chapter explores how to use commercially available tools to build a mainframe "programmer-friendly" development environment on a Windows 2000 Workstation. You will learn about some tools that you can use to develop mainframe applications on a workstation. Some of these tools can also be used to develop cooperative distributed applications that split processing between these two platforms.

Offloading mainframe development is beneficial in those cases where there is not enough mainframe time available for development due to production constraints. It is very handy in those cases where you do not have access to a mainframe—for instance, when you are on the road with your laptop. Workstation-based development can also be preferable when the development tools provided are more user friendly than those available on the mainframe.

This chapter includes discussions of a workstation-based mainframe-style text editor and a complete Windows-based tool set that can be used to develop mainframe applications without a mainframe.

SPF/SE

Much of a programmer's time is spent editing programs and other text files. The Windows 2000 Notepad is the only editor that comes with Windows 2000. It is safe to say that Notepad is not a very good editor if you are used to mainframe tools such as SPF. One way to make the workstation development environment friendlier to a mainframe programmer is to use a familiar text editor, such as one that mimics the TSO/SPF Edit and Browse facility. One such editor is SPF/SE from Command Technology Corp.

SPF/SE presents two user interfaces. For compatibility with the mainframe, it supports the familiar 3270 Edit/Browse window with line numbers down the left side, as shown in Figure 18.1. It also provides a more Windows-oriented GUI interface that can be used after you get used to PC development.

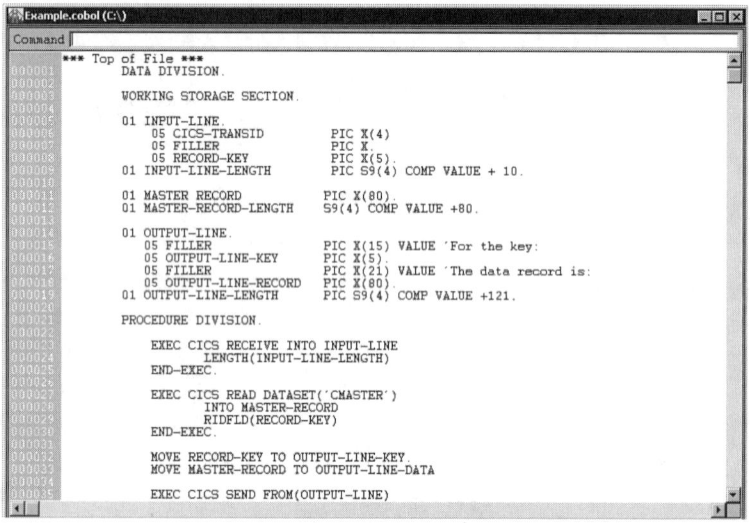

Figure 18.1 *SPF/SE.*

The SPF/SE editor supports almost all the expected primary area and line number area commands provided by SPF on the mainframe. It also supports the usual SPF function keys, such as F3 to exit and F5 to repeat a Find operation.

Mainframe Express

The rest of this chapter describes a product that provides an integrated environment for developing mainframe applications written in COBOL and Assembly Language with CICS and DB2. This product is Mainframe Express from Micro Focus. Mainframe Express can be used to offload the development of mainframe applications to a workstation. Although there are other products sold to perform individual parts of this process, Mainframe Express is the only product that I know of that provides them all in an integrated package. (While I was writing this book, Micro Focus merged with a company called Merant. Out of a long ingrained habit, I still refer to them as Micro Focus in this book.)

A Disclaimer

This is the first chapter in the book in which I felt compelled to issue a disclaimer. I am not an employee of Micro Focus. I have not been influenced by them in any way, except that I have been using their development products successfully for many years. If I seem overly enthusiastic about them, it is just that they have consistently provided the best and most complete sets of tools for developing mainframe applications on Windows (and some non-Windows) platforms. ◆

The COBOL Development Environment

To support workstation-based mainframe application development, a good deal of the mainframe development environment must be duplicated on the workstation. As every mainframe developer knows, it is not sufficient just to know how to program in COBOL to develop modern mainframe applications. You must understand JCL as well as how to use common utilities, such as IEBGENER, Sort/Merge, and Access Method Services. If you are developing applications involving database and transaction processing, you also need to understand DB/2, CICS, and possibly IMS as well.

Even when it comes to languages, it is not sufficient to just know COBOL. Many legacy mainframe applications also use Assembly Language subroutines for common functions. (For instance, many companies have date routines written in OS/390 Assembly Language.) A good development environment will have to duplicate a large portion of this mainframe environment.

The Mainframe Express Integrated Development Environment

Mainframe Express provides its tools in an *integrated development environment* (IDE). This IDE provides the same type of friendly development environment that Visual Basic and C programmers have come to expect from their development tools (see Figure 18.2).

Using the IDE to test a program consists of the following steps:

- Creating a project
- Adding files to the project
- Building the project
- Testing and debugging the project

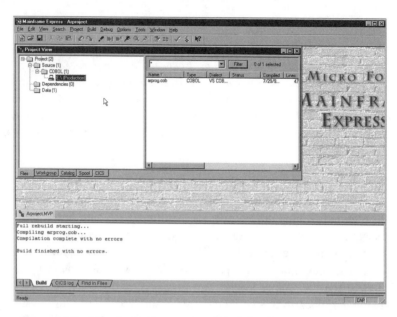

Figure 18.2 *Mainframe Express integrated development environment.*

Creating a Project

Mainframe Express is based on a project approach and its IDE reflects this organization. A Mainframe Express project is a collection of files describing all of your application's program and data files. The advantage of this organization is that you can load and work with all of an application's related source and data files as a group. Every MFA project has a project file with an .MVP extension.

This project organization is reflected in the IDE, which has multiple windows. Several of these windows have multiple display pages that can be brought to the foreground by clicking on a tab at the bottom of the window. When you start the IDE for the first time, the Project View window will be in the foreground. Figure 18.2 shows the Project View window with the Files page selected. This page consists of two display panes. The left pane shows a tree view of the project. By clicking on the plus signs in the tree, you can expand the collection of files at any point in the tree. When you select a node in the tree, the right pane shows a list of the files in that category. You can then double-click on the file in the right pane to open the appropriate editor for that type of file. Other tabs at the bottom of the top window can be used to display pages related to other options that are discussed later in this chapter—the Catalog tab, for instance, shows the files currently in the simulated OS/390 catalog (see Figure 18.3).

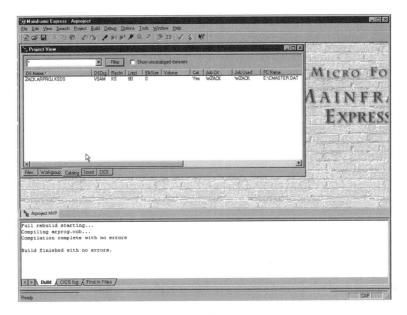

Figure 18.3 *Catalog view.*

You can add any files that you need to the catalog by right-clicking on the right window. When you do this, you will get a pop-up menu with file-creation options. At the time that you add a file to the catalog, you can specify an MVS filename and other OS/390 catalog options for the file.

Mainframe Express provides a dataset catalog that simulates the OS/390 catalog. This is an MVS-style catalog, which enables you to use MVS-style dataset names. It also supports dynamic TSO and JCL allocation of datasets. Using either JCL or the built-in GUI tools, datasets can be created, added to the catalog, and deleted. Supported catalog functions include the following:

- ALLOCATE
- ADD EXISTING DATASET
- DELETE
- RENAME
- UNCATALOG
- RECATALOG

The Mainframe Express development process normally begins when you download your source code and data files from the mainframe. Normally you would do this with the file transfer capabilities of a workstation-resident 3270 emulator, as discussed in Chapter 16, "Communicating with

OS/390." Micro Focus also sells a workstation-mainframe integration package, Mainframe Access Drag & Drop. If you have this package installed on your mainframe, you can also drag and drop files between two GUI windows representing files on the mainframe and files on the workstation. After the files are on your workstation, you can create a new project and add the files to it.

When it comes to downloading data files, Mainframe Express supports the simulation of almost every conceivable mainframe *dataset organization* (DSORG), including the following:

- Direct Access (DA and DAU)
- Generation Data Groups (GDGs)
- Indexed Sequential (IS)
- Partitioned (PO and POU)
- Physical Sequential (PS and PSU)

For these datasets, you can specify details, such as *record length* (LRECL) and *block size* (BLKSIZE). It supports most of the allowable mainframe *record formats* (RECFM) such as fixed, variable length, undefined, and spanned records (see Chapter 7, "Data Management").

Its support for VSAM files is pretty impressive as well. It supports the creation of VSAM files, from the GUI using an interactive AMS Define Cluster utility, or through the execution of JCL. Most of the VSAM parameters necessary for an accurate simulation of VSAM can also be specified.

Building the Project

The next step is to build and run your project. The IDE Debug menu on the menu bar provides options to rebuild only the components that have changed since the last build, or you can rebuild the entire project. (This is similar to the minimal Make facility used by C and Visual Basic programmers.) Note that Mainframe Express also "compiles" JCL and Clists prior to execution.

As the build proceeds, status messages are shown in the Output window (see the bottom of Figure 18.2). The build process creates work files to be used during execution and testing. If there are errors in the source, a Source window will open with the lines in error marked with a red *X* in the left margin. You can double-click on the error messages and move to the lines in error or just select them directly. You can then edit the program lines in the Source window.

The steps that Mainframe Express takes in building the project depend on the components included in the project. The following components may be included

- COBOL programs
- CICS COBOL programs
- DB/2 programs
- Assembly Language programs
- JCL
- OS/390 utilities
- Clists

COBOL Programs

The build process will compile any COBOL programs in the project. Because COBOL is the language most often used to develop mainframe application programs, having a good COBOL compiler and debugger is one of the most important requirements for a development environment. A good implementation must support the debugging of programs written in COBOL II and/or VS COBOL. Mainframe Express includes the excellent Micro Focus COBOL compiler. This compiler is the oldest and most widely used workstation-based COBOL compiler available for offline mainframe application development. It supports a half dozen dialects of mainframe COBOL including several versions of VS COBOL II, MVS COBOL, and OS/VS COBOL.

The compiler supports the compile-time inclusion of COBOL copybooks, including those that use the standard COBOL COPY syntax as well as those that use the INCLUDE syntax used by Panvalet and Librarian.

Debugging mainframe applications has always been a big part of a COBOL programmer's job. To assist in this process, the Micro Focus COBOL compiler in Mainframe Express provides a superb interactive debugger called the Animator. With the Animator, you can actually watch your program run line by line, set breakpoints, and examine the contents of various working storage variables. At a breakpoint, or when your program aborts, you can examine and change the contents of key memory locations and then resume execution by single stepping through statements, continuing to animate or to just run the program to completion. You can debug batch COBOL programs as well as COBOL programs including CICS, DB/2, and IMS calls.

CICS COBOL Programs

A large number of mainframe applications are transaction-processing programs written in COBOL with embedded CICS commands (see Chapter 15, "Transaction, Database, and Message Processing"). Mainframe Express comes with a CICS option that provides support for testing both single-tasking and multitasking CICS applications. This option is based on CICS emulation software that Micro Focus has also been refining for years.

This includes support for the development of *basic mapping support* (BMS) mapsets. You can develop maps on the workstation by using the built-in screen painter, or you can import downloaded mainframe mapsets or files from the CICS *Screen Definition Facility* (SDF). The local screen painter generates maps and BMS copybooks that can then be copied into your CICS program at compile time.

To facilitate downloading and testing programs, you can also import mainframe CICS resource definitions for tables, such as the CICS PCT and the CICS FCT (see Chapter 15).

When it comes to the debugging of CICS COBOL applications, Mainframe Express uses the same interactive debugger used to debug batch COBOL programs.

The CICS option provides a simulated 3270 window where the programmer can enter CICS transaction codes and see the output of the CIC program. In Figure 18.4, you can see the CICS example program from Chapter 15 being debugged in Mainframe Express. The black window at the bottom of the screen is the 3270 window. You will notice that the 3270 window shows a typical CICS error, just as it might be reported on the \ainframe during development.

DB/2 Programs

Mainframe Express supports two options for batch and CICS COBOL applications that include DB/2 calls:

- The SQL option
- The DB/2 option

A large number of COBOL programs involve processing data located in databases managed by IBM's DB/2 database management system. IBM sells a version of DB/2 that can run under several operating systems. If you have one of these products installed on your workstation, you can use it with Mainframe Express to debug COBOL-DB/2 applications.

If you do not have DB/2 installed on your workstation, you should use the integrated Mainframe Express SQL option. This option uses the XDB database management system that Micro Focus acquired when it merged with XDB Database Systems. XDB features strong mainframe DB/2 compatibility. (At one time, XDB was more compatible with mainframe DB/2 than IBM's workstation version of DB/2. Over the years, however, IBM has been gradually improving the compatibility of their DB/2 version for different platforms.)

Both of these products also support IBM's *distributed relational data access* (DRDA) architecture for supporting distributed database applications. Using the DRDA support in these products enables you to access DB/2 files on a mainframe as well as on other platforms that support DRDA.

Assembly Language Programs

Mainframe Express supports the testing of Assembly Language programs written in *High-Level Language* (HLL) Assembler with macros. These programs can also include CICS and IMS calls.

One interesting feature of the provided Assembler is that it can be used to generate object modules in OS/390's relocatable object module format. These object modules can then be uploaded to the mainframe and provided as input to the OS/390 Linkage Editor without reassembly on the mainframe. I know of at least one mainframe CICS product vendor who maintains his CICS-Assembler package on his laptop. If he needs to fix a bug, he just reassembles the appropriate module on his laptop, uploads it to the mainframe, and links it into his product.

The Assembler support in Mainframe Express also includes an interactive debugger similar to the Micro Focus Animator. This debugger, however, is more oriented to debugging an Assembly Language program with register storage displays, and machine-code instruction execution.

JCL

As discussed in Chapter 9, "Job and Task Management," the OS/390 JCL provides the interprogram glue that ties an application's program and utilities together. Mainframe Express provides a multi-step JCL engine that supports JOB, EXEC, DD statements, symbolic parameters, concatenated datasets, partitioned and generation datasets, and many other JCL features. It also supports in-stream and cataloged procedures using cataloged procedure libraries. For manipulating VSAM datasets with JCL, it also provides emulation of the OS/390 IDCAMS utility.

For job output, Mainframe Express provides output-spool emulation at the JES2 and JES3 levels. A Spool window can be used to view an entry for all JCL members used, jobs and steps run, as well as for output dataset (SYSPRINT and SYSOUT) created by the job. These spool files can be viewed using an SDSF-like spool capture-and-display facility included in the IDE (see Chapter 11, "Printer Management"). In addition, all job execution and operator messages are written to a log file similar to the console log of a real OS/390 system.

OS/390 Utilities

No mainframe development environment would be complete without a frequently used OS/390 utility programs. Mainframe Express includes most of the important utilities, such as IDCAMS, DSORT, and IEBGENER, as well as the ever-popular IEFBR14, whose sole purpose is to execute a null program so that you can manipulate datasets using JCL.

Mainframe Express also comes with a complete set of data-file manipulation tools that can be used to create, edit, and display data files of all types. This also includes a feature to display and edit data files in record layout format by mapping each record in the file with its copybook record description.

Clists

Mainframe Express also provides an implementation of the TSO READY prompt that enables you to execute simple TSO commands and Clists. It does not, however, include support for the REXX Execs. The Windows 2000 Resource Kit does come with a version of REXX for Windows 2000, but it is really not compatible with mainframe REXX.

Surprisingly, it does also support the IJKEFT01 utility that allows the batch execution of TSO commands and Clists in jobs.

Testing and Debugging

After a clean build, you can select a file from the Files windows to execute and select either Run or Start Debugging from the Debug menu on the menu bar to execute your program. If you are a perfect programmer, you will have no errors when you run your program. If you are like most, however, you will have some debugging to do.

If you are running a CICS program, there will also be a simulated 3270 window at the bottom of the screen. Note that this window arrangement is the default Mainframe Express IDE arrangement. You can rearrange these windows to suit yourself. One bit of advice, however. The screen can get quite busy during the typical debugging session, so it would be a good idea to set your monitor to high resolution, such as 1024×768 or better (see Figure 18.4).

As you can tell by this chapter, I am pretty impressed with this package. To my knowledge, it is the only full-function package that supports all facets of mainframe development on a Windows Workstation. It is the only package that enables me to "take my mainframe with me" on my laptop so that I can do development without being attached to a mainframe.

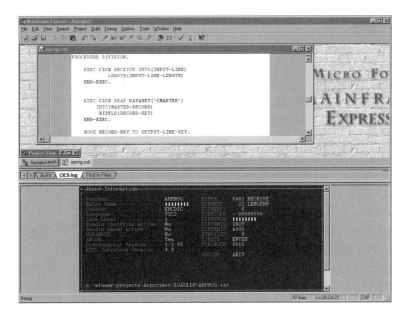

Figure 18.4 *Debugging a CICS COBOL program.*

This chapter has explored tools and techniques that can be used to build a mainframe development environment on a Windows Workstation. The next (and final) chapter talks about scalability and the future of Windows 2000.

19
Scalability

When I started this book, I decided to leave this chapter until last because I thought that I would have a hard time convincing you that Windows 2000 can scale up to challenge the raw performance of high-performance UNIX systems and even mainframes. Now, as I write this chapter, the challenge of persuading you of this seems smaller somehow. Perhaps it is that four-way and eight-way *symmetric multiprocessor* (SMP) x86-based systems and multicomputer clusters have already begun to encroach on the cost/performance realm once dominated by UNIX systems. In fact, the areas of scalability and reliability are the most rapidly changing aspects of the Windows NT and Windows 2000 picture.

Scalability is defined as the capability of a computing resource (hardware and software) to grow to handle larger processing volumes. If the resource has an upper limit, it can be said to not be scalable. It is not enough to consider the raw power of a computer system. Cost is always a factor. In the commercial environment, the cost of this scalability must always be considered. There are UNIX and mainframe systems that can achieve higher performance than Windows NT and Windows 2000 can on a specified workload. They generally do so, however, at a greater cost (as you will see later in this chapter).

The "traditional wisdom" of only a few years ago was that UNIX systems would never scale up in reliability and performance to challenge mainframes. Today the prevailing opinion is that Windows NT systems can "never" scale up to challenge UNIX systems. It is my opinion that the prevailing wisdom is wrong.

Back in the 1980s, UNIX was popularly viewed strictly as a minicomputer operating system. (Remember minicomputers?) That was until companies such as Amdahl and Bell Labs ported UNIX to System/360 architecture hardware. (The Amdahl version was called UTS for UNIX Timesharing System.) It ran fast! And it supported thousands of users.

I recently heard a rumor that a major computer manufacturer has ported Windows NT to run on a mainframe in their research labs. It is also reported to run fast. Note that I do not expect a mainframe version of Windows 2000 to be commercially available anytime soon; however, this is an indication of what is technically feasible. What I do expect soon, however, is the release of the Data Center Version of Windows 2000. This product, not even in beta testing at the time that I write this, is expected to ship six months after the shipment of the other versions of Windows 2000. The Data Center Version of Windows 2000 is being architected by Microsoft to challenge UNIX and possibly even mainframes in a data-center environment.

Mainframe Scalability

If you are reading this book, you probably come from an IBM mainframe environment. Even if this is not the case, you would have to have led a very sheltered existence not to know that the mainframe is considered to be the ultimate in scalability. For a price, you can have a mainframe complex capable of handling the largest and most demanding processing requirements.

Since the early 1990s, IBM mainframes have been built using *symmetric multiprocessing* (SMP) and the parallel sysplex clustering technology. Parallel sysplex clusters provide for two very important data-center requirements: scalability and availability. A parallel sysplex cluster can consist of up to 32 separate processors each running its own copy of the operating system (see Figure 19.1).

Each operating system manages its own resources and each operating system can run dedicated applications. Each processor running an operating system is said to represent one system image.

Although this chapter doesn't go into the different types of disk- and memory-sharing technologies used to build clusters, parallel sysplex uses a shared-disk clustering approach. In this architecture, disk resources are shared by all the cluster partners. In parallel sysplex, this is implemented via a high-speed *coupling facility* (CF) used to coordinate access to a set of shared DASD that can be accessed by all processors (see Figure 19.1). The CF is actually implemented as a special set of programs that can be run on a selected OS/390 processor in the complex. The DASD, in turn, is shared by being connected to a common data switch called an *enterprise system connection* (Escon).

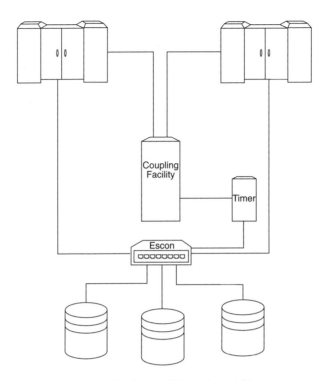

Figure 19.1 *IBM's parallel sysplex architecture.*

The CF is used to coordinate requests for common resources and to provide a place for things such as locks and buffers for these common resources. A set of highly optimized instructions have been added to System/390 to make access to cluster resources look as much like access to local resources as possible. In addition, OS/390 implements a distributed lock manager for controlling access to shared resources.

Disk storage can be partitioned to dedicate some disks to individual images, some to be shared by applications running on multiple processors, and some to be used as cluster control and optimization resources.

A Timer facility (refer to Figure 19.1) is used to synchronize events in the complex so that things such as transaction commit/backout and recovery can be synchronized across the complex.

OS/390 has been written to be cluster aware so that it can communicate with the other copies of OS/390 running on other processors. In addition, key OS/390 subsystems such as VTAM, CICS, IMS, DB/2, and JES have been modified to also be cluster aware. This allows them to provide both failover and load-balancing capabilities. For instance, multiple copies of

CICS running in multiple OS/390 images can share the transaction-processing load among them. If one processor fails, VTAM can automatically switch the processing load to one of the remaining processors. In the case where there is no failure, VTAM can also load balance the transactions across the multiple copies of CICS. This gives the appearance of a single image when, in fact, there are actually multiple VTAM and CICS images in operation.

In any cluster configuration, it is desirable to have the cluster appear to both users and administrators as if it is a single large computer system (or single image). IBM has gone to great pains to simplify the operation of a parallel sysplex cluster to make it appear to be a single system. This also gives the appearance of one larger system and contributes to scalability. A parallel sysplex cluster can be partitioned so that it looks like one big system or several smaller systems.

Other subsystems, such as DB/2, JES2, and the OS/390 operating system Workload Manager, have also been optimized to run in this environment as well. Thus, parallel sysplex clustering provides both performance and failover capabilities. The bottom line is that thanks to its overall design and cluster-optimized operating system and subsystem software, IBM's parallel sysplex achieves nearly linear scalability with the addition of multiple complex members.

As an example of this scalability, IBM quotes a 10-processor complex based on their largest available processor as providing an IMS and DB/2 transaction-processing rate of approximately 900,000 transactions per minute! (Reference: "System/390 Parallel Sysplex Performance," IBM publication SG24-4356-03). It should also be noted that IBM is notoriously conservative in quoting performance figures. Nevertheless, this serves to set the bar for measuring the scalability of all other systems. You will note, however, that nothing has been said here about cost per transaction. Mainframes are notoriously expensive, and this is a multimillion-dollar system complex that we are talking about here.

Windows 2000 Scalability

As in the case of mainframes and UNIX systems, there are two ways to achieve greater processing performance: use more CPUs per processor, or add processors using clustering. Windows 2000 uses both these approaches; as you will see in this chapter, however, Windows 2000 clustering is still in a fairly primitive state. Figure 19.2 shows Microsoft's current scalability vision.

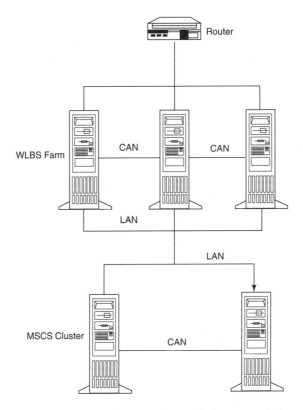

Figure 19.2 *Front-end and back-end load balancing and clustering.*

This vision consists of a front-end cluster of computers providing load balancing and failover fault tolerance for input transactions from a community of users accessing the computer complex via clients using Internet/intranet technologies, such as Web browsers. These front-end computers, in turn, make requests for processing and database services from a back-end computer cluster that also provides load balancing and failover. This is a nice picture and should scale well; however, it is not yet fully in place. In fact, it will not be completely implemented until sometime after the release of the Data Center Edition of Windows 2000.

The Windows Load-Balancing System

Currently Microsoft does provide front-end load balancing and fault tolerance using the *Windows Load-Balancing System* (WLBS). (Microsoft acquired WLBS from Valence Research, where it was originally named Convoy Cluster.)

A WLBS cluster can contain up to 32 nodes. These nodes each normally have two network adapters. One adapter is used to communicate heartbeat and status information between the cluster members via a *cluster area network* (CAN), as shown in Figure 19.2. The other adapter is used to communicate with a back-end MSCS cluster via a LAN. Typically the CAN is a high-speed network supporting a 100MBps data transfer rate. The LAN is usually a standard 16MBps Token Ring or 10MBps Ethernet network.

WLBS runs on each server. Incoming requests are routed via a load-balancing algorithm to the least-busy server for processing. When a node fails, the remaining nodes react to the missing heartbeat and adjust to take over the workload of the failing node. In addition to providing fault tolerance, this architecture also contributes to scalability. Adding a new node to the cluster automatically increases its capacity.

Microsoft Cluster Server

In the case of back-end clustering, however, the *Microsoft Cluster Service* (MSCS) solution (originally called Wolfpack) provides only two-node failover support (refer to Figure 19.2). It does not currently support load balancing. Furthermore, this failover capability works only on the basis of one failover node backing up one other node. Both nodes in a cluster can also process work as long as they have the capacity to back up each other. They can also provide mutual failover support for each other. Other vendors, such as IBM and Sequent, have recently demonstrated enhanced MSCS clusters that allow better than two-node backup.

You will notice that nothing was said about scalability in the preceding discussion, and indeed MSCS does nothing by itself to aid scalability. Microsoft does have plans to add load-balancing support in a future version of Windows 2000, but for now it is limited to just providing fault tolerance. This limits the scalability of Windows 2000 systems somewhat. You can add processors using SMP machines, or you can use software that naturally partitions a processing task across multiple processors in such a way that the workload is actually balanced by the subsystem or application software.

More About Clusters

The best, most thorough, and enjoyable treatment of clustering is In Search of Clusters, *by Gregory F. Pfister, Prentice Hall PTR, ISBN: 0-13-899709-8.*

For a good understanding of the Microsoft Cluster Server architecture and implementation, you should read Microsoft Cluster Server, *by Richard R. Lee, Osbourne-McGraw Hill, ISBN: 0-0788-2500-8.* ◆

Scalability Using SMP

Until recently, Windows NT had a fairly poor reputation concerning scalability using multiple SMP processors. In fact it was widely reported not to scale well beyond three or four processors. I do expect that Microsoft will improve this situation by the time that it releases Windows 2000. Even so, recent benchmarks of SMP systems have begun to challenge even the larger UNIX systems on the basis of raw performance and to blow them away completely when it comes to cost/performance (see "Recent Scalability Developments," later in this chapter.)

Scalability via Application Partitioning

Even without load-balancing clusters, some subsystems and applications do lend themselves well to application partitioning across multiple computer systems in a cluster where no data or memory sharing is required. (These are called "shared-nothing" clusters to distinguish them from shared-memory clusters or shared-data clusters, such as IBM's parallel sysplex clusters.) For instance, database management systems can have their databases partitioned such that queries can be spread over multiple processors. Each processor can then access a subset of the entire database in resolving a single query.

In fact, Microsoft demonstrated one such system as part of a recent "Scalability Day" demonstration. Microsoft demonstrated a system using SQL Server to access a 1.4-terabyte database partitioned over 324 separate disk drives. This feat, while impressive, was a specially contrived demonstration. Until a load-balancing version of MSCS comes out, general back-end scalability of Windows 2000 systems will have to be achieved by means of SMP systems.

Availability

You will note that I have not dedicated much space in this chapter to the subject of availability. It is true, however, that it is almost impossible not to consider availability along with scalability. No one wants a high-performance scalable computer system that is available only "some of the time."

In the area of availability, mainframes and specially built proprietary fault-tolerant systems reign supreme. These systems are often quoted as providing 99.999% uptime. To put this into perspective, consider the actual amount of annual downtime that each percentage figure listed here would provide. (Source: In Search of Clusters, *by Gregory F. Pfister, Prentice Hall PTR, ISBN: 0-13-899709-8.)*

continues ▶

▶ *continued*

90%	More than a month
99%	Just under four days
99.9%	Just under nine hours
99.99%	About an hour
99.999%	A little over five minutes
99.9999%	About half a minute
99.99999%	About three seconds

Mainframes are usually credited with "five nines" (99.999%) availability. Fault-tolerant systems, such as those provided by Compaq/Tandem and others, are required to do better than that.

Recently several vendors, such as Hewlett-Packard and IBM, have announced their intention to offer a 99.99% uptime guarantee on Windows NT– and Windows 2000–based systems. In one case, a third-party vendor, Marathon Technologies Corp, has even sold systems that the company is reported to claim offer 99.999% uptime. All these systems are based on clustering of one type or another. In fact, clustering Windows NT and Windows 2000 systems does even more for availability than it does for scalability. ◆

Recent Scalability Developments

As mentioned earlier, Windows NT originally did not scale well beyond three or four processors. Windows NT–based SMP systems are beginning to show better results. For the first time, a Windows NT–based system has appeared in the Top 10 list of the Transaction Processing Performance Council based on raw performance. In addition, Windows NT systems occupy all the Top 10 positions on their list of systems based on cost per transaction. (This is based on the status of these lists as of August 1999.)

The *Transaction Processing Performance Council* (TPC) is a non-profit corporation founded to define transaction-processing and database-processing benchmarks and to disseminate objective, verifiable performance data to the industry. (See their Web site at www.tpc.org.) Although they do state that their transaction-processing and database-processing benchmarks may not match the requirements of your applications, nevertheless they are reasonably well defined and do serve to allow a rough comparison of the performance achieved by different computer systems. The TPC has two benchmarks of interest to this discussion: the *transaction-processing benchmark* (TPC-C), and the *database-processing benchmark* (TPC-D).

The first system to crack the TPC-C Top 10 list for raw TPC-C performance was an NEC Express 5800 HV8600, which achieved a tpmC (transactions per minute for the tpmC benchmark) of 50208 running an Oracle database and the BEA Tuxedo teleprocessing monitor. This was reported in June 1999. It did this at a cost of only $94.05 per tpmC. All the higher-rated (and non-Windows NT) systems in the Top 10 list achieved their ratings at a higher cost per tpmC than this system.

In the list of systems rated by price/performance, all 10 of the Top 10 were Windows NT systems. There were (in no particular order) five Compaq Proliant systems, four Dell PowerEdge systems, and one AcerAltos system. The number-one rated system was a Compaq Proliant 5500-500-2M system, which was rated at 22057 tpmC at a price per tpmC of only $14.62.

This is the situation with respect to scalability of Windows NT systems as of August 1999. There is one other scalability architecture supported by Windows 2000. The Windows 2000 Terminal Server service, which is discussed in the next section.

Windows Terminal Server and Scalability

Windows Terminal Server is a service of Windows 2000 that brings Windows 2000 applications to computers and other devices that would not ordinarily be capable of running Windows 2000. These devices can be older computers running 16-bit versions of Windows. These client workstations do not have to be powerful enough to run Windows 2000 Professional by themselves. They could be legacy 386 and 486 PCs. They can also be devices called *Windows terminals* that only run software and/or ROM-based microcode necessary for them to boot up and connect to Terminal Server.

How It works

Terminal Server makes it possible for remote users to execute applications that actually run on the server. With Windows Terminal Server, only the GUI is remoted to the client device. The actual application runs on a Windows 2000 server. This allows older computers to run Windows 2000 applications.

It allows each remote client to run applications in its own session as if it has exclusive use of the machine. The client runs all applications on the server and just remotes the GUI interface to a client system.

Windows Terminal Server is based on earlier development work done by Citrix in their WinFrame product. Citrix also sells an add-on product that improves and extends Terminal Server to non-Windows desktops.

To accommodate this service, Windows 2000 essentially performs a terminal-emulation function much like the terminal emulation provided by PCs connected to a mainframe. This makes the Windows Terminal service useful for supporting task-based workers, such as order entry clerks or bank tellers who perform a few specific functions using inexpensive low-powered devices.

Performance Issues

Windows Terminal Server may seem to be too good to be true, and in a sense it is. Although you can run Windows 2000 and Windows 2000 applications on less-capable client equipment, the processing has to go somewhere else. In this case, it is the server that must have enough resources (processing power, memory, and disk space) to support all simultaneous Terminal Server users. In addition, there must be sufficient network bandwidth to support GUI updates as well as normal LAN traffic. A general rule of thumb is to allow at least 15–20MB of memory per simultaneously active remote client. This can require a pretty large server.

The current Windows NT Terminal Server performance leader may well be a 10-processor Unisys XR/6 system demonstrated by Unisys at PC Expo in June 1999. Although exact performance data is not available, Microsoft and Unisys have announced that this system did exhibit linear scalability across all 10 internal processors with reserve capacity to spare. (Unisys also offers a 12-processor system as well.)

If you want to know more about Terminal Server, you can read *Windows NT Thin Client Solutions: Implementing Terminal Server and Citrix MetaFrame*, by Mathers and Genoway, Macmillan Technical Publishing, ISBN: 1-5787-0065-5.

Windows 2000 Data Center Edition

This chapter closes with a brief discussion of the expected features of Windows 2000 Data Center Edition. The Data Center Edition will support up to 32 processors.

Vendors such as IBM that provide both the hardware and the software for a complete computer system can ensure that all these components work well with each other and that they are tested and certified together. In the case of Windows 2000, Microsoft provides only the software. They have little control over the quality of the components, such as device adapter and device drivers that users install in their computers. In fact, the experience of others and myself in the industry is that most serious reliability problems stem from the use of substandard or unapproved hardware components and buggy vendor-developed device drivers. (Of course. there is a Windows Hardware Compatibility List, which Microsoft makes available; however, users who want to cut corners often ignore it.) One of the features of the Data Center Edition is that it will be certified to run only on a specific and limited set of hardware and software components. This should increase its reliability.

The Data Center Edition will support up to 32 processors. It will also include support for up to 64MB of installed real memory via a special *Application Programming Interface* (API) that uses memory-windowing techniques similar to the dataspaces and hiperspaces of OS/390 and the extended and expanded memory once supported by MS-DOS.

It will include a Process Control tool, developed in conjunction with Sequent, which uses the Windows 2000 Job object to allow an operator to partition an SMP system to dedicate processors to specific applications, such as SQL Server.

In addition, it will also support both the load-balancing and clustering features discussed earlier in this chapter. It will also be the vehicle for the implementation of higher forms of clustering, including greater than two-node failover and advanced load balancing.

Those of us who are used to the high reliability and scalability of mainframes can hardly wait until the Data Center Edition is released.

Index

Symbols

(*) asterisk, Windows 2000 wildcard characters, 125
($) dollar sign (operator commands), printer management, 200
(//*) double slash asterisk, 154
(\\) double slashes, job classes, 148
(-) hyphen, dataset names, 112
(.) period, dataset names, 112
(#) pound sign, dataset names, 112
(?) question mark, Windows 2000 wildcard characters, 125
16-bit DOS processes, running VDMs, 80
802.2 connections (SNA Server), 329
3270 applet (SNA Server), 331
3270 screen scraping, 337
3270 terminal emulation, 253-254, 304, 316
   SNA Server, 319, 327-328

A

Access Control Facility (Computer Associates, Inc.), 22, 231
access control lists. *See* ACLs
access methods
   OS/390, types, 118-119
   partitioned access method (PAM), 135
   source-code control systems, 136
   resources, OS/390 RACF security, 233-234
access tokens (Windows 2000 security), 238
accessing
   files
      file access types, 117-118
      Windows 2000, 127
   resources, 243-247
account operators, 245
ACEs (access control elements), 247
ACF (Associates Access Control Facility), 22, 231

ACID transactions (CICS), 297
ACLs (access control lists), 12, 247
Active Desktop, 78
Active Directory
   DNs (distinguished names), 188
   domain trees, 189
   forests, 190
   GUI access options, 193
   namespaces, 179
   OUs, 188
   RDNs (relative distinguished names), 188
   replication, intersite, 192
   sites, 191
   subsystem, Windows 2000 architecture, 33
   UPNs (user principal names), 188
   Windows 2000, 178-179
      database, 180
      database schema, 180
      DNS operations, 182
      domains, 181
      global catalog, 181
      groups, 184
      partitions, 185
      user accounts, 184
   WSH access scripts, 194
Active Directory Services Interface (ADSI), 168, 194
Active Directory Users and Computers snap-in (Windows 2000), 248
active threads, displaying, 83
ActiveX
   Business objects, 308
   methods, 159
   objects, brokering, 309
   properties, 159
adapters, device, 95-96
Add Printer Wizard, creating logical printers on printer servers, 210
Address Resolution Protocol (ARP), 277

J

K-L

M

X-Z

New Riders Professional Library